Ian McPhedran is the Sydney-based natio... P9-DDR-241 Limited. He has been a journalist all his working life and has covered conflicts in Burma, Somalia, Cambodia, Papua New Guinea, Indonesia, East Timor, Afghanistan and Iraq. In 1993 he won a United Nations Association Peace Media Award and in 1999 the Walkley Award for best news report for his exposé of the navy's Collins class submarine fiasco. His first book, *The Amazing SAS: the inside story of Australia's special forces*, is a national best seller. McPhedran lives in Balmain with his wife Verona Burgess and daughter Lucy.

SOLDIERS WITHOUT BORDERS

BEYOND THE SAS
a global network of brothers-in-arms

IAN McPHEDRAN

HarperCollinsPublishers

HarperCollins*Publishers*

First published in Australia in 2008
by HarperCollins*Publishers* Australia Pty Limited
ABN 36 009 913 517
www.harpercollins.com.au

HarperCollins*Publishers*
25 Ryde Road, Pymble, Sydney NSW 2073, Australia
31 View Road, Glenfield, Auckland 10, New Zealand
1–A, Hamilton House, Connaught Place, New Delhi – 110 001, India
77–85 Fulham Palace Road, London W6 8JB, United Kingdom
2 Bloor Street East, 20th Floor, Toronto, Ontario M4W 1A8, Canada
10 East 53rd Street, New York NY 10022, United States of America

National Library of Australia Cataloguing-in-Publication data:

McPhedran, Ian, 1957–
   Soldiers without borders : beyond the SAS / Ian McPhedran.
   ISBN: 978 0 7322 8555 5 (pbk.).
   Includes index.
   Australia. Army. Special Air Service Regiment. Soldiers–Australia–Retirement.
   Commando troops–Retirement. Career changes.
355.114

Cover and internal design by Matt Stanton
Cover image of soldier by Stocktrek Images/Getty Images. All other cover images by Shutterstock.com
Maps by Laurie Whiddon
Typeset in 11.5 on 16.5pt Bembo by Helen Beard, ECJ Australia Pty Ltd
Printed and bound in Australia by Griffin Press
70gsm Classic used by HarperCollins*Publishers* is a natural, recyclable product made from wood grown
in sustainable forests. The manufacturing processes conform to the environmental regulations in the
country of origin, Finland.

5 4 3 2 1   08 09 10 11 12

For Verona and Lucy

ACKNOWLEDGMENTS

This book could not have been written without my wife, Verona Burgess. Not only is she an incisive editor, she is also a boundless source of ideas and inspiration. Once again we have been able to produce a book together and remain happily married.

Our daughter Lucy took the long absences of her dad in her stride and my stepkids Daniel and Jenna Cave were keen supporters.

I received generous help and guidance from several ex-SAS men, but none more so than Terry O'Farrell, who is a fine example of what the regiment is all about. The wonderful hospitality that I enjoyed from Terry, Lee and Liam made my trips to the Middle East feel like family visits.

Ken Webb was a source of encouragement and inspiration. Jim Truscott and Pete Tinley provided plenty of ideas. George and his wife 'Audrey' gave very generously of their time and friendship. I thank George for raking over some grim experiences.

Rob Jamieson in the UK provided insights and ideas. Thanks to Dave Harper in Dubai for his help and hospitality.

I am grateful to Terry Culley in Auckland for introducing me to many great blokes from the New Zealand SAS and thanks also to Pete Bradford and his wife Wendy.

I am deeply indebted to all the former soldiers who bared their souls, particularly the counterterrorism pioneers, who deserve closure.

David Horner's wonderful official history of the SAS, *SAS: Phantoms of War*, continues to be a valuable reference tool.

My sister Jane provided shelter during my many visits to Perth and thanks also to my other sisters Lynne and Cheryl, brother Shaun and dad Colin. Thanks also to my sister-in-law Adrienne Burgess and her husband, Martin Cochrane, for their kindness and succour at the marvellous Pimlico guesthouse.

Janette Doolan and Liz Kemp provided very professional and timely help with their transcriptions.

Once again I am indebted to my employer, News Limited, for its tolerance and forbearance.

Finally to Shona Martyn and her terrific team at HarperCollins, particularly Mel Cain, Jennifer Blau and Christine Farmer, many thanks.

Ian McPhedran
Sydney, June 2008

CONTENTS

GLOSSARY

1 SAS	1 SAS Squadron
2IC	second in command
2RAR	2nd Battalion Royal Australian Regiment
2 SAS	2 SAS Squadron
3RAR	3rd Battalion Royal Australian Regiment
3 SAS	3 SAS Squadron
ADF	Australian Defence Force
ADFA	Australian Defence Force Academy
AO	area of operation
ASIS	Australian Secret Intelligence Service
CCP	casualty clearing post
CDF	Chief of the Defence Force
CQB	close-quarters battle
CO	commanding officer
CT	counterterrorism
DFAT	Department of Foreign Affairs and Trade
DIO	Defence Intelligence Organisation
DRC	Democratic Republic of Congo
dust-off	troop extraction
Falintil	Army for the National Liberation of East Timor
FOB	forward operating base
GPS	global positioning system
HALO	high altitude low open
helo	helicopter
Huey	Iroquois UH1H helicopter
Kopassus	Indonesian special forces
LNG	liquefied natural gas
LRPV	long-range patrol vehicles
LUP	lying up position
MID	mentioned in dispatches
NCO	non-commissioned officer
NVG	night-vision gear
OAG	offshore assault group
O-boats	Oberon Class submarines
OP	observation post

PTS	Parachute Training School
PTSD	post-traumatic stress disorder
RAAF	Royal Australian Air Force
RHIB	rigid hull inflatable boat
RMC	Royal Military College, Duntroon
RPG	rocket-propelled grenade
RSM	regimental sergeant major
SASR	Special Air Service Regiment
SBS	Special Boat Service (UK)
SEALs	Sea, Air and Land Forces (US Navy)
SF	special forces
SOC	Special Operations Command
SOCOM	Special Operations Command
SOE	Special Operations Executive
SOPs	standard operating procedures
spook	secret agent
TAG	tactical assault group
TTPs	tactics, techniques and procedures
UAE	United Arab Emirates
UN	United Nations
UNAMET	United Nations Assistance Mission in East Timor
UNAMIR	United Nations Assistance Mission for Rwanda
USAF	US Air Force
WMDs	weapons of mass destruction

INTRODUCTION

One of the biggest challenges facing the Special Air Service in the uncertain post 9/11 world has been to hold on to its highly trained soldiers.

This extraordinary group of Australians work in a shadowy but tremendously rewarding occupation and taxpayers invest a huge amount of money in their special skills.

In my first book, *The Amazing SAS*, many men of the SAS opened up about their exploits from the time of the 1999 East Timor crisis to the 2003 Iraq War. Their personal tales and insights, which they shared with generosity of spirit, were about extreme soldiering and how to apply strategic force while maintaining humility and humour.

Yet since 2003 many of them have resigned to pursue other opportunities in a borderless marketplace where their skills are in high demand.

Ever since World War II there has been a trickle of special forces operatives who have moved out to pursue 'other interests' but that trickle has become a torrent in the early years of the twenty-first century.

In Iraq alone there are more than 40,000 private security contractors and the best paid of those are former 'tier one' special forces operators from Australia, Britain and the US. Hundreds more are working in Afghanistan, Africa, and South-east Asia and in many other parts of the world applying their unique abilities to a variety of highly paid jobs.

I wanted to know more about what our former elite soldiers were doing in these often obscure pockets of the world and how they were finding life beyond the SAS, so I raised the idea of this book with Terry O'Farrell.

Terry left the SAS himself in 2004 after a 38-year army career mostly spent in the regiment, including two tours of duty in the Vietnam War. He is now a full colonel and deputy commander of special operations for the government of the United Arab Emirates.

He liked the idea for a new book and he offered some unique perspectives. The Middle East is the current centre of the action for serving and former special forces soldiers and Terry and his team are right at the heart of it.

One of them was George, a senior operator whom we met in *The Amazing SAS* during his time in East Timor and Afghanistan and a ferocious networker.

Soon emails were flying around the world and my initial list of names jotted on the back of an envelope grew into a long catalogue of those who were prepared to share their stories, including some upon whom fortune has not smiled as kindly as she has on heroes of the most recent conflicts.

A strong theme quickly emerged. Wherever they are and whatever they do, these former SAS soldiers are linked by a bond that is forged during their time in the elite regiment.

The new information age has also enabled them to keep in touch as never before, contributing to the creation of a shadowy and increasingly valuable global network of former brothers-in-arms that reaches across generations and national borders.

It is a network that is made all the stronger by their common experience of the gruelling SAS selection course, which requires each successful candidate to leave his old self behind and step forward into a new life.

So as I set out in late 2006 to discover more about what ex-SAS men get up to after they walk out the gate of Campbell Barracks in Perth, I was very lucky to meet up again with some of the great characters whom I encountered as I researched the first book.

They were very generous with their time and hospitality as well as opening doors into the wider network. Whether it was in a small hamlet outside Hobart or amongst the concrete, steel and glass fantasy of Dubai or in a London pub, I found an incredible and ever-expanding network of these former troops linked together across the globe and all of them with terrific stories to tell.

That is how the theme of *Soldiers Without Borders* emerged. As one former SAS man told me, it doesn't matter where he is or what he is doing; a quick call on Skype will connect him to dozens of mates. In some places, such as Dubai international airport, they can literally collide with one another in the check-in queue.

The Chief of the Australian Defence Force, Air Chief Marshal Angus Houston, is more aware than most of how difficult it is to keep special forces soldiers stimulated and in the service of the Commonwealth.

'I hold them in the very highest regard,' he told me in March, 2008. 'I think they are arguably the best special forces in the world. They are certainly the crème de la crème as far as we're concerned and they do a magnificent job for us. And therefore I am very keen to retain as many of them as I can.'

Houston is a realist about the fact that the lure of big dollars in the global security market has taken a particularly heavy toll on the regiment, but he also knows that money does not always compensate them for the support network and the standard of professional excellence of the SAS. He is keen to see SAS operators re-enlist once they have tried their hands in the outside world.

He also recognises that keeping SAS soldiers interested and rewarded is a major task.

'They are very talented people, very highly trained and you don't get into special forces unless you are an adaptable soldier. And I guess the other thing about the special forces people is, they are always wanting to improve themselves. There's a great desire to achieve the maximum amount of self-improvement to attain higher skill levels. So their professional standards are very high and they are second to none.'

In conducting the interviews for this book I found that that desire for excellence continues to drive former SAS men — able-bodied or not — in their new lives, whether working as security operators in Iraq, crisis managers in Africa, corporate risk advisers, small businessmen, politicians, ministers of religion or even stand-up comics.

Their tales are diverse and fascinating, as are their reflections on the military life that made them the people they are today.

Every quote is genuine, chosen from dozens of interviews conducted during 2006, 2007 and 2008. Where possible I have used full names. Three — Ray Jones, Rob Jamieson and 'Audrey' are pseudonyms. George, Grant, Steve, Chris and Willy could only be identified by their first names for reasons of national security.

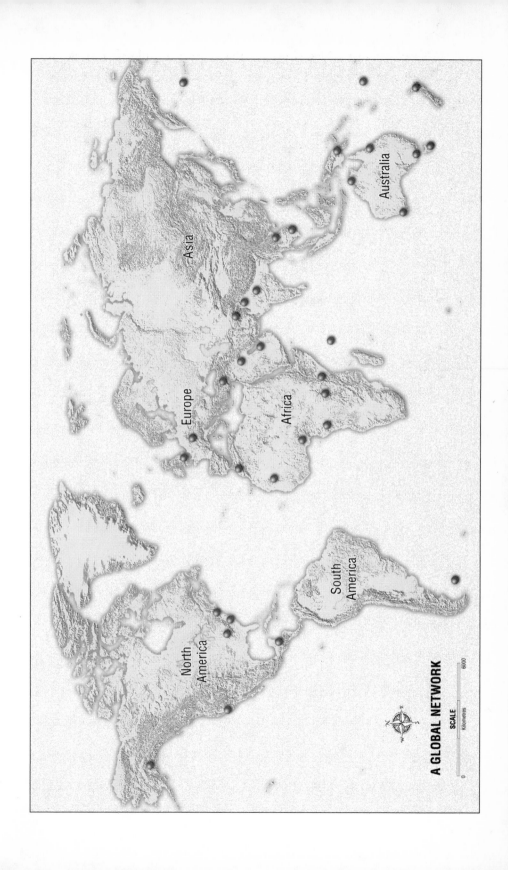

A GLOBAL NETWORK

SCALE

0   Kilometers   6000

Asia

Europe

Africa

Australia

North America

South America

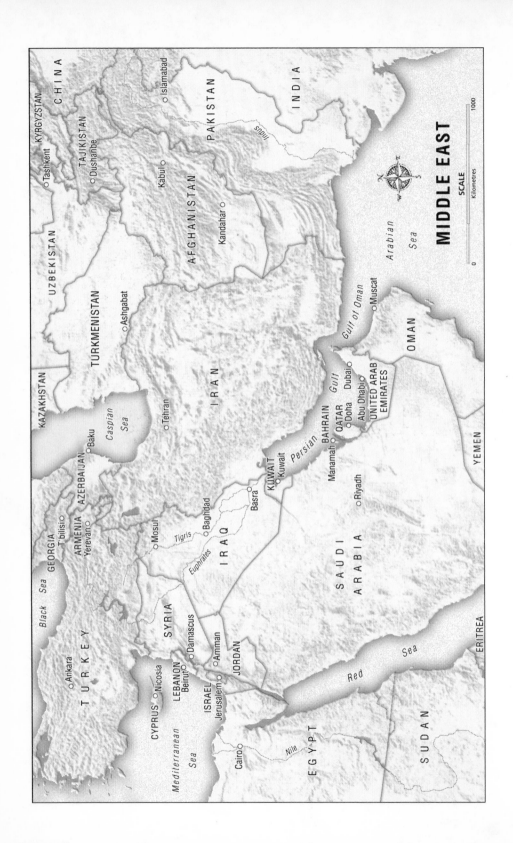

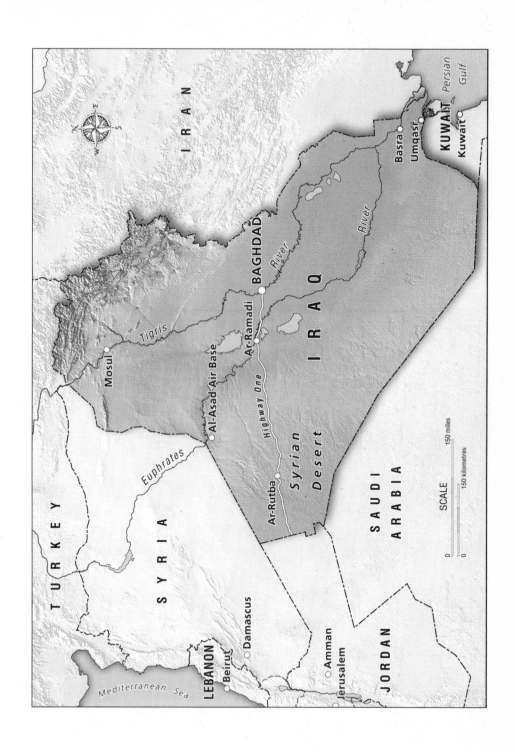

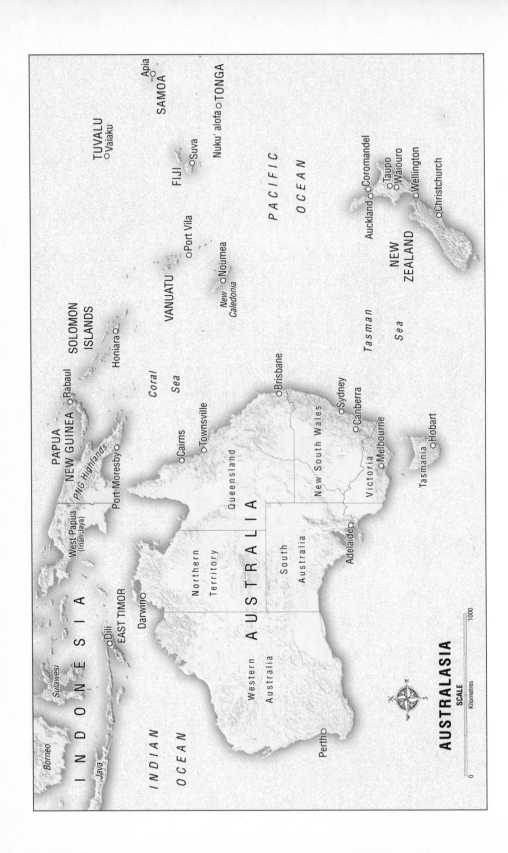

AUSTRALASIA

SCALE
0   Kilometres   1000

AWAKENING

The oily waters of the South China Sea lapped against the side of the tramp steamer as she chugged north towards her destination.

Standing against the rail, gazing out into the moonless night, Ray Jones wondered what the hell he had got himself into.

The former Australian SAS officer had only taken on the job as a favour to a mate, but it had been a shit sandwich from day one. Even the fact that it was a clandestine task, an important national security operation to collect a deadly secret military cargo on behalf of western governments, couldn't lift his spirits.

Jones knew the score with 'deniable' operations that were sanctioned secretly at the highest levels. If they turned to custard and the cover was blown, the powers-that-be would simply deny everything and disown all involved, from the military down to the spooks and, at the bottom of the food chain, hired guns like him.

After breaking down in the Java Sea, the vessel had safely negotiated one of the busiest and most pirate-prone waterways in the world, the Malacca Strait between Malaysia and the Indonesian island of Sumatra, and was now heading gingerly through the tepid, tropical waters.

Jones and his offsider were supposed to be the security detail on board, in case pirates or anyone else decided to raid it. Asia's seaways are riddled with gangs of marine criminals, equipped with fast boats, GPS and satellite phones, who hit private and merchant vessels and rob, kill or cast adrift all souls.

Jones wasn't too bothered about pirates; he had enough firepower at his disposal to dampen even the most daring swashbuckler sailing under the Jolly Roger. Besides, the government men who were on board to oversee the operation would provide plenty of muscle should he require backup.

What was eating away at him was the fact that here he was back on bloody gunfighter detail. He knew he should be in a boardroom somewhere, selling his education and military expertise to corporate high flyers or governments, not wet-nursing some half-arsed freighter and her motley crew.

The ship's master was a former navy man who, Jones thought, obviously couldn't cut it in Her Majesty's senior service and had washed up on this rust bucket. He had taken an instant dislike to Jones and his mate and had made life a misery at every turn, treating the security detail like deck hands rather than as the professionals they were.

Jones knew that keeping to himself as much as possible would be the key to getting through the weeks that stretched out in front of him. He decided then and there that this would be his final turn as a gunslinger.

The vessel arrived in port and the owners came on board. After a few days alongside, there was suddenly a sense of urgency. Several plain wooden crates were transferred from a nearby ship and stacked neatly on the wharf. Inside was a new missile system, ready to be transported supposedly to a buyer in the Middle East. The highly sensitive cargo was loaded onto the steamer and she put to sea on a westwards course towards an Arab port, but several days later she swung about and made for her real destination.

An agent from a western government's overseas spy organisation, under the guise of a Middle Eastern arms dealer, had brokered a deal with corrupt elements inside a foreign, potentially unfriendly military service to buy the weapon. Instead of heading to that troubled region it would be shipped to an allied power's research facility where its brand new guidance system would be investigated, isolated and stolen.

On this leg of the voyage Jones and his team were placed on intensive 24-hour watch, not just for pirates, but for any hostile government ships as well. Fortunately the voyage proceeded without a hitch and some time later the vessel hove to off a port. A fast, friendly navy vessel soon pulled up alongside and the cargo was transferred for shipment to allied laboratories where scientists waited to unlock its secrets. Within days valuable data concerning the weapon system would be on its way to its real western destination where countermeasures would be developed.

After more than two months on the hot, stinking vessel, Jones was delighted to bid farewell to the steamer and her bizarre skipper. While he kicked himself for taking the job in the first place, the contract had taught him many lessons, the foremost being that he was too old to be carrying a gun on dubious jobs.

'Essentially, I was no longer prepared to put up with idiots,' he says. He vowed that the boardroom and not the wardroom was where he would operate from then on.

Six years on, Ray Jones (not his real name) has built a successful international business and can laugh about his days on the tramp steamer.

In his new role as a chief executive he is always on the lookout for talent — former SAS colleagues whose qualifications might include extreme service in 'deniable' operations under deep cover in the post 9/11 hunt for Islamic terrorists.

These jobs are at the so-called 'tier one' end of the special forces spectrum, and include such tasks as providing security for agents from government overseas spying agencies and collecting human intelligence to help track down some of the world's most powerful terrorists through small para-military groups operating outside the diplomatic safety net.

Jones knows that it is only a matter of time before some of these tier-one specialists reach the end of their time in the SAS and start looking for opportunities elsewhere. He also knows that sooner or later a client will require an operative with this unique skill set.

In the post 9/11 world, many former SAS soldiers are working in hazardous or challenging jobs in new careers and businesses spanning the continents in a strategic environment that was unimaginable a decade ago.

They are part of a growing global network in what, to them, has become a borderless world.

WAR HORSES

chapter one

AFRICAN NIGHTMARE

The brand new white BMW 325Ci hits 160 kilometres an hour as it zooms along one of Abu Dhabi's numerous eight-lane freeways.

The fit, olive-skinned driver's eyes are smiling behind his designer shades and he has not a care in the world.

'Life doesn't get any better than this,' he says, as he speeds home to his luxury villa and his loving wife.

The handsome former Australian SAS sergeant looks for all the world like a well-heeled local and he works to a similar timetable: only 35 hours a week as a contract instructor with the United Arab Emirates Special Operations Command and earns at least twice his former pay. Just 11 years earlier, he was sifting through the rancid mud and filth of Kibeho in Rwanda, searching for survivors of perhaps the most savage massacre of the late twentieth century.

Pacing up and down with his Steyr rifle at the ready, George was almost daring the Rwandan Patriotic Army (RPA) soldiers at the checkpoint to take him on.

The tall, dark Australian SAS soldier was infuriated at having to stand by as these savages murdered and maimed defenceless men, women and children. He was itching for a blue.

'We could hear gunfire going off on the other side,' he recalls. 'So they were probably killing people that they'd rallied up. We were getting pissed off.'

George, a newly trained medic, was on his first operational deployment with the SAS and he and his mate Dominic were stuck at the checkpoint with the ambulance they were driving and a heavily armed infantry section from the 2nd Battalion Royal Australian Regiment.

The diggers were part of the Australian Defence Force Medical Support Force working for the United Nations Assistance Mission for Rwanda (UNAMIR). It was in April, 1995 when the appalling slaughter took place near a town called Kibeho in southern Rwanda.

The shooting had started 24 hours earlier and now three vehicles, a command Land Rover, George's ambulance and a Unimog truck carrying the 2nd Battalion security detail were trying to reach the victims. As an army medical corps officer negotiated with the RPA soldiers blocking their way, George and Dominic, another SAS soldier, moved to the far side of the vehicles and gestured to the African troops to have a go.

'These guys looked pissed and they looked young and they've got this vacant, distant look in their eyes,' George recalls. 'You can look at a bloke who is 15, 16 years old carrying an AK-47, you look him in the eyes and it is just blank, almost. And you think about what happened in the last year or six months and what part he had to play in it and then it makes you angry. You just look at him and think, "You're a piece of shit." And he doesn't care, he just doesn't care.'

George knew that if push came to shove then the hard-core boys from 2RAR would be up the guts with mud and smoke, but the fight never eventuated and the Aussies were allowed to pass.

Around the next bend, the small convoy motored into an apocalyptic scene. The massive camp that had held some 100,000 displaced people at first appeared deserted.

'We drove past hundreds of those UN blue plastic tarps strung over humpy-style twig huts, all empty,' George recalls. 'There were thousands of these things, all empty.'

They drove to the UN hospital in the centre of the camp that was secured by Zambian troops. Adjacent to it was a compound with a group of buildings and a cleared centre area. That was where anyone who had not fled the carnage was holed up.

There were about 300 people in the clearing and from within the crowd someone was shooting at the RPA soldiers. Many of these people were hard-core members of the Hutu militia, the Interahamwe, which was fighting against the RPA. For the displaced people caught in the middle it had literally become a choice between the machetes of the Interahamwe, which means 'those who fight together', or the bullets of the RPA.

'Through discussions with our translator we found that most of those people didn't want to be there. They were scared but they had no choice and it's really sad. Either they stayed because they were hiding the hard-core element that was there, or they would try to leave and be hacked to death. If they weren't hacked there they'd be hacked somewhere else, through word of mouth. So they had no choice.'

Born in New Zealand of Samoan parentage, George carries the relaxed air of his islander heritage mixed with the rugged determination and expert training of a special forces soldier. In April 1995 that training, including his skills as a patrol medic, would be put to the test on numerous occasions.

Prior to the Kibeho job, George and his small team had been driving ambulances in the Rwandan capital, Kigali. In a three-week cycle they manned aid posts at either the hospital or UN headquarters or else they just chilled out and sorted out their gear.

On 18 April they received orders to move to Kibeho, about a six-hour drive from Kigali.

They had already listened to the reports of reprisal killings in the wake of earlier mass murders and the UN's desperate attempts to keep the warring factions apart.

At the RPA checkpoint, anyone who looked suspicious or who didn't have the correct papers was simply dragged to the side of the track by the RPA and shot on the spot like a dog. It reminded George of the stories he had read about Hitler, Nazi Germany and the genocide of the Jewish people.

'Obviously the crowd's getting more and more unsettled about this because they're sitting there thinking, "Fuck, I've got to go through this and whichever way I answer a question is going to determine whether I live or die",' he says.

It was the rainy season in central Africa and the rain and mud simply added to the misery.

'All their worldly goods were in their hands so they are carrying little buckets and sheets of what-have-you. And there's a mass of people and more and more people, as they are processing through, are getting killed,' George says. 'They just start to get more and more edgy and, because if you can imagine it was a very hilly area, after a day or so of this rough justice, people started running over the hills and trying to get away. I don't know exactly what sparked that off but once the crowd started moving like that the RPA forces . . . just opened up on them and they let rip.

'They had anti-aircraft guns, light machine guns, heavy machine guns, RPGs and they just tore the hell out of them and I don't know the numbers because I didn't see them, but they reckon about 8000 were killed.'

By the time the medical convoy arrived at Kibeho some 24 hours later, it was confronted with death and injury on a biblical scale. The first people they met were fellow SAS soldiers Paul Jordan and Jon Church. A picture of the tall, fair-haired Church, also born a Kiwi, cradling a small Rwandan child as he carried it to safety had been published around the world. It was one of those defining images that came to symbolise the Kibeho massacre.

George was close to Church. The two had been on the same reinforcement cycle after passing the selection course for the SAS and had also shared their medic training.

He recalls that 'Churchie' was seriously affected by what he witnessed at Kibeho. 'When I first laid eyes on him, he had that thousand-yard stare on his face; he just couldn't believe what he'd seen because he was really a decent, honest, open person. You meet a lot of cynical people in the army, but Churchie so totally wasn't that, he really cared about people. I mean, I could see someone get hit or smashed or whatever and look at it quite objectively and go, "Fuck, I don't care!" Whereas Jon would care. He was a very empathetic fellow and, positive or negative, I'm not.'

George was angry that he had been stuck in Kigali on ambulance detail while Paul and Jon had been in the thick of the action.

'He [Church] was aghast at what he'd seen. I was talking to him about it and he kept saying he couldn't fucking believe it, "You wouldn't believe, they're just mowing — you just wouldn't believe that people could do that, just kill other people wantonly, absolutely in cold blood." I couldn't believe it either.'

At the Kibeho compound next to the UN hospital, George and Dominic were tasked with collecting the dead bodies from among the traumatised people and their meagre belongings.

'I remember mostly blue plastic basins, that's the thing that strikes me most — plastic bags and just the detritus of life. All their belongings, all the people's belongings that were lined up to go through that checkpoint earlier were just there, almost a metre deep on the ground,' George recalls. 'And another thing I remember clearly is human shit everywhere. They were living off corn and maize, whatever that stuff is, and just massive turds sitting everywhere with all corn and shit in it and you're going, "Fuck, what a way to live." I've got a photo of a turd sitting on the ground and a dead woman lying next to it, and it sums up the place, virtually.'

The team established a casualty clearing post manned by two doctors, a couple of nurses and the SAS medics.

In addition to their medical duties the SAS men assisted with security to ensure that the medical team was not in danger. They also had 'issues' with the Zambian troops securing the compound.

'We had a Red Cross element with us and they wanted to go in and take out anyone who was injured or dead, because [in] all that shit that I'm talking about, there were dead people lying everywhere and obviously it's not a healthy state,' he says.

The problem was that the Red Cross had asked for help, but due to their non-violent ethos, they refused to allow the soldiers to carry their weapons.

In a highly charged environment dripping with guns, machetes and hidden warriors, there was no way the diggers were going to agree to that.

'We said, "Well, we're not going to help you then because we're not going anywhere without weapons."

'"Oh, but we really need to go and get the bodies", they said.

'"Yes, we'll do that", and we started moving again.

'"Oh, but you can't take weapons."

'"Well, fuck. Either we come in with weapons or we're not going to help you." They are appallingly naïve in that respect.'

Eventually the Red Cross gave way and George and his comrades went in armed. They immediately established machine gun positions on vital points on the high ground.

'We moved into the core of the place and that was interesting in itself, because most people were aghast, just sitting there almost inert, wet, unhappy from the trauma that had occurred. But some — and you could see them absolutely clearly, they stuck out like sore thumbs — were standing there saying, "Get out of here, get out of here." We just pushed in by force, occupied the place and we started moving bodies out of there.'

Within minutes the soldiers had dug a huge pit and buried the first 50 of what would be many hundreds of bodies.

'The worst ones I think were the kids, little kids you could just pick up with one hand and move with. I remember clearly — and it is disturbing, I can understand why some people are pretty messed up with it — we wore masks and heavy, heavy plastic gloves,' he says. 'I couldn't understand how someone, either they're freshly dead or not, you grab someone by the arm and all the skin moves off, you know, sloughs off, and the smell was fuckin' heinous. The other thing that I remember very clearly was the amount of swelling that a body generates.'

As the men moved through the putrid mass of humanity searching for dead bodies or survivors, they were struck by the resignation of the victims. They would be cooking their corn over damp, smoky fires and simply point silently to a nearby pile of rubbish. The troops would shift the garbage and uncover yet another corpse.

'You move something and there's a face, and you pick it up and take it and put it in the pit.'

One of the most pathetic sights that George saw was in the hospital. It had been run by Médecins Sans Frontieres (MSF) but the doctors had fled when the orgy of violence began. Several people, probably those judged least likely to survive anyway, had been left behind in the beds.

Black humour has always helped soldiers cope with the worst aspects of war. In the SAS a good dose of black humour is never far away and as George and Dominic cleared the hospital they took to giving the dead nicknames.

'There was one we called the Donut Eater. I don't think he was a fat man but he was a fat man by the time we got to him, he'd bloated so heavily and his eyes were bulbous and his lips were enormous so we nicknamed him the Donut Eater,' George recalls. 'The other one was the Maggoty Cat and I'll never forget him for the life of me. We were walking through and Dominic's going, "Ah yeah, there's another one." I say, "Okay, I'll get the boys."

'Obviously he must have got out of his bed, fallen on the ground, crawled along a bit — he still had a tube coming out of his arm and he was just face down with an infestation of maggots out of his back, and he had an injury to his head. So there was a big pool of fluid coming, like black tarry slick fluid off his head, and for all purposes he was dead. So I stuck my foot, if you can imagine, he's lying there, my foot under his shoulder and just kicked to flip him over and have a look at him.

'And when I flipped him over — Dominic was standing on the far side looking into the next room — he went, "Arrgh", made this horrible noise that scared the absolute shit out of both of us. So we got the infantry, they took him back to the CCP (casualty clearing post) and he ended up in our ambulance, the old Maggoty Cat. He stunk like no tomorrow. We actually encouraged them to throw him in the pit because he was as good as, he was really fucked over, but they took him back to the hospital.'

For three days solid the men cleared bodies and searched for the living.

'We got to the point where death was no longer an issue, it was fucking commonplace,' says George.

They found people hiding in the oddest of places. Some had been almost submerged for days in the contents of a pit toilet or camouflaged under piles of rotting corpses. They would never willingly emerge from their hiding places either, so George and his mates had to coerce them and assure them there were no RPA troops nearby.

'Everything we were doing was shadowed by the RPA who had control of the area still and were watching. Every time we sent a helicopter out or an ambulance left, like with the Maggoty Cat, we would hide in the ambulance people we were trying to get the fuck out of there at the same time — you know, kids or whatever.'

RPA troops would search the vehicles and remove anyone who was not injured, so the Aussies took to bandaging all passengers to make them look badly hurt.

George describes the Kibeho experience in two words: 'wholesale slaughter'.

On the second day they were heading back to the massacre site when they saw a group of people on the side of the road. These people had been trying to escape and were set upon by bandits who had hacked them up and stolen their meagre possessions.

'They've got hack marks from where they've been holding their arms up. They've been hobbled because they've chopped their Achilles tendons so they can't run. But they wouldn't kill them,' George recalls. 'I couldn't understand that. These guys were just lying on the side of the road, had been hacked, anything they had was taken, and they were just lying there. We dressed them, treated them, and we took them to Médecins Sans Frontieres. Not much else to do.'

Once the fields had been cleared of dead and injured, George and the team moved into the hospital to assist wherever they could.

'We had some really good surgeons there. I helped with a couple of orthopaedic surgeons and whatever, they were really good guys, intensive care surgeons, taught us an awful lot of stuff. They'd sit and talk because there wasn't that much work to do. We'd have a laugh and drink or whatever and the next day you could be in there, scrub up and go and give them a hand.'

During one operation the anaesthetist was inserting a tube into a patient's throat. A video camera was set up nearby to record the procedure for training purposes.

'Oh Jesus he smells!' the anaesthetist exclaimed as he took a close look. 'My God!' he added as he started to pull a long worm out of the man's throat.

'And no shit, it was like four feet long,' says George. 'He's pulling it out and he says, "Did you get that on camera?" And they didn't get it on the camera. So he stuck it all back in his mouth, just laid it in his mouth and went through it again and then at the end, like, "Oh my God!" and then pulled this fuckin' worm out. So funny.'

Thousands of people died in the Kibeho massacre and this small band of Australians saved hundreds of lives as they swam against a deadly tide of tribalism, blood lust and murder.

Four of them, Corporal Andy Miller, Warrant Officer Rod Scott, Lieutenant Steve Tilbrook and Captain Carol Vaughan-Evans, were awarded the Medal of Gallantry for their extraordinary deeds.

chapter two

BLACK HAWKS DOWN

There were six Black Hawk helicopters in the air on that fateful winter's night. Two sniper machines were out in front, then came three more flying abreast carrying SAS troops, with the command machine at the rear of the formation. They looked just like wasps as they buzzed towards the target.

It was the night of 12 June 1996 and the SAS counterterrorist squadron was at the High Range Training Area west of Townsville. The tactical assault group (TAG) was practising the most dangerous activity of them all, one in which there is no margin for error: men simultaneously fast-roping from multiple helicopters and attacking a target at night.

'Normally we'd all fly in a line straight because it's safer — you're always next to each other and as you're jostling around trying to get into position, that's the best [way to] be until you are almost there and then you fan out,' George says.

'But for some reason, and I don't understand it because I wasn't part of any of that planning, they flew three abreast with the snipers up. Snipers up is not an issue, neither here nor there, because they're well separated and they're ahead. But normally these three would be in a line ahead. We'd practised this by day, three in line, coming around onto target and our target was a fire support base, FSB Barbara, which is virtually an artillery gun position on the top of a hill, but we'd put structures on it for us to attack.'

George, who was a lance corporal in the TAG that night, understood the mission scenario was to simulate the rescue of hostages from a hostile environment similar to the Khmer Rouge stronghold where Australian tourist David Wilson was killed in Cambodia in 1994.

'So that was our aim, to be able to be competent at resolving an issue like that.'

After practising the mission earlier that day they had paused for a hot lunch.

'Two very good friends of mine were killed there [that night] from my [SAS] selection — Glen Hagan, who was from the same battalion as me, and Jon Church, who I went to Rwanda with. I remember sitting eating — they bring out those army hot boxes, a little aluminium tin with a whole stack of trays of pre-prepared food — and sitting there talking, eating this shit, having a laugh with Glen.'

Hagan was sitting there taping a torch onto his weapon as they talked.

'We hadn't advanced to the point in the regiment yet where we were using M16s for this job because we were on-line for counterterrorism, which meant we were using primarily MP5s, 9mm weapons. At that point we hadn't got to the point of being able to have integral weapon mounts and whatever, so we were black plastic taping things all over the place. Now we do it with the M4s, we can put anything on the damn thing. I remember him doing that and lending him some tape.'

He also remembers standing beside Jon Church, talking to him and looking at the sunset.

'We were good mates, we travelled through Europe together when we had some time off from Rwanda, we went and drove for a week from Paris through to Berlin and back into Amsterdam and had a fucking whale of a time. I was talking to his father about it at his funeral, [how we were] just shooting the shit, having a laugh, and oddly enough not 20 minutes after that we're mounting on helos. And, as it should be for an exercise, the helos came in and landed on this hill; we're just attacking that hill, so they'd fly off and they'd do a circuit to come back around and on to target.'

George was on board the machine designated Black 3 on the extreme right-hand side of the three-abreast formation as they attacked the target in the pitch-black night. He has a crystal-clear recollection of the collision and the aftermath.

'We got to 30 seconds, and so everyone's up on their haunches, doors are open and you've got the rope and everyone's virtually leaning, ready to get out of the plane,' George recalls. 'We'd been given 30 seconds so we'd know for a fact — the helicopter flies differently, it slows down and it's cutting in ready to flare and stop. That's no doubt our biggest issue, is how long it takes him to get stable so we can get the fuck off the plane. We'd rather he just came in "boof!" and we got off. But they want to fuck around and that's why we do those exercises, to reduce the amount of time it takes them.

'I remember them saying in orders that they were going to drop mortars beyond the target as a preparatory action for us. And I knew we had people on the ground as safety but they'd be further back. If you can imagine ... the front's behind me, the two pilots, the loadies [loadmasters], and the right door's open.'

A dozen armed soldiers were sitting on the floor of the machine.

As it approached the target George glanced forward to see whether there was any strike from the mortars.

'It's actually very cool. It's like that movie *Black Hawk Down* — it's exactly like it. You know they look like wasps flying over, it's as cool as shit. So I really enjoyed that aspect of it too. So I'm looking forward, all you can see is the silhouette of the pilot, the green illuminated instruments as they're talking and flying and you can really see bugger all of what's in front. The pilots are flying on NVGs [night vision gear], it's very unnerving because by the time we get to 30 seconds, you imagine this time frame for a target, we're high, we go low and they just fly really hard, as hard as they can, low to the target so that it muffles sound, all that sort of shit. So they come popping up and then they're there. It's amazingly exhilarating and exciting but horribly, horribly dangerous in the same respect and more so if you're flying helicopters side by side.'

What happened next is as clear to him now as it was in 1996.

'I could see a green glow, which was another helicopter, which I thought was cool, and this is all in that 30 seconds. I'm looking at that and looking at the other helicopter and thinking about our proximity, and we were quite distant from him.

'I'm looking at it and just see this — it might have been inside the helicopter — a really faint red glow, something from the loadmaster and I'm watching that with interest and then a God almighty flash when the two helos struck each other. And we were right on the hill we were about to hit. I know; I went back there with a mate of mine.

'Flash! Our target was here, the helos impacted maybe 250–300 metres back, so they would have collided another 400 metres beyond that. So we were right on the fuckin' cusp of it. Everyone in all those three helicopters would have been up, ready and blood boiling, ready to go.

'You can imagine, there's nothing but noise, *whvv whvv whvv*, that sort of noise, you know what it's like in a helicopter, you can't hear shit and we had hearing protection on as well. So the world is whatever is in your mind. I had this kind of classical music sort of scenario going on. I saw this flash start and then like a falling star keeping moving. And until I got over there on the ground I thought it was only one helicopter, because I had thought seriously that a mortar had hit one of them, or something like that had occurred.

'So I saw this flash, and as we tracked, because we were so low in tracking into target, I saw it hit the ground. The one I saw at least hit the deck hit the way it should, wheels down, then rotated and the blades, I saw them disintegrate. This is all with the only light I had, the light generated by the flames from the chopper. The blades all fell apart. And this is horribly quick — we're still coming in on the side. So I saw that and I saw someone get up and get out of the thing and in retrospect that was Dominic [from Rwanda].

'Our pilot, and they must be well trained, was horribly quick — lights on, everything on, and landed and we just ran straight out of the plane over to see what we could do. And it wasn't until we got over there — the bird I got to had come back down and both of them [were] horribly on fire. There were already about six people on that aircraft pulling people off and I ran to the rear one, me and a couple of mates of mine from our helo. And by the time we got there, not that many people there, the thing's just horribly on fire and stacks of people inside. I know about the front one from what I've talked about to other people, but the rear one I remember clearly because I saw it. We honestly thought it was the right way up but it was actually upside down.'

Unfortunately the chopper's loadmaster was still hooked in.

'We couldn't understand, "Where the fuck is it because it should be above?", so it took us maybe a minute to work that shit out because it's a fucking furious fire, to get him out.'

Each SAS soldier is either a trained medic or signaller (chook). After the choppers hit the ground, the medics worked overtime trying to save lives, while the chooks carted bodies back and forth.

George worked on the loadmaster who had a broken hip and other serious injuries. 'The loadmaster, I remember he had a broken hip because they taught me this thing on the medics' course where you spring the pelvis, like when you're doing an overall check of someone. Bleeding in the pelvis, particularly in a traumatic scenario like that, is a bad thing,' he says. 'So you check fundamentally that bones are intact, all that sort of shit, and you put your hands either side of their hips and you just push. And we did that in training and everyone's like, "Yeah who knows what a fuckin' broken pelvis is like?" I do, it didn't collapse, it was him, he went, "Aaaagh!" The noise he made, it was fuckin' obscene, absolutely obscene but in a funny way I felt good — "Yeah, he's got a broken pelvis, send him off, write that on his card." So at least the training's good in that respect.'

He also found his good mate Glen, but he mistook him for another soldier. 'It wasn't until I took his armour off and undid his flight suit, he had this big eagle on his chest as a tattoo, that I recognised him. "Fuck!" But try as we might, when we did, a mate of mine and I did CPR, the classic — I'd do five beats, he'd breathe, but he was absolutely cactus.'

The helmets on all the soldiers inside the chopper had been torn free of their inner liners and George recalled thinking they looked like old

Russian tank commanders with their skull caps. The men had been badly smashed up by their weapons and other hard objects inside the Black Hawk. Many suffered broken limbs and ribs from their rifles and in some cases the force had completely bent the steel barrels.

'I grabbed [one man's] arm and it was jelly all the way along,' he says.

He began administering first aid as he had been taught for trauma victims. 'He was still breathing . . . but his chest was squishy as well and I knew his brain was shutting down. He was fucked up.'

After all the survivors had been dealt with, he and an officer swept the crash site searching for bodies. They covered them with blankets and placed glow sticks on them as they went.

'As we were going along we'd double check, make sure they were fucking dead. It's pretty poor form to leave someone there who's not.' George says.

The following day George and his mates had the sad task of clearing out the barracks at RAAF base Garbutt in Townsville. The base is home to the army's 5th Aviation Regiment which flies the Black Hawk fleet.

'Almost all of [SAS] land troop were either dead or in hospital,' he says simply.

It was a standing joke on those sorts of trips that 'every night's lady's night'. That means they worked hard and played hard. 'So everyone had all their gear ready to go out and large it up with the boys, so it was fucking sad.'

What struck him was the differences between the men's personal habits. Some had all their gear neatly folded on the bed ready to go, others had it scattered around like a pigsty.

The saddest thing for him was the impact of the tragedy on the families.

'They've never seen what they do and they don't understand it, whereas if you see it, you do it, you've got a good gauge of why and when and how. At least we could close it in our minds because we'd seen them dead, we'd seen the aircraft burning and stuff like that and it made sense because we knew exactly what happened and how it happened, whereas other people were sitting there thinking, and possibly imagining stuff that wasn't even real.'

George says nothing haunts him 'in his heart' about that dark night, but he does have stark memories of the tragedy that claimed so many of his good mates.

Despite the tragic outcomes of both Rwanda and the Black Hawk crash, he feels proud when he reflects on how he and his comrades performed.

'Everyone worked as they should have done and everyone did everything they could have done,' he says.

But there are aspects of the Black Hawk incident in particular that leave a bad taste in his mouth. The treatment of the commanders on the ground, particularly squadron commander Major Bob Hunter and his 2IC, Captain Sean Bellis, a former helicopter pilot, appalled George and the others involved in the crash.

Hunter and Bellis both left the military and another high-flying officer caught up in the tragedy and its aftermath, Ian Young, also left soon after.

chapter three

WHO DARES

Colonel Terry O'Farrell is resplendent in his army rig. He gazes straight into the camera with a hint of a smile for his teenage son, Liam, who is taking the photograph.

O'Farrell, whose campaign experiences with the Australian Special Air Service Regiment stretch from Vietnam to Afghanistan, wears a colonel's two stars on his shoulders, three rows of Australian decorations and a winged emblem above his left breast.

But this is not an Australian Army uniform. The sand-coloured beret and winged dagger of the SAS, which he wore proudly for 38 years, are nowhere to be seen. Instead, he is wearing the uniform of the army of the United Arab Emirates. It sits very comfortably on him in his current role as the assistant commander at Special Operations Command in Abu Dhabi and in his new rank of colonel.

With his long career in the Perth-based SAS Regiment coming to an end, old 'Steel Eyes' O'Farrell had seen it all. From two tours of Vietnam and being wounded in action twice, the boy from Coffs Harbour had risen through the ranks from private to major, but in 2004 he hit the wall.

Very few soldiers who are commissioned from the non-officer 'other ranks' under the Warrant Officer Commissioning Scheme reach the lofty heights of colonel in the Australian army. That is the preserve of the 'Ruperts' (officers) who graduate either from Duntroon or another officer training school. So 'Tof', as he is known to the SAS community, and his wife, Lee, faced some tough decisions.

Although he was as fit as a fiddle and possessed more corporate knowledge about the Australian SAS than almost any other person, it counted for little. The 57-year-old's days at his beloved regiment were fast coming to a close and he faced the inevitable journey to the 'retirement paddock' down the road at Karrakatta Army Reserve Barracks by the Swan River, not far from SAS headquarters at Campbell Barracks, Swanbourne.

'I just thought, "Fuck, that's not what I signed up for. I signed up to bloody soldier on",' he says.

But while the Australian Army was incapable of finding him a job that would put his accumulated wisdom and tactical expertise to good use, somebody else was watching and waiting.

One day while O'Farrell was acting executive officer of SASR, the regiment was notified that the Crown Prince of Abu Dhabi and deputy commander of the armed forces of the United Arab Emirates, Sheikh Mohammed bin Zayed Al Nahyan, would be visiting. One of the sheikh's private secretaries arrived with the advance party and O'Farrell spent the day with him.

As he was about to leave, the sheikh's man said, 'Are you thinking of separating at all in the near future?'

'As a matter of fact I am, and we're looking around for something suitable.'

'Would you be interested in coming to UAE?'

'I'll have to talk to the chief of staff [wife Lee] about it,' O'Farrell said.

When he arrived home that night he told her he had been offered a job.

Around the same time, a large industrial firm from Iraq had been in touch with him.

'We hear you're on the verge of getting out.'

'You blokes have got bloody good intelligence! Where did you get that from?'

'Oh, we just heard. So we'd like you to come over and run security for us.'

'They were involved in reconstruction of the oil fields,' O'Farrell says. 'So we tic-tacked on that for a while.'

Eventually they came back and said, 'Look, we definitely want you.'

The carrot was a package of US$160,000 a year and a contract working six weeks on and two weeks off. To an army major on about A$80,000 a year that was a large inducement but O'Farrell had seen dozens of men chase the big bucks to Iraq and it often ended in tears.

Working as a security contractor in post-war Iraq offered lots of money and excitement, but it carried a huge personal risk without the support and safety networks of the military.

'We thought about that for a while, we did.'

'No we didn't!' says Lee.

'In the end we sat out the back over a couple of tins and a few olives and said, "Nah, we don't want to be doing this rubbish where we're backwards and forwards and I'm in danger and all that sort of stuff. So let's take the UAE offer",' he says.

The job involved moving the family to Abu Dhabi, where the military is based, to become counterterrorism adviser to the Special Operations Commander, General Juma Al Bawardi Al Falasi. But by the time O'Farrell got there, that had changed.

'He didn't think he needed a CT adviser and so I went down to what's called the Special Operations Battalion as a special operations adviser, the first time that had been done in the command as a civvy,' O'Farrell says.

The family took to life in Abu Dhabi like ducks to water.

The UAE is made up of seven emirates: Abu Dhabi (the capital), Dubai, Sharjah, Fujairah, Ajman, Ras el-Khaimah and Umm al-Quwain. It has played a pivotal, albeit low-profile role in the campaign against terrorism. The UAE was a key US ally in the 1990–91 Gulf War, hosts some large US and coalition military bases and is a crucial staging post for the movement of people and supplies into and out of the Middle East area of operations.

If Dubai is the flashy younger brother of the Emirates, then Abu Dhabi, a reclaimed island about 90 minutes' drive south-west along the

Persian Gulf, is the solid older brother. There is money and plenty of it in the oil-rich emirate, but unlike Dubai, which has no oil but is the trading hub of the nation, Abu Dhabi does not feel the need to be ostentatious.

The family lives in a comfortable downtown apartment. O'Farrell leaves home for work at 7 a.m. in his sparkling new V8 GMC Suburban station wagon and is often back by 2 or 3 p.m. Liam attends the best international school in town and the family is plugged into an active expatriate social network.

Three months into the job, the sheikh's private secretary asked O'Farrell how he was enjoying it.

'It's good. Life's pretty cruisy, I go to work at seven and I'm home at two, no real responsibilities, all I have to do is give the commanding officer advice if he wants it; if he doesn't, well okay.'

The private secretary said, 'Sheikh Mohammed didn't really want you to come across and do that, he really wanted you to be prominent in the command. We'd like you to accept an offer of a commission. Come into the army as a colonel and run operations.'

'So I thought about that for about two seconds and said, "Yeah, okay"!'

That was in September 2005 and suddenly the former SAS Major Terry O'Farrell, who, if he had stayed in the Australian Army, would have been working out his time quietly at a reserve unit in Perth, was a full colonel and chief of operations in the special operations command of a key nation in the world's most volatile region. With Iran just over the water, the Saudis across the desert and al-Qaeda and its fellow travellers all around, old 'Steel Eyes' knew what he was signing up for.

His Irish/Sicilian ancestry, dark piercing eyes and olive skin, a soldier's weatherbeaten features and a well-groomed moustache meant he could easily pass for an Arab. He has sworn loyalty to his new masters and says this is absolutely genuine. He also knew there would be deep suspicions in some quarters back home, but says he would never compromise the security of Australia, including by divulging any unique tactics, techniques and procedures (TTPs) of the Australian SAS.

Fortunately, the UAE special forces already had their own procedures, largely based on the British SAS model.

Being the first westerner to be appointed a colonel in the UAE army threw up some unique problems. 'It's quite funny – they had to come to grips with the pay bit so they said, "We'll have to pay you as a UAE colonel", which is bugger all, peanuts. So I get my pay in two lots – I get an automatic payment through the banking system as a colonel and I go over to GHQ every month and get a fistful of cash! Which is a problem because as soon as I arrive home, this pair [Lee and Liam] are onto me – "Oh Dad! You're cashed up!" So they're in for their take.'

O'Farrell was confronted with some very sensitive live operations right from the start.

The UAE is a key member of the US-led coalition in the campaign against Islamic extremism, as well as being a very devout Muslim society. Its ruler and President of the UAE, Sheikh Khalifa bin Zayed Al Nahyan, together with his younger brother, Sheikh Mohammed, inherited a legacy from their father, the UAE's founding President, Sheikh Zayed bin Sultan Al Nahyan, which is taken very seriously. This is a benign and generous dictatorship which looks after its own, provided they don't get out of line.

The Emirates are increasingly important in the secretive world of special forces. With a 4000-strong special operations command and with close links to British, American and Australian SF units including the SAS, it is a substantial contributor. Its leaders have shown the political will to confront terrorism and UAE was one of the first Muslim nations to condemn the Taliban regime in Afghanistan. It also has special forces troops deployed there and it funds aid projects throughout the war-torn country.

How it has managed all of this without suffering a single terrorist attack on its soil from al-Qaeda or its offshoots remains a mystery. Being responsible for the country's counterterrorism capability means O'Farrell is as well placed as anyone to ponder why this is so.

'First of all in this country you only have a small local population. Out of the five-odd million people here, only 800,000 are Emiratis,' he says. 'And most of those Emiratis are very well looked after. So there might be a bit of dissent in terms of religious freedom and what's actually allowed to happen in this country but in a general sense that core population is very well off.'

Because of that, and the speedy and clinical silencing of any dissent, there is little or no room for terrorist groups to gain a foothold.

'They don't have that fertile ground that you have in countries where you have the conditions already set – poverty, everything that goes with poverty, corruption and all that sort of thing and it's just fertile ground, and a mass population. The rest of the [expatriate] population that is here is here for one reason and that's to make money and to enjoy life.'

In addition the sheikhs are constantly on the lookout for bright kids to send overseas to study.

'Dad comes along to said sheikh and says, "Look, eldest son here, pretty sharp at school. What are we going to do with him?" And so these kids are then sent off to America or Australia or England and they are given a world-class education and all that's paid for through the petrodollar. They are hardly the kind of guys that are going to turn around and attack the country and become dissidents. So there is quite a benevolent distribution of funds in that respect.'

The second critical factor is the security apparatus in the UAE, with which O'Farrell is intimately involved.

'There is a very, very physical presence here of security and it's layered. On all our vital assets for example, our waterways, our bridges, there are police, there are military forces on these things,' O'Farrell says. Plus, there are really good entry and exit procedures. In a general sense you fly into Dubai, okay you think it's pretty quick and you come through. But they've got a really good interconnected system with the world in terms of trying to identify people who might be suspicious.

The third factor is the one that is most difficult to quantify: money.

A massive amount of cash moves through the Emirates, mainly through the Dubai free trade zone. Property is one prime method of money-laundering the world over and in Dubai there are dozens of

40-storey apartment blocks standing virtually empty, despite every unit having been sold. At the new Dubai Marina it is an eerie feeling standing on a sixteenth-floor balcony at night, surrounded by towering blocks of luxury apartments with just the occasional lonely light flickering.

'There's definitely a lot of money that goes through Dubai and no one's quite sure where all that money comes from,' O'Farrell says. 'It might be just a case of you don't want to shit in your own back yard. I don't know.'

The UAE has become a vital ally and partner to the western special forces and intelligence networks. 'The UAE defence policy, although it hasn't been fully articulated in terms of a green paper and a white paper, in the general sense is non-expeditionary,' O'Farrell says. 'It's focused on home defence and the fact that we do have a special operations element in Afghanistan is not an aberration, I think it is a very good adjunct to the defence of this country in that . . . it's based on forward defence.'

The UAE provides the coalition with an Arab Islamic perspective on some intelligence hot potatoes and it enjoys better access than any other Arab nation to western intelligence. But that access is limited because of America's close and abiding links with Israel. A major strategic problem is that the United States military/industrial complex will happily sell weapons to the UAE, but the US State Department prevents many source codes and other vital data from being supplied to them. For coalition operations in Afghanistan that can be a nightmare.

'You're trying to get commonality, equipment and codes, crypt [encryption] data and all that sort of thing and all of a sudden you get, "Oh no, you guys can't have that", because the State Department won't release it. And this makes a huge problem when you're trying to bloody be part of a coalition. The American military understand it. But the laws of the land are exactly that.'

O'Farrell regards the close relationship between UAE special forces and their counterparts in the US and Australia as crucial.

'We have a large engagement, a big, comprehensive engagement with the American special forces. Primarily we're hooked up with Special

Operations Command Central, which is part of Central Command. We meet on a three-monthly basis, on the basis of a five-year training plan. And so there is a series of combined exercises we have with the Americans, both special forces and [US Navy] SEALS.'

'The other big bilateral relationship is with the Australian special forces and we have a similar five-year plan, and we engage with them on a yearly basis in a major training exercise and then we have a number of other issues or initiatives that occur. Last year we had a full colonel out there, he did six months' language training and then spent three or four months in the headquarters. They got him out to everything so it's a really good deal on behalf of the Australians – they're really working hard to get a foothold and maintain the links between those two forces.'

That foothold has extended to joint operations in the Chora Valley region of Afghanistan where the Australian Special Forces Task Group, made up of SAS troops and Commandos based at Tarin Kowt, has encountered some fierce Taliban opposition.

'The boys absolutely loved it because the Australians are really good in the way that they deal with them. They didn't exclude them from any of the intelligence that they had, they sat down with them and did the combined planning and the operation and they went out with them and they stayed with them. That doesn't always happen with other relationships. So that was a real eye-opener, I think, for them,' he says.

It is not easy for Muslim troops to fight in another Islamic country, but the Emiratis have worked in the US-led combined special operations task force. They have killed Taliban fighters, as have the French, German, Norwegian and Dutch special forces troops operating in the task force. Less well known are the Jordanian and Egyptian contributions, including an Egyptian field hospital at Bagram air base north of Kabul.

One of O'Farrell's first tasks in Abu Dhabi was to raise a new counterterrorism force. Along with a small band of UAE national officers, he built the concept and ran a series of exercises.

'It was full on, went into operations and immediately got involved in a number of quite sensitive operations, live ops, and they went off pretty well so that was a good start. Plus I also raised what's now called Joint Task Force 71, which is specifically designed for counterterrorism tasks, and they hadn't been able to do that.

'So that was good, it got me a foundation, got me a reputation around the place very quickly because I was out and about briefing people on the concept. I had to go and brief the chief of staff, basically the chief of the armed forces, I had to brief the sheikh on a number of those other missions as well.'

When O'Farrell arrived in Abu Dhabi there was a small number of expatriate Australian soldiers already there. Now there are 20 former Australian SAS men working for Special Operations Command.

O'Farrell vowed he would not poach any soldiers from the SAS. He promised the then head of Australia's Special Operations Command, Major General Mike Hindmarsh, that he would not head hunt and would only consider SAS men who were leaving the regiment anyway.

The accusation which O'Farrell finds more amusing than disturbing is that he 'cherry picked' blokes that he knows and likes.

'To a degree that's true, I have looked after guys that I've liked and worked with, but one reason for that is they're all professionals and good at their job. The other is that you've got to have harmony in places like this,' he says. 'You can imagine what it would be like if we weren't getting on. There's 20 of us here and if there was a splinter group in that it would just be hopeless.'

Places such as Dubai and Abu Dhabi offer significant advantages for expatriate former soldiers.

'The big thing is they come [here] for the family life. You don't get that in Iraq,' he says. 'And the money in Iraq, while it may be initially a bit better, there's also no guarantee your contract is going to be renewed. Plus, let's face it, you're in the bloody front line in Iraq. You could get knocked off any time and I don't know that a lot of these companies have thought through that piece, where [if] you do get bumped off . . . what sort of compensation and those issues — whether they've been really covered or not.'

Compensation is more a social than a legal contract in the Emirates. If an expatriate trainer is injured or killed there is an understanding that the family will be cared for.

'We lost a Brit guy last year who was on leave, he was paragliding in Cyprus, he had four kids, four boys. Sheikh Mohammed opened an account straight away for those boys and they will have their schooling paid for straight through until they finish university.'

O'Farrell compares this with his frustrations when dealing with the Department of Veterans Affairs in Australia after being wounded in Vietnam years ago.

He says General Juma is also very loyal to his contract officers. 'He will only get rid of them if they've been absolutely stupid and done something right out of the ordinary. But if he's hired you personally — mate, you've got to burn down the Empire State Building before you'll be gotten rid of.'

The Emiratis can also be ruthless but usually in a subtle, non-confronting way.

'People have arrived at their office and put the key in and the key doesn't work anymore. That's the signal that you're no longer wanted here. So they can be pretty ruthless here as well, whereas in the Australian system you've got to go through all that rigmarole of bloody trying to get rid of someone. Here it's either one way or the other.'

Many SAS soldiers reach the point where they are torn between family life and their job. Being away from home for months on end and missing key family milestones, such as a child's first steps, takes a heavy toll.

O'Farrell understands that better than most, having spent months and even years away from his first family. 'You go away and the child is crawling and you come home and it's running. You've missed all of that. And a lot of young blokes don't understand it at that stage, but they certainly miss it later on when they haven't really bonded with their kids or the marriage break-up occurs. It really cuts.'

chapter four

LEAVING SAS

'George, where are you? We're supposed to be there already,' says Audrey.

But George is lost in another world, gazing at his computer as images from his past life in the SAS emerge and fade on the screen.

Pictures of him and his mates amid the carnage of the Kibeho massacre in Rwanda; on patrol in Afghanistan; posing in East Timor; back in Perth parachuting; diving; clowning for the camera; focused on their weapons; up to their armpits in water and muck.

'It's funny, because I can just sit there for anything up to 20 minutes, staring, just watching images come up of my mates on patrol or things that I've done,' he says. 'I really loved being in the Australian Army but I am happy to be out of it now . . . It's a demanding lifestyle.'

For his first seven years in the SAS he was a specialist water operator. He had only retrained to become a free-faller (parachutist) as a way to wangle his way into Afghanistan as a patrol commander in 2002. For obvious reasons, there was no requirement for SAS water operators in the snow-capped mountains, fertile green valleys and arid deserts of that troubled country.

'I was quite happy with that once I'd changed; I was very happy with it.'

Funnily enough, his brother was an instructor at the parachute training school in Nowra, New South Wales, where George went to train as a free-faller.

Says George, 'I turned up at the PTS and I hadn't told him I was going. When I turned up he said, "What the fuck are you doing here?"

I said, "I'm in the SAS", and he got into the SAS the very next year. It was quite natural sibling rivalry.'

Water being George's natural element, some of his happiest memories are of working amphibiously or underwater. One of the most exciting exercises he ever did was diving on the Collins Class submarines.

'When the Collins subs came on station we had to validate what we used to do on the O-boats [the Oberon Class submarines], rig up little sets so we could switch from air to oxygen, [work out] how we're going to fit it in, how we're going to fit a force underneath the casing. We didn't have to change much but it's really amazing as it's going down and the sub starts to sink. They're blowing out all the air ballast from the side tanks, it's a horrible noise like something out of *Raiders of the Lost Ark*,' he says. 'You're sitting there entombed in this dark little cave and as the boat starts going down this water starts flooding in and you can see it all coming at you and, "Fuck, this is wild!" It's the sort of thing that you're really happy to be doing because who in the world sits outside a submarine when it's going deep seas? Great, it's really enjoyable.

'We were filming it to make sure we could get a record of all the drills so that it's easier to teach other people. We filmed ourselves sneaking way up onto the back of the submarine. The whole principle is, the sub would come up "x" distance away from the target, everyone would come out of the pressure hull under the casing, 'cause there's only so long you can tolerate being outside a submarine. There's only so long you can tolerate being on the air, because the system will run out. So "x" amount of distance from the target the sub will come up, we'll come out of the pressure hull then put ourselves in the casing and go on air.

'And down she goes. By rights the sub should come within metres of whatever your target is. So through a series of taps and whistles and knocks and whatever we communicate with them inside, and they tap, tap, tap saying, "We're getting close to the target", and we tap, tap back saying, "Okay, we're going to move up onto the back." So they slow down their speed so we don't just go peeling off the back. We have our little lines on there. And we swam out and lined ourselves up on the aft of the casing and I was hanging onto the fin and filming everyone and as they gave us the taps and everyone swam off, we swam way off and filmed the force.

'Then I stopped and turned around and filmed the submarine going away and the crew were really happy because they'd never seen what their sub looked like underwater. So for them it was amazing. I think they think we've got rocks in our head but it was cool, it was really cool. Everyone in that force, and that's the reason I turned around, as they were swimming away, three stacks of divers, the minute everyone was about 5 metres away they all stopped and turned around just to have a look at what the sub looks like going away from you. I really loved that job, things like that.'

George's first marriage did not survive regimental life. His ex-wife moved back to Brisbane with their two girls and as he was coming up to the end of his time in the SAS he went through a stage of feeling angry and bitter.

'I was thinking, my grand plan was, "Bugger this, I'd better go to Iraq and kill as many [insurgents] as I can." You know, sort of crazy. I'm glad I didn't do it! Fortunately I met Audrey and that changed a whole lot of my life.'

He had loved being a senior soldier in the SAS but he believed those days were numbered.

'The more senior I got, the more I saw myself doing jobs that took me away from the job that actually I wanted to do on the ground with the boys, to become more an administrator or an operations room person and I really didn't want to do that. So the last job I got in the army was [out of the SAS] to be an instructor at parachute training school [PTS] because at least you're still hands-on with people.'

One of George's other motivations was to 'get the hell out of Perth'.

'When you're there your identity [with the SAS] is so hard to divorce yourself from. When I went to PTS I just snuck out of the army, literally.'

Aged only 39 with another 25 or more years of working life ahead of him, he wanted to do something relatively different but knew he needed to use his military skill set. To his mind, it was the only thing he had that was saleable or useful.

'But so many options for me in Australia weren't really viable and the other options I had in Australia were to go away for a month and come back for a month and I really didn't want to do that,' he says. 'There was Iraq, of course, but I really wasn't interested in that. I figured that if you run with the devil long enough he's going to catch you and fuck that, I don't want to be just driving down a street and get a hole in my head for no good reason. No amount of money is worth that and you're not really using your skills in that job either. I know blokes who were enjoying that for the adrenaline rush but it seemed pointless to me.'

Other options were training as a sky marshal or going to South-east Asia. 'My brother had been working overseas in Indonesia running security in a tin mine. I think he got that through Bobby Hunter, and then he freelanced himself.'

The bottom line was that, apart from his daughters, George's relationship with Audrey (not her real name) was now the most important thing to him, and he did not want to compromise it.

Then the opportunity came along to work in Abu Dhabi as a special forces trainer.

'Two of my very good mates had been here. One had left and gone back to Australia and I talked to him for a while; I knew other guys who had come over. I just rang one of the guys who was here and asked him if there were any places open and there were,' he says. 'Terry [O'Farrell] was a big factor. I know they like Australians, but at least with people like him in that position he can virtually pick and choose people he thinks are competent or worthwhile in the job here. So it was a pretty rapid decision. In fact I talked to Audrey about it and I think within two weeks I'd rung over here and we'd come to at least an agreement on getting a job.'

She says: 'Neither of us are really long-term planners. We just thought, "Oh, that'll be different."'

Part of the adventure was that neither of them had lived out of Australia before. The comfortable expatriate lifestyle and being able to spend most of their time together were also major incentives. Another was that Audrey really needed a break from her full-on career in media sales.

'I was fed up with work and this was an opportunity. We couldn't have afforded to live on one salary in Australia, not the way we live here,' she says. 'You'd have to be earning $250,000–$300,000 in Australia by the time you pay tax, rent, water, electricity, medical and so on. We have no living expenses whatsoever except food and that's ridiculously cheap here.'

It was in 2005 when George first agreed to go to Abu Dhabi. But the decision kicked off a massive steamroller.

'I did it all transparently,' he says. 'I approached the army with everything I was thinking of doing. So I was talking to the CO of the PTS and told him what I wanted to do and he gave me his approval and that was great. And I was ready to take long service leave to come over here and start working and absorb that leave over time.'

Audrey resigned, said her farewells and was sitting at the hairdresser's 'absorbing a bit of lifestyle' when George called to say there was a snag. The army wouldn't allow it, because while he was on long service leave he was still serving.

'So I had to cool my heels in Australia and Audrey had to go back to work,' says George. 'I was very busy for six months doing nothing.'

Well, not quite nothing. A job for a month on a super yacht owned by a super-rich IT mogul came up and he didn't look a gift horse in the mouth.

'He was shipping it from Durban up past Madagascar to the Seychelles and off to the Maldives and then over the Horn of Africa,' says George. 'They needed some security fellows on board, so I got paid 20 pounds a day less than the people were getting in Baghdad, for sitting on this massive yacht.

'It was quite funny because the crew were generally good but the first officer absolutely hated us because we threatened his manhood just because we had alpha male smartarse attitudes and ignored everything and just did our own thing. I think he felt a bit threatened by that. So he was running some subversive, "Security this, security that", running us down.

'The captain was a big boofy Pom bloke and he's never done

anything in his life other than drive yachts and that sort of business and he's a real tosser. And his cabin was up at the top and he used to get the girls to send his washing up through this dumbwaiter [lift]. He couldn't be bothered walking down three floors to get it.

'We'd just sailed, I think we were eight hours out of Djibouti. He opened the doors to the dumbwaiter, and the elevator was stuck half way up because one of his shirts had become entangled in it. Rather than be smart and try to get it out he stuck his leg in and kicked it, and broke a cable and the elevator smashed down and broke his leg, smashed his leg to pieces. It was horrible, ripped his skin and everything.'

Djibouti had a French garrison and a good military hospital, but the skipper couldn't be evacuated immediately because although there was a chopper on board the pilots had disembarked at the Maldives.

'Anyway it was me and another guy, Harry, we both used to be medics in the regiment. We heard the call, he's panicking over the radio, so we ran around to see what's happening. The crew are running all over the place and the first officer's going, "So much for the security! The skipper's just been attacked by pirates! We let someone on at Djibouti!"

'But we came around and found him and crowbarred him out, hit him up with morphine and all that sort of business. Because they didn't have a decent medic on board, they had a system where you ring, talk to a doctor and they tell you what to do. Whereas at least we laid him out clean, gave him antibiotics and morphine and looked after him, then stole some cigarettes out of his cabin.

'The fellow who had hired us was very happy, because he was copping some stick because of how much it was costing to have us on board. So that was his argument, "Well, you got more than you paid for." We sailed back to Djibouti in the end. I had to get off there though, because I had to look after the captain and come through to Dubai and fly home because he had to get off the ship. Everyone else went off through the Suez and into southern France.'

Eventually, George and Audrey arrived in Abu Dhabi.

Looking back, he says he feels well satisfied with his 20 years' service in the army and that he achieved everything he had wanted to.

'I've got nothing but really warm positive feelings about the regiment and particularly my closing years I found were so rewarding. To at least become a patrol commander, which was something I'd wanted to do, but then to have operational service in Timor and Afghanistan, which was arduous and demanding but massively rewarding and the blokes who I worked with are still really good mates of mine, I've been nothing but happy. The experience of leaving the army was a positive one. They were nothing but helpful to me and it fills me with great pride, having been in it. And when I see it, when I was in Afghanistan recently [strictly in a training role], looking at them, listening to them, seeing what they're doing, they grow, develop this smartness, it's a positive thing. I don't feel like I want to go back in there because I'm satisfied with what I've done.'

He loved the eight-week trip to Afghanistan. As well as catching up with what the Aussies were up to there, he says, 'It was a nice little kick back into getting my head back into an operational mode.'

Audrey, on the other hand, hated it.

'It was just awful. Because, much as he enjoys what he does, we're not here for that,' she says.

'Although I did have a good time over there,' George adds with a guilty laugh.

Audrey had never been a regimental wife, having to tolerate months of absences. 'I wouldn't have liked it, I wouldn't have enjoyed it. I can see why so many families split up.'

Well into their first two years in Abu Dhabi, everything is going well.

'At the moment we're thinking we'll stay here a minimum of six years and see how we're going from there,' says George. 'This job came so rapidly, anything is possible and Audrey has started working again.'

They have thought about setting up a business — there are plenty of opportunities — but George says, 'I'm quite happy to sit here and cool my heels. You can start a business and there are a lot of risks involved in that, about whether it will happen, and you have to work hard to achieve it. I'm actually content just to mellow, to mellow out . . . I'm a bit too relaxed to think about it.'

He is enjoying meeting people who have no idea about military life and who don't even talk about it. The fact of living in a global village was driven home to him when they met up with the Hash House Harriers [running and social club].

'I've never done it before because I've always trained with the military. A guy comes around and he's taking names and he recognises my surname. Anyone who has that name is related to me and it turns out he used to play rugby with two of my brothers in Darwin. Here in the middle of Abu Dhabi I meet this bloke!'

He has even gone camping for pleasure.

'I swore I'd never go camping, not ever in my life again: "I've been in the army for 20 years, it's ridiculous, I'll never go camping." And I was flicking through a camping book we got when we bought our jeep, and as I read it I thought, "There are some wonderful places we can go and look at, out in the desert or up into [the] mountains or off to Oman and look at the sea." And we've been twice now out camping and really, really enjoyed it — it was a really cool experience. There are huge mountains and wonderful seascapes — you'd think it's just some big sandpit but it is remarkably diverse. There are areas where it's mountainous, and big wadis with running water and things like that.'

It was rather different from camping in Afghanistan with his SAS patrol and having people trying to kill him. But old habits die hard.

'I tried to show Audrey what it was like with water rationing, but it didn't wash too well.'

She says, 'Seriously, the first night we went camping George didn't sleep because he was worried, obviously, about whether there would be anybody around. He couldn't relax. It was close to freezing . . . the middle of winter out in the desert is actually freezing. But we had to sleep with the fly of the tent open just in case!'

'I felt uncomfortable. I couldn't sleep inside a tent; I've never slept like that before. I've always been where I could see,' George explains.

After four or five nights he got to the point where he could relax.

'With a few Scotches under my belt,' he adds.

'Originally there was no fire,' Audrey says. 'He'd say, "You can't have a fire 'cause people can see you." The transition from hiding to openly camping!'

Whatever happens, George says, they will end up in Australia. 'I absolutely love Australia, plus the kids are there. We'll retire there. Once we're free of financial obligations and we've set ourselves up well enough, it is our aim go to back and live in Australia and relax and enjoy ourselves.'

He feels his horizons have broadened. 'I learnt a lot when I met Audrey. She was a very successful young lady. And as I talked to her I opened my eyes up to a lot of things that I had shunned or didn't know much about — "What the fuck would they know or how important is that?" But all of that is important.

'It wasn't until the sixteenth to twentieth year [in the army] I started thinking more, because I was getting closer to getting out and I was thinking, "Fuck, I'm going to be out in the world soon, I'd better start to have a look at it and see what it's like." Because it is so different. It's easy to hide all your life in the military, I think.'

Two years ago, Abu Dhabi was the last place he imagined himself in.

'Audrey and I often laugh about that — it just happened so quickly. I suppose getting divorced and getting out of the army were the two pivotal things that changed my life completely. But I'm very, very happy.'

He believes his life in the SAS will stand him in good stead forever. 'Having endured, done things hard like that in life, you can appreciate a lot of normal life, chilling out, relaxing. Putting up with hardship if you need to is not really an issue. Some people think the hardest thing they've got to do in their life is pick what colour underwear to wear or answer the phone 10 times a day. I often would think about something like that. It could always be worse. Life could get a lot worse than whatever hardship you're facing.'

chapter five

THE SULLIVANS

Russ Sullivan works for Terry O'Farrell as a contract training supervisor and, just like him, the former RSM (regimental sergeant major) of the SAS reached his use-by date and was lured to Abu Dhabi.

A laconic and cheerful 49-year-old Queenslander, 'Sully' lives with his wife Jo and their son and daughter in a large villa in a new suburb on the outskirts of Abu Dhabi that has been reclaimed from the desert. Their small patch of green lawn and struggling shrubs provide a stark contrast to the drab desert grey surrounding them.

'My time was pretty well finished as far as the regiment was concerned, so I thought, "Well, if I move out of the regiment [to the regular army] there is a loss of pay, then after three years you lose your special forces allowance", so it was only downhill from there.'

He had first applied to go to Abu Dhabi back in 1995 but did not go.

'I got the go-ahead in October that year, but about six weeks before that I was asked if I wanted to be Squadron Sergeant Major of 2 Squadron and I thought, "I can't miss that",' the 27-year SAS veteran says. His decision to stay gave him the opportunity to experience the high operational tempo of the next decade.

SAS troops are trained to adapt to change and not become set in their ways, which makes forced retirement or being put out to pasture even harder to bear.

'The regiment is always changing; if you're not changing with it, you just get spat out,' Sully says. 'If the regiment would keep you, we'd all stay there. To be quite honest I can't think of anything else in this life to have belonged to. I've looked at other jobs that pay more money but it is not the same excitement. You are never doing the same thing as years go by, equipment changes, men change, tasks change and the great thing is we don't get set into doing something one way. It is part of the ethos to look at every possible way of doing something. The youngest and newest guys, except when it comes to the crunch, have as much say as anyone else as to how things should develop.'

So after reaching the pinnacle of his career as the senior soldier of the SAS, and after a record-breaking period of operational activity, including a final tour to Afghanistan, it was time for the Sullivans to forge a new life. Like O'Farrell, there was nothing left for Sully at Swanbourne.

He had asked O'Farrell to let him know if and when anything was coming up in Abu Dhabi. An offer wasn't long in arriving and he resigned from the Australian Army.

'Once I'd signed that final form, they took my ID card off me and gave me a retired serviceman's ID, I knew it had come to an end. I've been around long enough [to know] that once you walk out that [Campbell Barracks] gate, that world closes on you, never to open again. So the people still serving only talk about the things they can because they are so busy in there. The society is closed.'

Getting a job with UAE special forces allowed Sully to ease himself onto civvy street. 'I think I cheated a little because I've got into a similar job working with people I know and working with people from other countries with similar backgrounds, so it's like a halfway house,' he says.

The big difference is that he is home by 3 p.m., he generally doesn't take work home, has his weekends off and he can finally be an involved father before his kids leave the nest. That family involvement includes skiing holidays to Austria for Christmas and other trips that would be much more difficult to afford from Australia.

'Because of the age of the kids we can only expect to have them around another couple of years so we wanted to spend some time with them, show them some places before they move on. Otherwise their whole growing up life would be, "Dad was in the army and always away."

Even when I was home, I was gone when they woke up and then [they were] doing homework or watching TV by the time I came home in the evening, so it was a hard life for them, there is no doubt about that,' Sullivan says.

One interesting aspect of life in Abu Dhabi is bearing witness to the astounding transformation taking place across the Emirates.

Photographs from the mid-1950s show the city as a medieval-style mud fort. Oil and independence have brought great wealth and extraordinary change. Office towers, hotels, shopping malls, cheek-by-jowl with domed mosques and new residential areas are springing up almost overnight. It is almost as if the desert has been irrigated and is sprouting buildings instead of trees.

Not far from their home is the Grand Mosque, named after the former ruler of Abu Dhabi, Sheikh Zayed bin Sultan Al Nahyan. Its 70-metre dome and 115-metre-high minarets jut out of the earth in white marble splendour.

With just 800,000 Emiratis across the seven emirates, the population has had to be boosted to about five million to cope with the oil- and trade-fuelled boom. Many of the immigrants are poor workers from South Asia who sweep the streets or labour in the hot sun to send home undreamed of wages to extended families in Bangladesh or Pakistan. Among the influx are large numbers of western professionals who are transforming the desert from a sandy wasteland to a modern city-state.

Once their daughter has completed high school, the Sullivans will probably return to Perth so she can attend university. Sully will join his brother in their Asian-based eco-security business, which operates mainly in the jungles of South-east Asia, training local rangers and police to protect forests and endangered species such as the Asian tiger.

As the business grows, he expects that the global special forces network will come in handy. 'Now with the internet it is easy to get word out on the street to track people down to do this sort of work, mates you might not have seen for 15 years. We all know someone who knows someone to track down, so the network is immense.'

Jo Sullivan loves and respects the SAS, but she is relieved that Russ has been able to build a life outside it. A legal secretary in Perth, she met him when she was having a mini career change in 1979 and took a job as a waitress in the mess at SAS headquarters. About three weeks later Sully showed up in uniform.

'I thought, "Oh great, this is good", Jo says dryly. 'I didn't want to have any social interaction with the guys there, because I didn't want the guys not showing respect for me. I think at the time there was only myself and two other women on the base . . . you were branded a tart regardless of whether you went out with one of the guys [or not] so it was a bit difficult to start with,' she says. 'As we got to see more of each other and got more serious, they were good.

Their son Matthew was born in 1987 with the disability Asperger's syndrome.

'It was really difficult when he was first born,' she says, 'so I encouraged Russ to move on and do something else and spend more time together. But the one thing I've never done with him is say, "Look, I don't want you doing this anymore", because I've loved that regiment as much as he has. I know a lot of guys and their wives, too, say, "Oh, I'm glad he's out of it, don't want any more to do with it", but if it wasn't for what they did there and what the regiment gave them they would not be doing the work they now do. They just wouldn't have the capabilities.'

When the first job offer for the UAE came along in 1995 she knew that Sully wasn't really ready to move on, so she supported his decision to stay in the regiment and that paid off in spades.

'I know he, as a soldier — and I think I speak for many of those guys — they ultimately joined that unit because they wanted to fight and go off and do what they do. In the last 10 or 15 years, these guys have managed to do a fair bit,' she says. 'I know there are many who got out [earlier] . . . who are a bit bitter because they haven't been given that opportunity.'

When the time came to leave, she admits to being a little apprehensive. The regiment wanted Sully to commit to another year as RSM, but he was exhausted and said no.

'Those two years as RSM knocked him about. He is just starting now to look better. [It was] the intensity of the work and he didn't have a PA — they don't even have a secretary to answer the phones, it is constant. We just didn't see him at all.'

Yet despite the stress she believes the Australian military does a better job than most of looking after its people.

The move to Abu Dhabi was a huge step for Russ and the family. 'It is a very scary decision and even now I really quite miss the unit in a way. I probably miss it a little bit more than Russ will admit to, but I think [that's] because he's so busy here, doing pretty much similar sort of stuff. If he didn't have this, I think he'd probably miss it.'

But from a family perspective it has been good to live a normal life. 'The kids haven't had it before. They love it; it's been great for them. For 19 years they had none of this.'

She says the biggest challenge for the wife of an SAS soldier is understanding and accepting that you will always be wife number two. She says some women can never accept that they come second to the job.

'Even when they leave they never leave it, so it is always that first love they never get over and that is what it is all their lives. So you just have to accept that is the way it is and move on, because they just don't have the time to sit there and worry about how you feel. In saying that, I think they also have to learn — and that is where the wife has to remind them — you are still around. Sometimes they just don't know how to give things to both sides; it is a difficult thing for them and for the wives and families, trying to find the happy medium. A lot of times the [wives] blame the regiment. I know many cases where [the marriage] was doomed right from the beginning, but they are quick to blame something else rather than themselves. So sometimes that's not fair, but a lot of times it is the regiment, just the life. It is just too much for some and I can understand that.'

chapter six

SKULL THE FIXER

In most military units there is a fixer, a person who can put his hands on anything, or who at least will know someone who knows someone who can.

In the SAS that person was Peter 'Skull' Boyd.

Skull was the regimental quartermaster before he decided to call it quits in 2005 after 28 years in the army. The short, bald-headed bloke is one of those people who seems to know everyone. He is also one of the least likely looking SAS soldiers you could ever meet.

If something needed to be procured, the catchcry in the SAS was 'Call Skull, he'll know what to do.' Now he travels the world as a private operator peddling his wares and catching up with old mates, especially in the Middle East where his talents can be put to good use.

A classic example of the fixer's craft occurred at a coalition staging base prior to the invasion of Iraq in early 2003, when he was still in the regiment. He was managing the logistics chain for the SAS task group and was keen to upgrade their facilities. They didn't have a recreation room and he had his eye on a plentiful supply of American lumber, but he knew the Americans would not hand it over for that purpose.

'The Americans had all this timber, plywood and lumber, and wouldn't give it out. So I went and told them I was building a chapel for the padre so they could all go to church,' he recalls with an evil grin. 'They gave us a truckload of this timber so we had to knock something up that looked like a church and we gave it to the padre who gave a great speech. "Oh fellas, you don't know what this means." We said, "You've got to look at the sign, Padre." It said it was the soldiers' chapel and it had been built by such and such, but it would not be handed over until a date 12 months away. So we used it as our rec room and all the guys would come and watch movies in the "chapel".'

The fixer was on hand again when the Aussies moved into the American forces' Camp Victory close to Baghdad's airport. As he passed through the terminal he had noticed some very nice leather furniture and a large portrait photo of Saddam Hussein. After the diggers had cleaned up their new digs, Skull realised there was nothing to sit on and no decorations.

'I told the boss I wouldn't mind going to the airport to get some furniture to put in there,' he says.

He took some trucks and a security detail and made the short but potentially hazardous drive down to Saddam International Airport where he found an American captain asleep on the large leather sofa.

'It was a really big leather lounge that made a half circle. I said, "Look, we've just fought our way up from Kuwait with you guys, you've got an area to relax and you've got all this and we have got nothing. You've got two lounges, how about giving us one?"

'In the end I bludged it that hard that the guys were saying to the captain, who was lying on this thing, "Come on, sir, these Aussies have been here all the time", so we lifted it with him on it. In the end he said yes. I got this lounge, loaded it up with all this other furniture and we had this nice villa with all this leather furniture.'

Somehow he also managed to acquire the portrait of Saddam in a gold-leaf frame and it took pride of place back at the camp.

Skull Boyd hails from the Blue Mountains west of Sydney. He was one of 11 children raised by a single father who had been a prisoner of war in World War II. There was never a lot of money, so young Peter left school at age 16 to undertake an apprenticeship as a butcher. After two years on the knives he was laid off so he applied to join the army. Following recruit training at Kapooka he was assigned to the Transport Corps and his first posting was to the specialist air dispatch unit based at Penrith just an hour from his home at Blackheath.

Air dispatch are also known as the 'biscuit bombers' because they provide aerial delivery of everything from rations and ammunition to heavy guns and vehicles.

Aerial resupply is a crucial element of special forces operations so he was exposed to men from the SAS regiment early on in his career.

'I did my basic parachute course in 1980 with an SAS selection course and met all these guys and they scared the crap out of me. They were all these big SAS blokes, but as it turned out I became mates with most of them,' he says.

Skull is one of those men who become mates with most people he meets. In 1981 he was posted to SASR as an air dispatch driver.

'I turned up at Swanbourne. I was what was referred to as a "black hat" (non SAS qualified soldier), and worked in transport. I had a set of air dispatch wings on my shoulder that no one else had, apart from my buddy who turned up with me, so that was pretty unique and the guys treated us pretty good.'

In 1984 he transferred back to air dispatch, but after two weeks decided his heart was now at Swanbourne so he applied for SAS selection.

'I just thought, "There is no way in the world I can put up with this crap, the general mundane army",' he says. 'Even though air dispatch was different to a lot of units, you had a specialist job and the work was interesting, it was still the green army, "Yes sir, no sir."

'With SASR there still is a structure and discipline, but you know who's who in the zoo to talk to and how to go about it. It is a more relaxed attitude and even back in those days you could tell that if you weren't a dickhead people treated you well. A lot of the green army tend to come down hard on people because they can, without thinking a lot about it.'

His first attempt at selection is best described as a debacle. On the day in question he borrowed some new-fangled quick-release webbing and was introduced to the joys of the energy drink Sustagen. It was mixed with water and milk and he gulped it down just minutes before he undertook the 5-kilometre run in full gear as part of the barrier fitness test.

Unfortunately he only made it around the back of the gym before the Sustagen reappeared and a few hundred metres further on the quick-release webbing fell apart.

'The first time I knew it had come apart was when I was nearly knocked unconscious by a water bottle thrown by the RSM that hit me in the back of the head,' he recalls.

He fronted the selection board and the commanding officer told him his heart was in it but his stomach and webbing weren't and to try again the following year. So in 1985 a better prepared Boyd successfully completed selection and joined the SAS.

He didn't see himself working as an operator so he asked to go back into transport. After finishing his patrol course he changed his mind and became an operator, but six months later he badly damaged his back and was offered another job, either as a clerk or in the quartermaster store.

He thought, 'I'm a bit of a wheeler and dealer. I'll give the Q store a go.' He stayed there for the remainder of his career, rising from private to warrant office class one and regimental quartermaster of the SAS. Twenty-four of his 28 years in the army were spent with special forces.

'People knew that if they wanted something I could get it,' he says. 'You don't have to do things dishonestly to get it, [but] by approaching people and bartering. There are things that I've done that were probably not by the book, you would get into trouble because of the way you did it, but it was purely for the benefit of the soldiers to make sure that they got what they needed.'

That would extend to providing luxury items whenever possible. During the Iraq War the resupply packages often included iced parcels of soft drink or biscuits and fresh bread.

'[I'd find] something that is not going to melt and tie it on and hope that it gets to them all right and a lot of the times it did,' he says.

On one occasion an order came back from the troops in the Iraqi desert for some Cuban cigars. That was a difficult one, but eventually some cigars were found and duly delivered with an aerial resupply.

A key skill for a good quartermaster is an ability to barter. 'I've learnt on operations there is a big market out there if you can barter,' he says. 'If we've got kit the Americans or different people want, you do a deal. For instance, I think we have the best cooks in the world, on exercise or operations, and the Americans, the poor bastards, their fresh rations aren't very good at all. So you invite them to our mess where we are doing fresh rations and they come in and have a feed, they will appreciate that and then you can hit them up for stuff later on.'

He put his wheeling and dealing skills to good use in Afghanistan in 2005 when he upgraded the Australian base, Camp Russell, at Tarin Kowt. Named after the SAS Sergeant Andrew Russell who was killed in Afghanistan in 2002, the camp was a partly built dust bowl when he arrived. Within weeks he had acquired timber and hessian for the buildings and he had convinced an Australian contractor who was building the road to Kandahar to provide some hard stand for the troops.

'In the end these boys came in and laid a tarmac, a helipad for us, asphalt, they put the roads in and built it all up, compressed it down, because they had all this stuff left over,' he says. 'If they left it where it was, the Afghans would have just come in and stolen it and probably sold it and it could have ended up anywhere.'

During this period he was contemplating his future. His time at SASR was coming to an end and he could either apply for another warrant officer job somewhere in Australia, or he could undertake the Warrant Officer Commissioning Scheme and move to the dark side to become a captain. His other choice was a discharge.

'I didn't think I was officer material; it wasn't something that I aspired to do. Why go from the top of the heap to the bottom where you are just another bloody captain?'

So after 28 years of service he decided to quit the full-time army, join the active reserve and go into business for himself.

He joined forces with a mate and formed a company called Extreme Procurement Australia Pty Ltd which sources and supplies military equipment. Working from an office in Perth and from his family home in a nearby suburb, he now travels the world wheeling and dealing for himself.

He was at the massive IDEX arms bazaar in Abu Dhabi early in 2007, networking with old special forces mates, and there were plenty of them there, looking for a deal. He was back in Perth later that year organising the major event of the regiment's fiftieth birthday celebrations, the Saturday night ball for 2500 people. In typical fashion, and after much bartering and networking, the event went off like clockwork.

After 28 years with a regular pay packet and being kept by the army, being in business for himself brought some tough lessons. 'It's a hard game and you understand when you've been in it for a while why more people aren't doing it because it is so bloody hard,' he says. 'It's the old peaks and troughs. You think you've got something lined up and then it falls over, but you have to just keep at it and eventually you'll crack it.'

Now it is a matter of networking and knocking on doors and sourcing products that the military might need.

'I feel that I'm pretty good at networking and I know a lot of people around the world and it's helped me a lot,' he says. 'There are a lot of ex-regiment and army guys in jobs around the world who know me. When they find out what I am doing I get a lot of guys calling me asking me to supply everything from body armour through to helmets, vehicles, rations, the lot.'

Skull believes the world will remain a pretty unstable place for some time to come. The focus of his efforts is the Middle East for obvious reasons and he has interests in several countries there. It has been helpful that his old mate Terry O'Farrell is second in command of special operations in the UAE.

'Terry has been great for us. What he has been able to do is facilitate meetings and then it's on our own back,' he says. 'Terry wants to see the UAE progress, their military there, the special operations command, he is not one to just sit there drawing pay thinking, "Gee, this is a great life and in a couple of years I'll go." Terry really wants in his heart to leave a legacy when he walks away from that job, that he set up a professional special operations command with soldiers that know they can do the job.'

Like many Australian businessmen, Skull finds the Arabs quite different to deal with. 'The problem with our Arab market is you never know what they are thinking or what they are going to do,' he says. 'They are good people to deal with, but very hard to deal with. You think you've got it and then it falls over or you think you've blown it and we won it. How do you work that out?'

The other complicating factor is that many Arab nations have been dudded in the past by western carpetbaggers, especially in the military market.

'They've been taken for a ride so many times in the past that they have got harder with the way they deal with things, and they make sure you are doing the right thing by them,' he says.

A big plus is that they like Australians and particularly Australian special forces.

'Unlike some of our American and British friends, the Aussies will sit in the dirt with them, they'll eat with them and train with them and I think they really appreciate that,' he says. 'It goes back to the old Australian thing: if you are a dickhead, you're a dickhead; if you're a good bloke, you're a good bloke.'

chapter seven

THE 'OASIS'

Sitting on the porch sipping a cold beer with the soothing sound of sprinklers watering the perfectly manicured lawn and fragrant, flowering shrubs, this could be a five-star tropical resort or even a back yard on Sydney's leafy north shore.

But it is not. The sub-tropical garden is in a man-made residential oasis built in the desert east of Dubai and kept green with desalinated water pumped from the Persian Gulf.

In a city of brazen extremes, the gated 'Green Community', as it is called, is right up there. Just when you think you have seen it all in Dubai, this residential community blooms like a rich flower out of the drab, grey desert.

Upon entering, one can imagine what the Bedouin must have felt as they led their camels into a natural oasis with clear watering holes surrounded by date palms. The vista of beautifully landscaped villas separated by lush green parkland, clear, cool streams and bubbling fountains is overpowering and absolutely out of place in the harsh environment. The children of local rich families frolic on emerald-green lawns as their imported nannies gossip on park benches. A modest landscaped three-bedroom, three-bathroom villa in the community would set you back a cool $1.2 million.

Dave Harper leans back in his chair as his girlfriend Mariette's maid delivers another platter of food. The ex-SAS officer moved to Dubai in 2006 and lives in a less opulent but still up-market, brand new high-rise executive apartment block at the man-made Dubai Marina. The streets below are crammed with all manner of luxury cars, from Porsches to Ferraris.

This five-star lifestyle is a long way from Harper's modest upbringing in a flat in Coogee. The youngest of four and only son of an army officer, he excelled at St Joseph's College and was accepted into medicine at the University of Sydney, but he turned down the offer.

Young Dave Harper's first love was flying and he had aspirations to be an air force pilot. So he applied to join the air force.

'Academically I had no problems, psychometric tests no problems, I did the pilot aptitude test, this hand–eye coordination test.'

Unfortunately he misunderstood the instructions and failed miserably. He sat it again 10 years later and blitzed it, but by then he was an SAS officer and his dream of flying was but a memory.

Thwarted in his first desire, he turned to the army. During his later high school years his father Brian had worked for the Rhodesian army and young David had spent his holidays in Salisbury observing the Rhodesian bush war from close quarters. So off he went to Duntroon.

Harper served as a platoon commander until he undertook SAS selection in mid-1983. He passed the arduous course but again fate intervened when he won the prestigious job of Aide-de-Camp to the Governor-General, Sir Ninian Stephen.

Harper rates the distinguished judge as one of the finest men he has met.

'I openly say, of all the leaders I've worked with, military, private sector, he had it all, this guy was amazing,' he says. 'He had great intellect, decisive leadership qualities, he could see all angles, he would canvass widely but in the end he would make the decision and [was] extremely understanding. He could engage with anybody at any time on any matter for at least five minutes and he could hold a conversation with anybody anywhere.'

On one occasion the GG was due, as commander-in-chief, to attend the Chief of Army's conference at Canungra Barracks near Brisbane.

'I'd been briefed and I wrote into his brief that at a point in time they would play the various tunes for the army, and those officers of those corps, if they were still serving, would stand up to their corps tune,' he recalls. 'I knew his military history during the Second World War so we stood up first for artillery. They all thought it was fantastic — "He is one of us." — Then he stood up for the intelligence corps, then the signals corps and I think the infantry corps.

'I could just feel all the death stares at me, like, "You are an idiot, you have just embarrassed your boss, you haven't briefed him correctly."'

But the joke was on them because indeed Sir Ninian had served in all four corps during the war.

'I said to him, "You know I'm going to get belted for this, don't you?" He said, "Don't worry, it's okay", and he had a great time. At the end of the night, he said, "Dave, I've had a great night, go and party with your friends." He was a nice guy, a really nice guy.'

Harper would accompany his boss to dinner with the generals and it was the first time he had been exposed to his father's peer group.

'They had been his peer group for 40 years and they'd say, "You are Brian Harper's David, are you?" So it became not, "I'm the captain, I'm the general", it became, "Oh, we remember your mum and dad . . ." It brought back to me the humanity of it all. Just like me as a young cadet, like my dad was 30 years earlier, they talked about what they did and their memories of my dad and mum, so that was a nice thing.

'I think that generation of military are a different crew, different people. Most of them were obviously war babies or shortly thereafter and they have a different perspective on life.'

After this wonderful experience Harper joined the SAS in 1984 and was posted to 3 Squadron under Lieutenant Colonel Don Higgins, who would later command the regiment and special forces command.

Three years later he was at Land Command in Sydney and decided to take a break from the military and try merchant banking. With his new bride he went to Melbourne and they lasted nine months before he re-enlisted and moved back to Perth. After a six-month stint with the reserve battalion at Karrakatta he was back in the SAS as assistant operations officer.

This was a lean period for the regiment and there were suggestions that it might even cease to exist. To ward off the barbarians the counterterrorism role was honed and the regiment was marketed as an elite killing force capable of taking down any hostile force.

'My perception was, we marketed ourselves incorrectly,' Harper says. 'We'd get these politicians and decision-makers across to the west and we would destroy everything. We'd show them how well we could shoot and blow heads off buildings . . . If I was a politician and never had any exposure to the military I would drive out the gate and go, "That is very clever, but we can't let these guys go anywhere because they are going to destroy the lot and kill everybody and that would be an absolute disaster."'

Around this time some enlightened thinkers realised that the regiment had to promote its other skills.

'These guys can actually go out and spend time with people and talk to them and sway them. You don't have to do all this hard stuff, but they can cover a whole bag of tricks,' he says. 'A lot of the smart thinkers, not only in our community but in decision-making land like Canberra, were saying [that] there are other things this capability can be used for.'

After several staff courses and a promotion to lieutenant colonel in 1995, Harper was posted to Manila as deputy military attaché while he attended staff college there.

Unfortunately he contracted malaria so was sent back to Perth with his wife and two-year-old son, the first of two boys.

In 1997 the family moved to Canberra and Harper knew the writing was on the wall. He was not going get his dream job as the CO of SAS, so rather than yield to a life of staff work and desk jobs, he quit the army once and for all.

He joined a stockbroking firm in Perth, but soon realised the ethics of the financial services industry were a long way removed from his military training. The next step was a security consultancy for a couple of years with some former special forces mates before he fell in with what he describes as a 'shyster' in the high-tech field. That didn't work either, so he went back to Perth to run another risk management consultancy. During this time his marriage failed and Harper moved to Dubai in June 2005 with a woman whom he thought was the love of his life. It was not to be. The relationship ended three months later, but he stayed on as a consultant.

In March 2006 he joined the UAE Special Operations Command as a training adviser. He is now the deputy contract manager for western contractors, looking after the 100 or so westerners working for the command.

'What I have learnt from the military side, particularly special forces, is you don't need a big system,' he says. 'Most of the customers here are western focused and that suits the locals because a lot of them have been educated or experienced the west and they want to import and apply those systems with a local flavour to it.'

Harper says he has no problem working for a foreign government from an ethical perspective.

'They operate under ethical guidelines, rule of law, all those sort of things that are prevalent in any developed, mature society; they are all here. In any mature society, sometimes people get it wrong and I'm sure they get it wrong at times, but their intent is to develop world-class systems and processes which are logical and sustainable.'

He says if it ever became a question of the locals doing the wrong thing in terms of international law then he and, he suspects, 99.9 per cent of the expatriates working with him would be out of the door.

'There are some significant pluses here, great experience, travel, quality of life. There are pluses and minuses,' he says. 'The sheer frustration of doing some things here that you think would be simple can be like climbing Mount Everest. Just to get a piece of paper signed or whatever it is can be absolutely frustrating and at times you want to punch your hands through the wall, but that is the nature of life here and doing business, not just where we are, but doing business here overall.'

Such frustrations are part of the challenge and the positives outweigh the negatives. He says the quality of the former Australian SAS men throughout the Middle East is generally first-rate and their ability to operate in chaotic environments is outstanding.

'These guys have been to one of the best finishing schools in the world. Now some would say, "This guy's on drugs, he's mad! They are just teaching people to do horrendous things!" Not at all. I just go back to the intent as I see it. The individual needs to be able to survive by himself. Whether it is a hard environment, or a soft environment, or a confusing environment, you will see all these guys have translated their experiences, their skills and their personalities to complement the system to go forward,' he says. 'The guys are doing things they would not normally have done in Swanbourne: dealing with somebody . . . [for whom] English is not their primary language is not uncommon for them; the concept of buying something, selling something, training on something that is not a military item, it might be a piece of technology which they never would normally deal with; or training a third party they might not [otherwise] have anything to do with; it is a skill or a capability you've got to have. They are just so experienced at chaos and complexity.'

When employing foreign instructors, the special operations command looks favourably at settled and experienced family men.

'The type of guy you'd want needs to be of a certain seniority,' Harper says. 'Even in a junior instructor's position, you need to have a guy that has had at least five or ten years' experience in the old firm at home.'

Those are exactly the sort of senior soldiers, sergeants or warrant officers that the SAS and the wider Australian Army can ill afford to lose.

He concedes that the issue presents a conundrum, but he believes that people make their own decisions based on what is best for them and their families. He, like many others, says that when SAS men reach 35 or so years of age they hit a hiatus and with the expanding global network the opportunities are there for them to do something else with their lives.

Harper says that while he will eventually move back home, he is in no hurry to leave. His two sons are settled back in Perth. The younger boy suffers from autism and is in an excellent program. The elder has another year of high school to go in a top school. Such things do not come cheap and the tax-free UAE salary is a big help.

'For me, obligation number one is to make sure my kids are okay, and by association my ex-wife is safe. They are housed, want for nothing, they are in a safe and secure environment, they have health care, a good education and opportunity. I think you will find that is a common thread through all this community.'

chapter eight

NEW TRICKS

Cultural awareness, patience, diplomacy and the ability to win hearts and minds are all skills that are drummed into Australian SAS soldiers.

Along with their highly geared physical skills they are essential traits for the SAS's primary role of long-range patrolling, surveillance and reconnaissance.

The former SAS men working with the UAE special forces draw upon these people skills daily to devise culturally suitable ways of training and developing their new charges.

Terry O'Farrell is in the rare position of helping an allied non-western country build its special forces from within at the highest levels of command and control.

He quickly realised when he arrived that one crucial area in the UAE special forces that needed strengthening was the ability to describe the commander's intent. They needed help in developing their doctrine, ethos and a more professional approach at that level.

'They weren't so good at describing their intent and therefore you never knew what was really required,' he says. 'You had to ferret it out and quite often you'd go down a few blind alleys before you realised, "No, no, this isn't what he wants."'

'And they're not good at describing what they want because sometimes they don't know themselves. So they'll come in with an airy-fairy suggestion and then you've got to try and make that work and there can be some false starts.'

He found that difficult at first because in the Australian Army, like all the so-called 'ABCA' armies (American, British, Canadian and Australian) the first thing that is described, and described properly, is the commander's intent.

'You know where your left and right are, you know what you're doing, what you're meant to achieve, but you're given the means to do it, you're not told how to do it. Whereas here they're more likely to tell blokes how to do something, not give them the full story. That's coming, it's a matter of education. People are beginning to understand that you've got to get on, you just can't have everything coming in to the commander to do.'

But he knew he and his hand-picked team of former Australian SAS operators would get nowhere without diplomacy. Fortunately, they found the Emiratis were especially responsive to the Australian approach.

'We treat them just like we've been treating our own guys. There's no pretence, nothing. They really do seem to like us because of that approach we have. Plus you don't realise how well you've been trained in the Australian Army until you come out and you see situations like this where our guys have got so many different skills.'

The worst thing would be to take a condescending attitude.

'If you go around thinking of them as second-class citizens you're on the wrong track, mate,' O'Farrell says. 'They're every bit as good as you are, every bit as sensitive — more so in some ways. You've got to be careful with them. And of course they're very — when you get to know them — very demonstrative people. They come in and the old nose-kiss and big hugs and all that sort of stuff, you've got to be able to do that. You can imagine a bunch of Aussies racing up to each other and rubbing noses and blowing little kisses!'

He has a belly laugh as he remembers one culturally challenging occasion that occurred years before when he was doing a stint of training in Thailand.

'We had a bloke, he went to the toilet and he came out and he said, "Guys — I've been assaulted in the dunny!" We said, "What do you mean?" And he said, "Some old bastard jumped on my back!" We said,

"No, he's the masseur in the toilet — what did you do to him?" He said, "I beat the shit out of him!" Poor old bloke, we raced in there and he's lying there. We gave him some dough and straightened him up, took a couple of the boys to explain what happened — "There's been a misunderstanding! He thought you were a bloody She-male." "Oh no no no!" God it was funny! Yes, you've got to be culturally aware.'

Russ Sullivan says, 'We are trained in the experience of going overseas and training people, so once again this is not new. I've only seen so many of these people before but it is not dissimilar to other places I've seen, and when you think of it the cultural differences, given that Malaysia and Indonesia are both Muslim countries, even that aspect is not new to us. Afghanistan, the prayers, the religious festivals, attitudes, we've already encountered.

'It's not terribly unlike a training mission from work anyhow, especially when you are working with the same people. What we have to offer is, we know we've all been trained by the same system, the way we speak, the way we write. I guess they are quite lucky here in that they don't have to train us, we bring the complete package. The Australian taxpayer has made us very marketable.'

Fifteen months into his contract George says, 'I really like these guys, I like their culture, so I feel much more comfortable. I love the guys I'm working with, they're great. They're very similar to Thai people, just a bit more arrogant. They've got a good sense of humour, they're definitely strong in their own culture and attitude, they've almost got a juvenile sense of humour but what they like and what they laugh at is funny.

'They do on the whole want to improve and want to be good but by the same token they're quite happy to relax under the rules of their society — "One o'clock? Oh, let's take it easy." It kind of makes sense, it's so hot it's ridiculous and I think it's just a natural mechanism that's ingrained into them.'

George had to readjust his expectations.

'It's a funny job because . . . if you come here with the expectation that you really care too much about training or you want to train people into a certain product that you can in Australia it's fraught with disappointment because the locals — what's that saying, "Softly, softly catchee monkey" — you've got to get into their mindset and chill out a bit in order to achieve anything.'

One big issue is the lower levels of fitness and physical endurance of the local special forces soldiers.

'They're quite soft,' O'Farrell says. 'Their commando training does probably harden them up certainly more than the rest of the armed forces do. In the SAS you trained through umpteen bloody hardships to accept hardship. We would think nothing when I was in patrols of marching 60 or 80 kilometres a night. You didn't [stop] because you had to get to the next place. Well these blokes couldn't do that. It's just not in their mentality. It's, "Where's the vehicle, where's the aeroplane?"'

'So all that hard living and rigorous [SAS] discipline where you're freezing cold, you want to go to sleep but you've got to stay awake because you're on stag, all that sort of thing, that's not necessarily part of their nature. Whereas it used to be, that's the sad thing about it. They used to be hard as nails, live on bloody camel milk and dates and a bit of water if they could get it and do that for months on end.'

O'Farrell can drive his men hard because he drives himself hard and says they respect that. But he is part of the chain of command, whereas the Australian contract trainers are in a more difficult position.

'That's because they're actually dealing with the troops and it's will against will and they don't have the authority to do what I do, which is to say, "Well, get over there and get it done." They've got to cajole, to try and convince, they've got to try and win these blokes over. So they're in quite difficult positions . . . it's all about personal relationships and, obviously, leading by example.'

Unless they succeed, the trainers do not gain the respect of the local troops.

'That's the other issue. You've got to be able to do it. They may not be able to do it but they expect you to be able to do it. You've got to make sure that, if you're teaching shooting, you've got to be a bloody good shot. You've got to know the rules backwards and so on.'

That is one of the key reasons why he is so selective about who he hires from Australia. 'Since I've been here we've been able to vet the guys who've come in here and we're happy with that.'

His ideal choice would be someone who was about 35, had been in the special forces for a while, knew his job, was around the senior corporal or sergeant level, married with a couple of children, a good steady hand, able to develop rapport, get instructions across and maintain a good even temperament.

'You can't be volatile here because if you lose your temper in front of them you lose your face. They can lose their temper but you can't. But rarely will you see them lose their temper. I've seen officers just come into the commander's meeting almost an hour late, it's, "Salaam . . . kief halik [how are you], how's the family?" and so on. Now there will be a black mark go down but there's no outward show of anger, whereas if you walked into an Australian generals' meeting and you were an hour late it would be, "Where the fuck have you been? I'll see you later!" No bullshit about it!'

As the deputy unit and training adviser for the UAE Special Operations Command, Dave Harper reckons that the biggest obstacles to effective training of troops in the UAE are culture and language.

'The . . . [people] you are working with have a different cultural view of life,' he says. 'What we think is hard and what they think is hard at times can be worlds apart.'

While most of the students speak reasonably good English, virtually none of the trainers speak good or even passable Arabic.

The foreign trainers teach in English using translators for both the written and spoken word as well as maximising visual teaching methods.

'If they are teaching people a system, whatever the gadget may be, it is, "Explain, demonstrate, practise, do this, do that, now you do it." So it is a visual learning system,' he says.

Harper concedes that teaching some of the more complex skills to senior people can become a little tricky. 'There is a lot of reinforcement involved and simple is good, complex is not good and it really is an intricate process. The hill is not steep, it is a long slow gradient. If you try to push too fast, too early, you lose them very quickly.'

First impressions are often not correct ones.

'It may be that you are talking to somebody in a group of five who appears to be the most junior in age and rank in a military sense. But socially that person may be way up there or well connected, so that person may have the lead in the discussion you are having. You have to be sensitive about who's who in the zoo and who is in the room.'

The complex Arab etiquette of courtesy can also present challenges. You might put your case and think you have agreed on a decision when really the person may be saying what they think you want to hear as a way of being polite.

'To get a result you might need to revisit it sometime later and put the issue back on the table and that can be frustrating,' Harper says.

While concepts such as refreshing, practising or refining skills are difficult to sell in the Arab context, Harper believes the Australian trainers have the best chance of imparting the crucial messages.

In his experience both the expatriate trainers and the local troops do their best to accommodate one another. 'There is no such thing as a perfect system. It can be easy to become disparaging, but we wouldn't be here if we didn't believe there was a need to develop the capability,' he says.

The fact that the UAE is using the Australian SAS 'brand' when they can afford to buy any brand they want to achieve the capability is a compliment to the regiment and the Australians.

George also believes that the locals like and respond to the Australian attitude.

'The Yanks and the Poms do very similar drills in terms of counterterrorism but there's an attitude to how you go about business. I find the Americans are very condescending and the Poms like barking at people, whereas Aussies actually get in and do it with them.'

He appreciated doing a stint with the men in Afghanistan, although strictly in a non-combat training role, because it provided an opportunity to look around at what other coalition forces were doing and make sure his operational skills were up to date. It also allowed him to catch up with some old SAS mates who were in base at the time.

'Here there are only so many people with skills. Whoever is willing to come over can be kingpin.'

He is aware that some older expatriates who have been in the Emirates for years essentially belong in an 'old school' era.

'They're stuck in a different army because the army's changed so much. When I did my patrol course we were going to sleep at night everyone would just rack out and you'd sleep for 12 hours every night, 'cause there was nothing to do at night. Now we've got NVGs, [night vision gear] most of our work happens at night,' he says.

'The gear we've got is miles ahead and more capable than anything we ever had. So some of these old guys are way out of date but they've got some loyalty to people here, they don't want to sack them, they want to keep them on the books and just move them about.'

Like all the contract trainers, George is forbidden from undertaking operational service with the Emiratis, even if he wanted to.

'We're not part of their army and when I was last in Afghanistan we were told clearly we're not allowed to go out anywhere, we're not to engage in anything along those lines. I think the only way they'd ever use us is to advise them.'

George is attached to an operational battalion of the UAE special forces.

'Within that battalion they have different areas of expertise, similar to Australia, but they focus solely on that and people don't move from that area, like amphibious, counterterrorist, close protection.'

He is working with the counterterrorist group as an instructor.

'Anything from weapons to room entry drills, stuff like that, and planning, the whole gamut of what they need to do. You can think about it like intellectual property. Definitely I use whatever I've learnt in Australia but they've got all their own formats and that was something that troubled me to a degree, thinking, "I don't want to sell out anything that I know from Australia." But they were already running a British format here, it's got its SOPs [standard operating procedures] and its structures so we just bolt straight in.

'We don't teach them anything that's beyond the scope of what they already know — nothing that we have in Australia that they are not using. I'll never give up my loyalty to Australia at all, one iota. We comply with what they already know and were doing. It's not too different from what we were doing in Australia but [the Australians'] is an improved version of the British and the American.'

Any doubts George might have had were quickly overcome during his trip to Afghanistan.

'Having gone to Afghanistan and having worked with them, and seen that they were working side by side with Australians, at least made it feel better for me, because I'd rather they were up to speed if Australians were relying on them and working with them and they were on our side in the coalition situation,' he says.

'With complex operations they'd be an integral part of it so they'd be relied upon. I've got no reservations about doing this because when these guys go out into the field with coalition forces, they were previously literally bolted on to part of the Australian initiative and relied upon to do their job. So I'm quite happy that we need to train them to a decent level.'

He is proud of the way Australian special forces do business because they do not have an exclusive attitude.

'They'll take on anything and listen to people. Whereas the Poms would shun us totally and do everything their own way, the Aussies will take what's good and get rid of what's irrelevant and not good, and they morph — part British, part American, and they turn that into a wholly Australian thing.'

One big difference with the UAE army is the method of entry to the special forces. In Australia, those aspiring to the SAS have to really want to do it and go through the unspeakably tough selection course. In the UAE the pool from which they are drawn is inevitably far smaller.

'There's not so much of a selection process as [there are] people who've agreed the army is their job. And those who are fitter, I think, they push towards special forces and within special forces they'll filter down. We're one part. The special operations battalion is one part; they've got a commando battalion, and amphibious raiding battalions so they'll virtually put people into the job, not people [who] want to go for it.'

This results in a very different kind of motivation.

'When I first got here I went running with the company that I'm working with and within about 300 metres two guys had just stopped and started walking! And no one raised an eyebrow or waved or anything. They had excuses for them rather than the Australian way, [where] you'd rather have blood coming out of your eyes than stop doing anything that everyone else is doing.'

So he had to develop different motivational tools.

'In Australia you can motivate people by aggression or the outcome of what you're going to do — "We're going to get in there, take out these guys, this and that." You can't say to these guys, "I want you to get in there and kill everything in the room", because they're opposed to it by the very core of their being. They're not really interested in killing everything. They're interested in doing their job but I realised that it'll change [according to] the people you're talking to — some of them aren't too friendly to westerners — and you've virtually got to coerce them, make them feel good about themselves, that it's all their idea. Then they'll encourage the other people to do it.'

Flattery goes a long way. 'You've virtually got to come through and tell them everything was good and then try and, "Oh, something we need to look at is maybe improve this, improve that", but they lose spirit pretty quickly. However they are compelled to do well and I've found it very satisfying training them and watching them improve and develop.

'I was doing some night training and they've got a killing house similar to what we've got in Perth, with some minor differences. I worked with them one day and then I came in, in the evening, and somebody had been training with them. They'd go through the place the same way every time. It had the capability of changing the doors and directions or whatever and I was standing up on the rail watching them walk through and I walked around the other side and looked at them getting ready to rehearse and they were choreographing exactly what they were doing. Again and again and again, doing exactly the same thing.

'And I thought, "Bugger this, they're not learning anything." So I kicked them all out and I shoved furniture everywhere, put a sofa in front of the door so it wasn't a door anymore and they were getting really angry, they were up in arms and really animated. And I said, "What's the problem?" And they were really worried that they would look stupid. I said, "Don't worry, I want you to make mistakes. All I want you to do is talk" — because they were no longer talking about what they were doing, which is one of the principles. If you want to get into a room, if I'm facing this way a guy needs to tell me there's an open door over there, and that was what I was trying to hammer home.

'After maybe three run-throughs, and I changed it every time so they couldn't choreograph it anymore, it dawned on them that what they were doing was progressive at least and they actually started to enjoy it. So I think it was just fear of looking stupid. And they thought all I wanted to do was make them look foolish, as though I was a mighty fellow.'

SECURITY

chapter nine

THE MAN FROM WOODSIDE

Bill Forbes had just arrived back in Perth from Casablanca, Morocco, in August 2005, when he received a call saying there had been a military coup in Mauritania, West Africa.

Mauritania's President Taya had been overthrown by the military in a bloodless coup when he was out of the country attending the funeral of Saudi Arabia's King Fahd.

Forbes's response was to jump on the first plane and head back to Casablanca.

The former SAS officer is general manager of security and emergency management for Woodside Petroleum, Australia's biggest oil and gas firm, which has 3500 employees on four continents.

A coup in an unstable West African nation, where the company runs the Chinguetti offshore oil operation, carries very high risks for the West Australian giant.

'My aim, on behalf of the executive committee of Woodside, was to get into the country as soon as possible, liaise with our people there and to see what the circumstances were, and [decide] should we remain or should we evacuate,' Forbes recalls.

His earlier mission had included assessing whether or not Casablanca would be a viable transit location for expatriate staff travelling in and out of Mauritania.

That was suddenly put to the test when Forbes faced his first challenge: how to get from Casablanca to Mauritania after the closure of the international airport in the capital, Nouakchott.

'I did a little negotiation with Air Tunisia in Casablanca and they were able to fly a plane in. And I and a half a dozen other people got off the plane in Nouakchott about 12 hours later,' Forbes says in his typically understated way.

A 747 jumbo jet landing at a closed airport in a troubled West African nation and disgorging a handful of white men onto the tarmac would normally arouse some interest.

'They didn't exactly put the gangway up to the plane so you could do that, so you dropped onto the tarmac and moved to the edge of the airfield to meet our in-country security people,' he recalls dryly. 'We had a security presence there that was assisting Woodside anyway, a group of ex-special forces, British, French Foreign Legion; I met with them, met the country manager and spent the next few weeks in Mauritania.'

The Chinguetti project generates about a quarter of Mauritania's national budget and at the time Woodside had some $750 million invested in it. Subsequently there had been a dispute between the military regime and the company over the terms and conditions of the drilling contract.

Forbes undertook an extensive security survey of the city: 'How many people are on street corners with their weapons and were their weapons cocked or not cocked? Were they prepared to shoot in the event that you went down the street at the wrong time of the curfew, what was their level of hostility, was there a lot of tension in the town?'

He studied all the options for getting Woodside's people out in a hurry including by road, sea and air.

After making his own assessment and consulting with other security professionals, including some from the Australian, Israeli, French and US governments, he recommended that Woodside continue to operate in 'stand fast' mode. That meant employing a smaller operational footprint, staff remaining indoors and reducing their workloads and waiting to see what direction the new government would take. His consultations included a call to an old SAS mate in Canberra who was well placed in the national security chain. The contact was pleased to receive a first-hand assessment, particularly since there were no Australian diplomats in Mauritania at the time.

'Our conclusion was [that] it was appropriate to remain, concurrent with looking at the options to leave if the coup was to turn bloody,' Forbes says.

Fortunately it didn't.

The worst nightmare of any company operating in the Third World is the loss of expatriate workers. It is the one issue that keeps Bill Forbes awake at night.

'The sort of people who work at Woodside are bright and energetic; they see opportunities, they seize them, they're sensible. But to be fair, in some instances the most intelligent individual and the most experienced traveller can still be caught in the wrong place at the wrong time,' he says. 'You could be in the middle of the wrong street in London or in a New York building or a Bali bar and it just happens. I hope that what I'm trying to build at Woodside lasts long after I'm gone. It's a case of security is everyone's responsibility; it's not just the person who is the general manager security and emergency management.

'It goes back to my roots, to my SAS days. Every person in a five-man patrol carries his load, everyone's looking after everyone else's back. It's a suite of responsibilities you have in a SEAL team or an SAS group no matter how large or small it is. It is the same sort of approach I'm trying to ensure exists within an oil and gas company called Woodside.'

High-quality information is a valuable commodity for corporate security operators whose recommendations to company boards can affect massive investment decisions in some dicey locations.

At times Forbes has gone to extraordinary lengths to recruit the right person to provide sound information and even to manage the situation, such as when Woodside was doing some exploratory drilling off the coast of Kenya in East Africa, close to the border with Somalia. In that volatile part of the world, where Islamic militants and local warlords operate alongside gangs of ruthless pirates, the security challenges are immense and it was imperative to find the right person to handle security.

Forbes knew of a former British Royal Marine Special Boat Service (SBS) colonel who was a white Kenyan by birth.

At that time the former colonel, who was fluent in several Kenyan dialects, was employed by the Democratic Republic of Congo (DRC) to train squads of anti-poaching police. Poaching is big business in Africa these days and many ex-special forces troops are working there to combat the illegal trade in exotic animals and their body parts. Every day unmarked huge Antonov air freighters arrive at obscure airstrips in the Congo, Kenya, Uganda, Tanzania and elsewhere across the vast continent, to spirit away valuable animal cargoes.

'He was a fellow who on paper had the credentials to look after our offshore maritime security requirements,' Forbes says.

Along with four other ex-British special forces troops, one of whom has since migrated to Australia, the colonel was working deep in the jungle in one of the least accessible places on earth. But Forbes needed to talk to him, so he swapped his business suit for some hiking gear and rode into the DRC via Uganda on the back of a motorbike.

'A guy dropped me off at a rubber plantation and he drove off into the sunset and I hoped that in a few hours' time I would be met by another group of people who would pick me up and take me elsewhere,' he says. 'It might sound a bit Boys' Own Annual, but there were certain prearranged rendezvous and arrangements set by me, but you still cross your fingers and hope like hell they'll come off.

'So after a couple of days I arrived at an ex-Belgian gunshot-pockmarked 1960s military camp on the edge of the White Nile and found four ex-British and one ex-Australian special forces person training about 300 Congo anti-poaching brigade people with weapons. We had a couple of days talking about the whole challenge back in Kenya and it was a most interesting interaction. He came back and did 12 months' work for us and he now runs his own security company in Kenya working for a lot of companies throughout Africa.'

Forbes, who spends most of his time in the office or travelling, is happy that he can still have these occasional forays into odd and interesting places.

★ ★ ★

An explosive charge is detonated on the training ground at SAS headquarters at Campbell Barracks in Swanbourne, near Perth, Western Australia.

SAS soldiers in training at Campbell Barracks, Swanbourne.

SAS trooper George (front), an experienced water operator, on an SAS training exercise.

George (centre in blue helmet) during the search for survivors of the Kibeho massacre in Rwanda during April 1995.

Ex-SAS trooper Gerry Bampton (centre in wheelchair) who was rendered a paraplegic in the 1996 Black Hawk tragedy with a gathering of former counterterrorism operators in Perth, 2007.

AUSTRALIAN WAR MEMORIAL NEGATIVE NUMBER P00966_097_1

Ex-SAS major and two-tour Vietnam veteran Terry O'Farrell on patrol during the Vietnam war.

Terry O'Farrell in his colonel's uniform of the United Arab Emirates army.

Dave Harper close to his apartment in the Dubai Marina. The former SAS officer traded his army career for a senior job with the United Arab Emirates Special Operations Command. In the background is the exclusive Burj Al Arab Hotel.

Head of security and emergency management for Woodside Petroleum and former SAS officer, Bill Forbes and friends during a security assessment mission in Kenya.

'I will die climbing, I am sure of it.' Ex SAS major and guerrilla warfare expert Jim Truscott testing his prediction on a sheer rock wall.

LEFT Ex-SAS officer Tim Curtis in the captain's chair on board the North Korean drug smuggling ship *Pong Su* in March 2003. Curtis led the SAS raid against the ship off the NSW coast. RIGHT Curtis has worked closely with the UN offering security services in Afghanistan.

Former SAS commanding officer James McMahon (second from right) with (from left to right) West Coast Eagles coach John Worsfold, captain Darren Glass and club chairman Mark Barnaba.

LEFT Then Major General Duncan Lewis in December, 2002. The former SAS commander is now deputy secretary in the Department of the Prime Minister and Cabinet in charge of national security. RIGHT Commanding officer of the SAS between 1982 and 1985, retired Brigadier Chris Roberts, at home in Canberra.

The young RAAF pilot Pete Bradford in the captain's seat on board a C-130 Hercules transport aircraft.

Forty years after he ferried the Kiwi SAS patrol and their dead commander Graham Campbell to safety in his RAAF Huey chopper, Pete Bradford (far left) meets survivors Mac McCallion, Sid Puia and Bill Taare at the Waiouru army camp in New Zealand in 2008.

Terry and Ellen Culley at a black tie event. The couple met and married after the former SAS major was told to manage her family's case after her first husband Graham Campbell was killed in action in Vietnam.

Former regimental sergeant major Fred Barclay found his SAS training invaluable in his new role assisting in the development of Great Mercury Island on the Coromandel Peninsula in New Zealand.

Auckland-based Anglican minister and former New Zealand SAS officer Kevin Herewini is pictured with the SAS *Pou Pou* (carved pillar) in the army *Whare* or meeting house at Waioru camp in New Zealand's North Island in January, 2008.

Bill Forbes's military career took him around the world from the tropical battlefields of Vietnam to the frozen Arctic.

He was born in Melbourne, the only child of a police detective and his wife and after completing his education at Scotch College was called up into the army in 1970. The army quickly realised that young Forbes, a cheerful and quietly focused bloke, was officer material and packed him off to the officer training unit at Scheyville north-west of Sydney, which catered specifically for national servicemen, or 'nashos'.

In early 1972 he left for Vietnam as a reinforcement platoon commander.

By Christmas the newly elected Whitlam Labor government had brought the troops home, but Forbes and some of his platoon stayed on to oversee the repatriation of goods and equipment from Saigon to Australia. He was one of the last Australian soldiers to leave Saigon in 1973 and, signed up for a further five years, he went to the infantry centre at Singleton.

He had encountered many senior SAS soldiers during his stint at Scheyville and in Vietnam.

'I obviously respected the sort of thinking that a lot of them had, and found that there was an appeal there based on the individuals I had met,' he says. 'They demonstrated to me the sort of characteristics that I aspired to demonstrate.'

So, along with 153 other soldiers, he took on the SAS selection course early in 1974. Just seven of them — Forbes, another officer and five diggers — passed. After reinforcement training he became commander of 'B' Troop, the 'Beagle Boys', which was the unconventional warfare troop.

Two years later he was posted to Sydney as aide-de-camp to the land force commander, Major General Donald Dunstan. Unlike some other army generals, who wanted the SAS disbanded, Dunstan was a strong supporter of the regiment. He went on to become Chief of the General Staff and later Sir Donald, Governor of South Australia.

After a year there, Forbes was selected to go on exchange with the United States Navy special forces unit, SEAL Team 1 based in San Diego,

California. The US Navy SEALs, which stands for Sea, Air and Land forces, are the navy's special forces, whose roles include guerrilla warfare, counterterrorism, special reconnaissance and direct action.

The SAS had established training links with the SEALs during the Vietnam War and those links, along with the relationship with the British SAS and SBS, have flourished ever since. The modern-day SAS also enjoys close ties with the top-secret US Army special forces unit known as Delta Force, which was formed during the 1980s.

In the mid-1970s, SEAL Team 1 was heavily involved in cold weather operations, or arctic warfare, with a focus on the Aleutian Islands chain in the Bering Sea between Alaska and Russia. The Cold War was at its height and the Soviet Union was the enemy, along with China and of course North Korea — all situated geographically fairly close to the Aleutians.

After initial cold weather training in the frozen mountains of Colorado and Utah, Forbes deployed to Alaska and then out to Kodiak Island in the Aleutians to sample arctic warfare training first hand.

Coming straight after the jungle environment of Vietnam and the hot and dusty outback of Australia this was fascinating and challenging stuff. Jumping out of planes onto pack ice or into freezing seas to be picked up by a submarine, or swimming off a US nuclear sub in extreme cold water below the ice and cutting an exit hole through the frozen sheet was fantastic and often very dangerous work.

The 25-year-old Forbes was also very excited to be with the SEALs at a time when they were pushing the envelope of extreme cold weather operations. He had worked with the Oberon Class submarines in the warm waters off Australia, but nothing prepared him for the sheer scale of the US nuclear boats.

'When these things surfaced on the ocean at night you saw something that looked like a city tower block coming up next to you,' he recalls. 'Or you were swimming towards something that got very much larger than an Oberon Class submarine did when you got close to it! And the method of getting onto them differed from the method with which you used to get on and off an O-boat.'

They also worked with swimmer delivery vehicles or mini-submarines that were steered by a group that were part of the US Navy Special Warfare capability.

'It was a fascinating period and a physically challenging period. For a young officer from Australia, leadership was a prime responsibility, so as well as pulling your weight in a physical sense you're in there getting your hands dirty as much as they are.'

His time with the SEALs was far from what young Bill Forbes had expected when he was drafted into the army as a raw 20-year-old.

'I was doing a lot of parachuting, a lot of diving, a lot of shooting, a lot of work with grenades and other weapons,' he says. 'It was exciting stuff and I was also working — as I had with SAS — with a bunch of very committed, very dedicated, in the main very fit young blokes who wanted to be part of a capability that was profound. It was the same as the SAS professionalism, to be as good as you can be. And it exists today across the Pacific and across the Atlantic with the other special forces elements. Everyone in that sort of group who wants to and struggles hard to get into that sort of capability generally gives their all when they get in there. So, yeah, there were no clock-watchers.'

During this period the Americans were also starting to hone their skills in applying military force to the counterterrorism role.

'It hadn't yet come to pass that there was a formal group, but certainly the special forces group that I had the opportunity of working with were practising for not just warfare, but selective surgical operations countering terrorism either in continental USA or wherever else American interests were.'

Forbes was in a leadership role with SEAL Team 1 which culminated with him and an Australian SAS sergeant also on exchange being asked to help develop a land warfare capability for the US Navy Special Forces operators.

Just like the SAS, the SEALs were desperate to expand their expertise and redefine their role following Vietnam. The men set up camp about 160 kilometres east of San Diego and proceeded to teach the SEALs the art of close-quarters battle in a non-supported land environment. Each SEAL team is made up of several platoons of 14 men, which on operations break down into teams of seven, which is very similar to an SAS patrol.

'We would take a SEAL platoon out there and endeavour to teach it as much as we were able to teach it in terms of close-quarters battle . . . when you're in a small group you don't necessarily have the support of a larger group like a company-size force or a battalion or a brigade,' Forbes says.

Whereas the reconnaissance mission dominated the role of the SAS, the SEALs had become the force of choice for some of the most daring military missions such as snatch and grab or hostage rescue. Because of their unique multi-skilling they can be used for a wide spectrum of missions including hostage rescue and, these days, for direct action against al-Qaeda targets in Afghanistan or insurgents in Iraq. The SEALs maintained their long-range reconnaissance capability, but they were increasingly involved in covert operations requiring immense firepower.

During his exchange with the SEALs, Bill Forbes also operated with US Army Special Forces and with the British SAS.

He had also married his Perth-based sweetheart, Susan, beginning an enduring and well-travelled partnership. She worked for Hamersley Iron, just down the road from his present-day office at Woodside in the Perth CBD.

'It might sound a bit trite but my greatest asset has been Susan, who's given me total freedom of movement. She lives with and has lived for over 33 years with my absence sometimes at short notice, sometimes of short durations and sometimes of very many weeks. And sometimes she's been particularly concerned I know but she doesn't lay it on me about anything else except, "Look after yourself."

'She's got a great deal of trust that I'll make sure, if I'm on my own getting on or off a motorbike in the Congo or getting on a plane to somewhere, that I'm not doing stupid things without considering the risk.'

He believes that the wives, partners and families of special forces soldiers do it particularly tough. Because of the commitment that

Australia, Britain and America have made post 9/11 to send troops overseas, the men sometimes have to work back-to-back or quick succession deployments at the expense of family circumstances.

'I think that a lot of wives have been given a lot more of a burden than they thought that they would, not just in the period post 9/11, but in all military circles. It's a bit of a tough life for the families of someone who chooses to do 20 or 30 years in the military.'

Forbes returned to Australia from the US to work in Canberra for the then director of Special Action Forces, Colonel Mike Jeffery. A former SAS commanding officer, Major General Jeffery would become Governor of Western Australia and ultimately Governor-General of Australia.

This was a period of great uncertainty for the SAS. The Hilton hotel bombing had occurred in Sydney in February 1978, but still some generals and politicians were not convinced about the need to employ the SAS in counterterrorism operations.

That all changed after the Iranian embassy siege in London in 1980 when the British SAS successfully ended the standoff in front of a live global television audience.

In response the Fraser government decided to develop both an onshore and offshore counterterrorism capability within the SAS. Bill Forbes was tasked by Jeffery with identifying and procuring some of the specialist weapons and equipment. He often flew into Perth with some unusual weapons in his luggage for the operators at Swanbourne to trial.

After two years in Canberra, Forbes returned to SAS headquarters as adjutant and then commander of 3 Squadron, a war-fighting squadron. The mid-1980s was a very quiet period operationally for the SAS, but they conducted some major exercises across northern Australia and South-east Asia.

'As the SAS focused on developing a counterterrorism capability, you wanted to be sure that the war-roles capability didn't suffer either, that you didn't suddenly become a regiment of black-clad super-soldiers capable of assaulting aircraft or ships or boats or trains or planes to do rescue operations at the expense of having a good capability that has since been tested in Iraq, Afghanistan, East Timor and Bougainville.'

From there, Major Forbes went to the US Marine Corps training academy at Quantico in Virginia and was posted out to various units up and down the east coast of the US, accompanied by Susan. The couple then returned to a staff job in Melbourne before Lieutenant Colonel Forbes was sent to Greece in 1991 to help organise the fiftieth anniversary celebrations of the battles for Greece in Crete. He was also awarded an Order of Australia for training and operations.

The one job that he did not get was CO of the SAS Regiment.

'Oh, everyone aspires to that,' he says frankly. 'Anyone who serves [in the SAS] who doesn't aspire to command it is a strange character and there's no one I know that doesn't. But it didn't come to pass.'

Instead, he was posted to Darwin as commander of the North West Mobile Force (Norforce). The SAS has close links with both Norforce and the Pilbara Regiment, which are employed in long-range surveillance roles across northern Australia.

'The role that they had was similar to the surveillance and reconnaissance role of SAS, so we had transferable skills and we transferred those into Norforce,' he says.

After Darwin he was posted back to Perth to a desk job, his final job for the army. In late 1997, after 28 years of service, Bill Forbes resigned his commission.

The army tried hard to keep him with several enticing offers including to go to Fort Bragg, North Carolina, the home of Delta Force, but Forbes could not be swayed.

A job advertised in the newspaper for the director of risk management with the West Australian Fire and Rescue Service took his eye. He won the position and just three months later was promoted to executive director and, shortly afterwards, as executive director of the WA Fire and Rescue Service.

In 2004 he became acting CEO of the Fire and Emergency Services Authority (FESA) where he had about 40 former SAS men working with him.

'They used to enjoy going down the side of buildings and they'd delivered a lot of capability into the fire and rescue service,' he says dryly.

Because the emergency services tended to operate along pseudo-military lines with similar chains of command, the job was a natural fit for former soldiers. So was the 24/7 nature of the work.

'I still had a pager on my hip, as I'd had in the military. We had 33,000 incidents a year, so you had to balance what you got excited about and what you didn't. It was very important to know how to set priorities and maintain a balance with regard to the daily or weekly challenges.'

There were two key differences. One was dealing with unions, a new experience for Forbes because the military does not have trade unions. The other was working with 30,000 volunteer fire fighters.

'So there was a lot of negotiation, both in an industrial and semi-industrial circumstance. There were wage circumstances, there were industrial agreements to strike, there was a suite of circumstances I'd had no exposure to,' he says. 'I believe in the reasonableness of man. I'd had exposure to a lot of reasonable people in my time in the military and I found if you were reasonable to most people in life, in turn they would be reasonable to you. So if you negotiated an enterprise bargaining agreement and you put your cards on the table in a frank way, the other side representing their union members would do similarly and you somehow reached a satisfactory midway point.'

After eight years with the state's fire and emergency services it was time for him to move on, so when the opportunity came along to join Woodside he jumped at it. It is a job he believes draws all the strands of his previous careers together.

The company's global operations were expanding into some challenging security environments and the need for sound risk management had become a core function. Up to then Woodside had hired consultants to provide the advice, but now it required in-house expertise. So in March 2005 Bill Forbes became the inaugural general manager security for Woodside.

He is responsible for securing a diverse range of activities, from offshore and onshore drilling platforms in West Africa and the Middle East to shipping LNG (liquefied natural gas) through the Malacca Strait and the Sulu Sea. A vital part of his job is plugging into the network that was established during his military career, though that process is not quite so simple once the uniform has been discarded.

'There was certainly a need to break ice and a need for you to point out that your . . . inquiry was based upon a commercial company as opposed to representing the Australian government or anything like that,' he says. 'Once that was clarified, the information that came to me and still comes to me is as a consequence of relationships that are of a personal nature, that have perhaps grown out of the professional relationship that existed when we were all wearing uniform together. And some of my colleagues that have worn a uniform of a different shade from mine have moved into like positions in international companies too. There's not a lot of new things under the sun with regards our subject area.'

After a year with Woodside he had emergency and crisis management added to his security portfolio. Crisis management has become big business for former special forces officers around the globe and for Bill Forbes it is a valuable network. He knows men who are former SAS, SEAL, Delta, Foreign Legionnaire or other SF operators in pivotal positions with companies or consultancies from Latin America, the Middle East, Africa, Asia and the Pacific.

'It's a suite of relationships that Woodside looks to me to make sure work when they need to work in a circumstance of some challenge. But they also have every expectation that those relationships are fostered.'

Those relationships extend to governments as well. Men like Bill Forbes might report back to their mates in government about activities they have witnessed in some dark corner of the world where there is no diplomatic presence. The network can also work in surprising ways. On one occasion the head of Woodside had to be escorted during a Middle

East tour, so Forbes made the arrangements from Perth. The man who met him at the airport was not aware that Forbes had made the arrangements so he asked the boss if he knew Bill Forbes.

'That particular person, who had attempted to get into SAS some 20-plus years before, remembered vividly that Bill Forbes had been the assessor on the selection course and had said to him, "Choose a different profession or choose a different stream of the military because you're not going to get into SAS." And here he was 20-plus years later, relating the circumstances that had happened in Australia during a selection course to my CEO. I thought, "There's a unique star alignment — when you think that those dots would be connected."'

His CEO came home and said, 'I've just met one of your traumatised ex-students that tried to get into the SAS 20 years ago.'

'I have since met the guy and we've reminisced about that.'

While he gets into the field as much as possible, the very fit 58-year-old is more often dressed in a dark suit attending a corporate meeting, though he has to be prepared to leave the comfort of the office at very short notice.

'I have to ensure that our people are safe and our information is secure and our assets in places like the Middle East or Africa or Latin America are as secure as they can be. The only way to do that is to go out and eyeball people and to look at the space and say, "This is safe or it isn't" — do a security risk assessment.'

His brief is to ensure that all Woodside staff are as prepared as they can possibly be for the environments they go to, '. . . that the items they carry are not going to expose them to higher risk,' he says. 'If they've got a Rolex, it's not on their wrist. If they've got some nice diamond rings, they are at home in the safe. If they've got baggage, it's locked, and whatever the hotel is, be it five star or three star, that they're staying in, that they are as secure as they can be, that they get into the right taxi, that they are trained to make these decisions and no one has to hold their hand.'

Forbes is constantly amazed by the places and the jobs in which he finds former SAS soldiers.

'Guys who are managing dozens and dozens of people who are in front-end circumstances in Algeria, Afghanistan, Iraq; these are blokes that back in the Australian military context I've known as lieutenants, warrant officers, corporals and colonels,' he says.

His own decision to move on came with the realisation that the sharp end of special forces is a young man's game.

'The biggest challenge we've all got in life, I think, is to recognise our use-by date in a professional context; not many of us actually identify it accurately,' he says.

In 1978, Bill Forbes was awarded the United States Navy and Marine Corps Medal for Heroism. At the time he was posted to the United States Naval Special Warfare Task Group at Chinhae, Korea, when he rescued five Korean women trapped in a blazing apartment block at the Chinhae Naval Facility.

Captain Forbes tried several times to enter the smoke-filled apartment from within the building. He eventually scaled the outside wall and rescued the five hysterical women.

The citation from the US Secretary of the Navy reads, 'Captain Forbes' courageous and prompt actions in the face of great personal risk undoubtedly saved several lives; thereby reflecting great credit upon himself and upholding the highest traditions of the armed forces.'

chapter ten

BAGHDAD OR BUST

There was a war on in Iraq, and Gordon Conroy wasn't part of it.

The ginger-haired former SAS major had left the regiment after the 2000 Olympics, intent on setting up a post-military business in international risk management.

Now the Americans had been true to their word and invaded Iraq and it was on for young and old. His former regiment was up to its ears in the action while he, once the commander of the SAS counterterrorism squadron, was on Civvy Street in Dubai.

It was no coincidence that he was there. The build-up to the invasion of Iraq had been going on for at least a year. Conroy had headed to Dubai to set up a consultancy as part of a plan to expand his business further afield from South-east Asia into the hotbed of the Middle East.

Now he knew that he had to get to Baghdad, and fast.

This war was a conflict that would break new ground in the privatisation of warfare. He knew that the Americans would require help from privateers to secure the strife-torn country. They had already offloaded many of their military functions to firms like Kellogg Brown & Root (KBR), a subsidiary of the US giant Halliburton, which between 1995 and 2000 was run by Dick Cheney. Cheney subsequently became US vice-president under George W. Bush and one of the architects of the 2003 war. The company employs more than 14,000 Americans in Iraq, managing billions of dollars' worth of projects for the US military.

On the back of this privatisation, the independent security industry in Iraq would grow to more than 40,000 contractors. This private-sector growth would help spare the already stretched US military but it would also bring a whole new set of problems, and who better to get his foot in the door to help manage them than a determined former SAS officer?

Conroy's immediate challenge was how to get into Baghdad, where the security situation was freewheeling in a post-invasion vacuum. A mate came to the rescue.

'I can put you on a truck, but you'll have to go as an engineer,' he told him.

'No problem,' Conroy said.

'So I snuck up to Baghdad and spent a couple of weeks there,' he recalls.

When he got there, he camped on a floor and wrote reports for some major banks to pay his way. Before long, the firm Unity Resources Group was born.

Dubai is one of the most bizarre city-states in the world. Where else could one watch the world's tallest building grow, ski down an indoor snow field, take tea at the world's only seven-star hotel (Burj Al Arab), shop at Harrods and retire for aperitifs in the lush gardens of a villa, all on the edge of the desert?

One place in this Arabian Las Vegas where visitors can still catch a glimpse of the old city and the vestiges of its Arab trading heritage is at Dubai Creek. A trip across the creek in a local water taxi called an *ara* takes passengers past dhows that have plied the waters of the Persian Gulf for thousands of years and minaret-topped traditional mosques that are dwarfed by concrete, steel and glass towers.

The creek is also home to the Dubai Creek Golf and Yacht Club, which offers respite to expatriate families who are otherwise locked down in their air-conditioned villas as the desert bakes in 50-degree heat.

For Gordon Conroy and his business partner Neil Marshall, their wives Gabrielle and Jo and children, the club's outdoor dining area and huge pool provide a measure of relief from the desert and the tepid waters of the Arabian Gulf.

As golfers drive past in their electric carts to do battle with the lush, sculpted fairways and greens, maintained year-round with desalinated water, the Conroy and Marshall families settle in for brunch.

Both the shorter, ginger-haired Conroy and his tall, dark Kiwi partner carry the confident air of military officers.

As their kids dart around the deck area between sips of orange juice and nibbles of bacon and eggs, the families exude prosperity. Business is booming and Unity Resources Group is growing strongly and making lots of money, thanks largely to the Iraq War. Their journey from army officers to successful businessmen has been one of high risks and hard work.

Conroy, born and raised in Melbourne, is a graduate of the Royal Military College, Duntroon. Neil Marshall was born in Scotland and raised in Christchurch, New Zealand where he left school at fifteen to become a boy soldier at sixteen. By nineteen he was a second lieutenant.

The pair met when both were posted to the Brisbane-based 5/7 Battalion.

Conroy had passed the arduous SAS selection course in 1989 and in 1995, after his stint with 5/7, found himself in London at the British Directorate of Special Forces. He worked on the counterterrorism desk and with NATO before returning to Australia to command the SAS CT squadron. There he was involved in the preliminary preparations for the regiment's substantial role in the Sydney 2000 Olympic Games.

But then his father was diagnosed with terminal cancer. Conroy took long service leave and went home to Melbourne. After his father died he went back to Sydney to join the Sydney Organising Committee of the Olympic Games.

'I thought if I was going to transition out of the military into the private sector then having the Olympic Games under my belt would be . . . a good gig to have, to throw that card out,' Gordon says.

At the Olympic security command centre he worked with the New South Wales Police Olympic Games security supremo, Paul McKinnon. His final Olympics job was project director in charge of dignitary protection, which included athletes and, specifically, protecting a member of the Indian hockey team who had been subjected to death threats. He loved it.

'I had the pass, I could go anywhere, any place, any time, back of house, field of play. Unfortunately I didn't see any events, but the Olympics was such good experience.'

During this time Conroy met another former military man who was running an event security company and the pair decided they should be looking at the bigger picture, especially the international risk management field.

'We had to go offshore. Before 9/11 Australians had a healthy disrespect for any risk management principles,' he says. 'In Indonesia we did some consulting. They do take it seriously there, and it is really tangible stuff. You are talking to presidents and CEOs of companies about how to maintain their business continuity if things start to turn pear-shaped for them. That is rewarding work . . . But Australians, until something happens, even now don't understand risk management.'

He also managed to fit in a few adventures, such as one occasion when, as a freelance job, he was asked to go to the Solomon Islands to meet a former prime minister of the country.

He arrived at the island of Gizo in the west of the tiny, troubled island nation to find a note directing him to a hotel.

'Go to the upstairs room and someone will contact you,' the note read. In due course his contact met him in the hotel bar, but it was obviously not very secure. So they arranged to conduct negotiations at a private island off the coast.

'I was told to meet a boat at the dock in the morning and there was a little banana boat with a driver with red, betel-nut-stained teeth. I was a bit nervous going across the open ocean. If they wanted to get rid of me they could just hit me over the head and over the side I'd go,' Conroy says.

At the end of the trip he advised his hosts that declaring a separate state of Gizo was probably not such a great idea.

Neil Marshall transferred to the Australian Army in 1988 and was welcomed — despite his personal concern that he wasn't from a Duntroon military college or Portsea officer training school background — with open arms. 'It was never an issue, it was all performance related which was a great opportunity . . . and I probably attained command before I would have in the NZ Army.'

He stayed until 1994 and then bought his own security company in Brisbane. He had been approached by the Kiwis to try for SAS selection and he was sorely tempted because two of his best mates were troop commanders. But he knew it was time to move on from the armed forces, so he turned down the offer and has never regretted it.

Marshall applied himself to his new career with zeal and tenacity, learning the nuts and bolts of the business.

'I did all the jobs like a security guard in the malls. I had to learn my own business so I had to do all the work, but I was fortunate that I got into electronic alarm monitoring early and four years later my business had grown substantially.'

Then an American company bought him out.

'We managed to give all our people away [and] I worked for them for eight months, which was an experience, learning about American culture,' he says. 'Then I restarted with a commercial electronic business on the Sunshine Coast. We had government contracts and high-end CCTV integrated access control.'

Sometimes Conroy would be on the phone saying they needed someone to go to Aceh or elsewhere to sort something out. 'I used to disappear up and do these little jobs from time to time. So we stayed in touch over the years.'

He moved to Hong Kong in 2002 working for a multinational chemical company as area security manager. 'Gordon asked me to look at Indonesia to see if we could run something. So we put together a business plan, rejected the first one, went back to the drawing board for a few months, revamped it and then we started that and once that kicked off I came across in early 2005.'

Marshall became regional director of operations in Asia and soon had the business humming. He is now Unity's director of global operations and Conroy is CEO.

'We made an acquisition which gave us China, Hong Kong, Singapore and that quickly expanded. Then we were looking at diversifying into Iraq and that was when I came across here as the director,' he says.

From 2005 the company grew to have offices in 12 countries including the UAE, Indonesia, Hong Kong, China, Jordan, Iraq, Dubai, Turkey, Afghanistan, the US, Australia and Kenya. It also operates in the Sudan where it employs 10 expatriates and about 250 locals, in total employing upwards of 1500 staff in a dozen countries.

Iraq in 2003 was the major catalyst for the company's growth.

Once Conroy had got himself into Baghdad on the back of the truck in the guise of an engineer, he quickly scoped out the business environment in Iraq. Within weeks he had strongly advised the consultancy he was with to get in there. But they hesitated about the price.

'I said, "Don't worry about the price. If it gets us in there, it gets our foot on the ground. We will find out all the hoops we have to jump through in setting up a company, with licensing, getting weapons to do business."'

Within a month, clients for whom he had been conducting a security audit decided that they needed to boost security.

'We need more people here,' they said. 'Do you have more you could bring in?'

'Yes, we do,' Conroy told them. 'These are ex-SF guys from Australia.'

'I took this back to the consultancy,' he recalls, 'and they said, "No, we won't have a bar of that."'

So he took matters into his own hands and before long had a team of 10 former SAS soldiers ready to move into Iraq to start work.

That signalled the coming of age of Unity Resources Group. Their first contract was worth in excess of $20 million. 'We seized the opportunity there, and then really that program just started to grow and grow.'

Conroy saw a lot of greedy companies in Iraq operating cowboy outfits that left their men dangerously exposed. He was determined to set a steadier pace.

'It was eight months before we took on another contract and they came to us because they heard we didn't have to go out and we weren't aggressive in our marketing. We made sure we got those processes and systems in place; we were running a really safe operation.'

Like many army officers, Conroy had studied for an MBA. The combination of special forces training and business theory stood him in good stead for navigating the fraught world of the Middle East security industry and Arab business practices.

'We come from a military background so with the business, when we initially started, we were very operationally focused, with the operational tail wagging this business dog,' he says.

They were very conscious not to be perceived as a couple of ex-army guys working out of the back of a Land Rover on green field notebooks. 'In Iraq you could be perceived as that because that was the sort of environment it was. We wanted to be corporate. We saw a real need to diversify our market base and work in risk management consultancy in Asia. So we set that up.'

Fortunately their third partner came from a tight margins business background so his business acumen kept a lid on the outgoings.

The company now has about 20 staff at its corporate headquarters in Dubai and 160 expatriates in Iraq. Of those, about 40 per cent are former Australian or Kiwi SAS and the rest are made up of 23 nationalities. In addition, Unity has up to 800 locally engaged staff on its Iraq payroll.

Former special forces operators are vital to the success of the business, but sometimes they need to adjust their attitude.

'We honour a lot of the SAS skills they bring to the table and while that has been incredibly good and healthy for this environment, it does come with its baggage,' Conroy says. 'It's important they come in and realise the commercial reality of doing business on the ground, out of special forces and away from the blank cheque syndrome. In the SAS you are well resourced, you are getting the best equipment, you are getting really good intelligence, which makes your job a lot easier. When you come into the commercial sector like us, we won't cut corners on safety, but there is a business and commercial aspect to it.'

Most of the men are flexible, but in his view there is an element of having been very spoilt in the SAS.

'When you come into the commercial sector and commercial reality . . . comes into it, you know you are not spoilt anymore and the client won't pay for the niceties that the Australian taxpayer will pick up. So it's, "Welcome to the big bad world of business."'

The biggest challenge facing foreign security firms in Iraq is avoiding the 'cowboy' tag because of the actions of a few, led most notoriously by the big American firm Blackwater Worldwide, which has killed dozens of Iraqi citizens.

Blackwater lost four of its expatriate operators to brutal insurgents in Fallujah in March 2004, triggering a terrible cycle of violence. The men's bodies were mutilated and paraded by frenzied locals and images were plastered across front pages and TV screens around the globe. Since then the company has adopted a hard-line approach culminating in September 2007 when Blackwater staff fired into a crowd in a Baghdad square, killing 17 people.

It hasn't been all smooth sailing for Unity either. Despite some high-profile successes, including a leading role in the freeing of American *Christian Science Monitor* journalist Jill Carroll, there have been controversies.

Unity has dealt with several kidnap and ransom cases such as that of aid worker Margaret Hassan, who was kidnapped and eventually murdered. Conroy regards her death as a political assassination aimed at pressuring her aid agency, CARE International, and the United Nations to leave Iraq.

But by far the most appalling and potentially damaging incidents for Unity have involved the killing of innocent locals.

Conroy likens the streets of Baghdad to a scene from a *Mad Max* movie, a dog-eat-dog world of suicide bombers, snipers, trigger-happy American troops in Humvees, private security convoys and local motorists chancing their arm as they move around the city. Well-trained operators wait until the last second to fire at a vehicle and then aim for its engine block rather than the occupants. But hesitate too long and an explosives-packed saloon could be killing you and your client.

In March 2006 Unity employees fired upon a vehicle in Baghdad after it refused to slow down while approaching a checkpoint. Inside was 72-year-old university professor Kays Juma. The dual Australian-Iraqi citizen perished in a hail of bullets and Unity was in the headlines for all the wrong reasons.

Shortly afterwards the company was in the news again when staff shot dead two women in a car as it approached some of Unity's vehicles in downtown Baghdad.

Marshall was in Dubai and Conroy was in London when it occurred. Knowing it was so soon after the latest Blackwater debacle and its accompanying media frenzy, they were braced for a public relations firestorm.

Marshall was able to react instantly. 'I knew intuitively where [Gordon] would want to take us and was then at least able to get things moving,' he says.

They engaged openly with the media and followed their well-established guidelines for dealing with fallout, involving days of round-the-clock activity and a massive effort to distance Unity from the likes of Blackwater. Nevertheless, media reports inevitably lumped Unity in with Blackwater and others.

'As soon as anything like [a shooting] happens we inform the Ministry of Interior, the Iraqi police, we inform the regional operations centre that runs the multinational forces and we get all those people in,' he says. 'We've engaged the families. That is just par for the course when working in those environments, you would expect nothing less with it.'

The firm has also strict hiring policies to mitigate the risk of a 'trigger happy' collateral damage incident.

'We've got guys who have seen the odd angry shot [in the military] so are very mature by virtue of being special forces trained,' Conroy says. 'It is a round peg in a round hole stuff, so when things are happening around you that would probably make a normal person feel uncomfortable, you are in your element . . . So we go to real pains to select the right guys to head up the countries, as country managers.'

Unity has conducted thousands of missions all over the country and was the last private operator to pull out of Basra when the southern city became too dangerous.

Conroy and Marshall concede that they could be making more money in Iraq doing the most dangerous and lucrative job of all, convoy escort, but they refuse to do it.

'We could be doing convoy work. People die in large numbers, guys make good money. But we wouldn't sit in a truck in a convoy in Iraq and run it, so why would we ask anyone else to do it?'

Unity's expatriate operators work to a strict roster of nine weeks on and three off. 'We are one of the few companies that have very little turnover. Attrition is low; we are very stable,' Conroy says.

There is no shortage of talent coming on to the market. For example, in late 2007 Neil was seated next to an older Australian man on a flight home from Hong Kong.

He asked the quiet grey-haired Australian what he did and when he told him he was a serving senior military officer, Marshall knew he had to be coming to the end of his time in the Australian Defence Force.

'What are you doing after that?' he asked.

'I think I'll probably be heading over this way,' the officer said wryly.

Unity runs its own intelligence department so that the company can know which risks are worth taking.

'We have very good collection and analysis; we use that for the protection of our people, we use it for mission planning. If we are taking a client somewhere and the indicators are there's something wrong, then we don't go. We tell the client, "do not go", and it is actually a carefully considered operational thing.'

They are aware of the shelf life for security firms in Iraq. 'We were mindful not to name the company a security company. It was called Unity Resources Group because we didn't want to be pigeonholed,' Conroy says.

While most of their work is still in security, they are diversifying into the lucrative areas of procurement and supply chains, as well as critical life support, and building and supporting refugee camps. They also have contracts with the Australian Defence Force to fly two aircraft a week from Dubai to the Australian base at Tarin Kowt in Afghanistan.

The men expect the global focus to soon shift from Iraq to Afghanistan. 'We are sort of strategising for that now,' Conroy says.

Neither expects to be working in the crisis industry directly in 10 years' time, but they know that global uncertainty means that the work will be available for as long as they want it.

chapter eleven

SON OF THE FATHER

Tim Curtis has soldiering in his blood. His father Rod is a former commanding officer of the SAS, so Duntroon was a natural fit for the young man.

Some had expected Curtis to follow his dad's path and to eventually command the SAS Regiment. Instead, the MBA-qualified former SAS officer is in Dubai, working in the thick of the security industry.

'My father's influence in having been CO was probably enticing me to stay to take the position of CO, probably for the wrong reasons. In the end I just simply decided that I had done all I wanted to do and that I didn't want to be CO SASR; I didn't like the look of what the CO did and was quite concerned about an inability to [ethically] lead through the politics that seemingly consumes the position,' he says.

Now, 90 per cent of what he does is business.

'About 10 per cent of what I do is probably leveraging off my security pedigree. At the end of the day my unique selling point is I'm an ex-SAS guy with an MBA,' Tim says.

In the boardroom that is what they want to hear and in the field, particularly in a dangerous trouble spot, that is what they want to see.

To understand business and be able to protect yourself and your clients in the event of trouble are premium skills. Like Gordon Conroy and Neil Marshall, Curtis is making hay while the sun shines, based with his young family in the secure environs of Dubai. He is chief operating officer and vice-president Africa, Middle East and Asia for the UK-based firm Edinburgh International (formerly Edinburgh Risk).

The company was started by a Scotsman and former British Army officer, Simon Frame, who went to Baghdad soon after the city fell in mid-2003. When Curtis joined in late 2003 Edinburgh had about 160 employees. It has grown to about 900 and since 2006 he has been responsible for diversifying and growing the business.

'Most of my focus was spent on building the business outside Iraq because everyone was hypersensitive about how long Iraq would or wouldn't last, with increasing amounts of regulation and legislation,' he says. 'The only sane way to do that was geographically diversify and diversify lines of business as well, so 2006 was pretty much me using the networks and my understanding of Afghanistan.'

He had also spent a fair bit of time in Sudan.

'We [had] about seven people in Afghanistan when I joined the company. Now we have 456. In Sudan, we had one, now we have 126 — some significant growth.'

His key role is to execute the business via program managers on the ground in each location. 'My core function is firstly to make sure the programs are achieving some level of success: building business, building clients, dealing with clients and their concerns or wishes, and also looking at new markets. So Afghanistan and Sudan are not the end of our outlook as we build this in other locations,' Curtis says.

He says the business has changed dramatically since the heady days of 2003 and 2004 when security operators could simply stand on the footpath in Baghdad and someone would throw a contract at them.

'That doesn't happen anymore. There is definitely a price war going on so things have become very, very difficult. There is a lot of competition and clients know it; it is certainly not as simple as it was a few years ago and the nature of the industry has changed. It has now become far more regulated; in a business sense it is far more professional.'

The stereotype of the soldier of fortune is also far from the reality, he says. 'It is not the group of mercenaries often depicted. You look at some of the organisations turning over hundreds of millions, if not billions and what sits at the top are not ex-security professionals, but knowledgeable businessmen. So I think there has been a lot of maturity in the industry in the last few years.'

Unlike many ex-soldiers Curtis not only understands but also lives and breathes the business bottom line. 'The army is quite charitable in its approach to money and a lot of guys come and join security companies expecting the same level of approach. Clearly that is not feasible if you are trying to make your business profitable,' he says.

Edinburgh employs about 15 former Australian SAS soldiers, mainly in close personal protection and protective security details.

'In one project in Iraq for a telecommunications client, all the ex-SAS guys are in the project management team, the three members of leadership are ex-regiment guys and out of the core management team, four are ex-regiment,' he says. 'That is our flagship project and the guys have just done a phenomenal job on developing the structure and architecture to create an environment where the clients feel safe to go and do their job. They are extremely professional, you certainly can't question that.'

Curtis says former soldiers who join the high-risk security industry are looking for three core requirements. First and foremost, they want like-minded and trained individuals whom they can work with and trust. Second, good equipment that won't let them down (preferably the same weapons as the SAS provides) and third, money. 'They want to be well remunerated for what they do, so they would be the three core aspects of someone coming to work for us,' he says.

Recruitment is mostly done by word of mouth, using the small and very tight ex-SAS global network.

'Most of the recruitment onto projects is done by fellow project members who realise that someone is available and he is a quality operator. They provide the advice and we recruit them.'

He tends to recruit men from a variety of backgrounds and nationalities, choosing horses for courses.

'For jobs that are high risk, that are very demanding both physically and mentally and you have to deal with a considerable amount of stress, plus your skills proficiencies have got to be phenomenal, then you will gravitate towards "tier one" special operations guys,' he says. They are men who have served in either the SAS (British, Australian or Kiwi), the Royal Marines Special Boat Service, US Delta Force or Rangers special forces troops or other SF units such as Germany's KSK, the Dutch KCT, South Africa's SFB or Russia's Spetsnaz. Tier one operators generally require a high degree of challenge to keep them interested, whereas jobs such as static guarding usually fall to operators from police or private security backgrounds.

'They [tier one] want to work with people who are like-minded and dynamic in interesting type jobs. So there is a contrast, I guess, between things they would be interested in and things they are not,' Curtis says.

Part of the equation from an employer's perspective is how well the men are looked after, not just in terms of pay rates, but also insurance, leave time and, of course, equipment.

'We look after our guys very well. The standard of gear they have on their projects, I am talking now about the ex-SAS guys, is probably the same standard as they would have back in the unit. They get a phenomenal amount of say on what type of equipment they want on that project and that is really only governed by cost in the end. Superimposed is what I think is a very, very good insurance package which is up to US$400,000 for death and disability and they are probably the best paid in the industry.'

As a consequence the firm has enjoyed retention rates of around 95 per cent. Most who leave say they have to get Iraq out of their system or that their family pressures are too great. Some have returned to the SAS to go back on operations.

Edinburgh has also introduced a sabbatical scheme to allow its operators to take five or six months off and then return at the same level.

'The ex-SAS guys that are on the Iraq projects, generally speaking . . . have been with us for some years and they are now at the stage where they have a level of financial stability and . . . are starting to want more flexible leave arrangements, more time out of country,' Curtis says. 'In the early days you would have seen the reverse being true, people wanting to spend time in country, because that is when you get paid.'

The firm does not poach soldiers and Curtis maintains a positive relationship with the SAS Regiment, staying close to many of his old mates in the network.

'It's funny, but you always generally know where people [still inside the military] are. At any one given day I could find out probably within a couple of hours what they happen to be doing and the location in which they are working.'

Another aspect of the regiment's culture that Curtis draws upon is the ability to talk frankly and honestly with people at any level. 'I think that is something directly transferable into the business environment. When you sit in the boardroom you are able to pitch the language at the right level,' he says. 'I think that is something the regiment does very well, the hard skills speak for themselves, the guys have an exceptional level of collective skills, but it is the softer skills, the people skills mostly that are done very well.'

Less tangibly, he believes SAS training equips the men to 'speak inside their own minds' to solve problems. He thinks this is because SAS junior officers and soldiers are expected to be involved in sub-tactical planning and briefing their bosses.

One of the most satisfying aspects of his job is watching men grow outside the military culture.

'They do become more business savvy, they get more business acumen, they are given far more responsibility in many ways outside the military in this industry, particularly those that have project management roles. They are largely very independent in the way they run their projects, so in that way they have to grow business acumen, they have to understand the language their clients speak because the client won't respect the language they've learnt from their military time. That is one of the fantastic things to see the personal and professional growth in guys that I've spent time in the SAS with.'

chapter twelve

CLIMB EVERY MOUNTAIN

Former SAS major Jim Truscott is a ball of energy who moves through life at warp speed. Ideas come to him like breaths come to most people and he works at a breakneck pace, whether climbing a mountain or selling crisis management to corporations and governments.

Apart from his family and his work, Truscott's two greatest passions in life are the art of guerrilla warfare and mountain climbing.

The wiry, bespectacled former SAS officer has used both skills to transform himself into a successful businessman. Business is what he calls his 'second battlefield', his first having been his 26 years in the army, with stints in and out of the SAS Regiment and with 2 Commando Company.

His fascination with the black art of guerrilla warfare culminated with the United Nations intervention in East Timor in 1999, when the fluent Indonesian-speaker gained first-hand experience alongside the Falintil resistance movement.

When he first passed the SAS selection course in 1980, however, guerrilla warfare took a back seat to counterterrorism, which was then coming to the fore of the SAS's business.

'In fact it dominated SAS life in the 1980s,' he says. 'Guerrilla warfare was still seen as something important but less important given the priority given to terrorism in the 1980s. And it wasn't until the 1990s when the terrorism capability had been developed and was up and running and in more of a steady state that the focus went back on to other forms of warfare. So it was maintained at a cadre level or just a bare bones level.'

Its focal point was the secretive Swan Island, near Geelong in Victoria, essentially the finishing school for unconventional warfare.

Shrouded in mystery, the island houses some of the most shadowy training facilities in Australia. It is run by the Department of Defence, but is utilised by a variety of government agencies including army special forces, the government's foreign affairs spy agency, the Australian Secret Intelligence Service (ASIS), Federal Police, Customs and others. Established in 1877 as a fort to protect Port Phillip Bay, the island is accessible only by a single-lane bridge. It was from that bridge that a vehicle carrying three senior SAS soldiers plunged in 2007, killing the men.

The island was also a repository for some unconventional weapons including World War II 'spy' weapons — such James Bond-style paraphernalia as cuff-link dart guns and pen pistols. Legend has it that following the bungled ASIS 'raid' on the Sheraton Hotel in Melbourne in November 1983, when armed ASIS agents invaded the hotel without telling anyone including the police, many of the 'special' weapons were dumped at the bottom of a lake before Royal Commission staff could find them.

Says Truscott: 'It [Swan Island] was only for people who were senior in rank, senior technical officers, officers who had already done a lot of other things, rounding off all the other military skill sets that they had.'

There was no formal selection other than that people who had already proven themselves, were seen to be at the peak of their trade and were able to operate in this very difficult environment.

'Guerrilla warfare is literally when you are by yourself or in very small parties doing things, surrounded by people who may not be sympathetic or supportive to you. It's an out-there form of warfare.'

He nominates rapport and the ability to get on with indigenous people and people of other cultures as essential traits for this underground kind of work.

'Inherent in that is the ability to speak another language, although that wasn't a prerequisite,' he says. 'It was more important that you be able to work with other societies in difficult circumstances and be able to influence and convince them to do some form of action, normally military action or it could be political action. Because when we are talking about guerrilla warfare we're talking about operations across the spectrum of social warfare, economic warfare and psychological warfare. It's all forms of bringing down an opposing power.'

Learning from the past is an important aspect of the training of special forces soldiers and at Swan Island they had an impressive line-up of guest speakers, many of them World War II veterans. One of the most inspirational was the legendary Nancy Wake. The New Zealand-born Australian woman had been number one on the Gestapo's most wanted list. She had a bounty of five million francs on her head at the height of her exploits with the French Resistance in 1942 when she was known by the code name 'White Mouse'. After her betrayal and narrow escape, she joined the forerunner to modern-day special forces, the British Special Operations Executive (SOE), and was parachuted back behind enemy lines in 1944 to re-join the fight.

'We drank a lot of whisky with Nancy. She was very interesting. She's a tough old biddy; her face would light up with glee when she talked about machine-gunning Germans,' Truscott says.

When he first went to Swan Island, jungle warfare was uppermost as a legacy of the Vietnam War. 'We were very much focused on those types of insurgencies in rural or semi-urban environment [and] while it wasn't government policy, we were providing government with the capability to mount that style of warfare if it wanted to.'

While many see it as dirty warfare, one argument is that making underground links with insurgents early in the piece can prevent a bigger conflagration later.

'It's a very efficient form of war fighting. It's not necessarily one that generals and admirals like because there are no ships to manoeuvre or stuff like that,' he says with a chuckle. 'You've just got small pockets of people doing things that can't necessarily be measured or even spoken about. It's not what we call deniable, but it wouldn't be admitted to.

'Australia's intelligence agencies, they operate underground now. That's their reason for being. They go and pay people — that's classic underground stuff so to an extent Australia has always been doing it, it's just the violence side of it has never been used,' he says. During the 2003 Solomon Islands intervention, SAS troops carried a large box of cash to Honiara on a navy ship. 'Although when it came to East Timor in 1999, in the six- to nine-month build-up to that activity we were able to see classic guerrilla warfare being enacted by the Kopassus [Indonesian special forces], where they were caching, where they were setting up the militia to act in that sort of way and they were trying to get the population to support them. So we were able to use those skills to counter what they were doing.'

Because of information picked up by intelligence agencies months out, the government had a very good picture of what was happening in East Timor.

'Indeed, if the documents ever get released you should see the concept paper we put up to try and achieve peace in East Timor. It was, basically, separate the people from the militia physically and by all forms of psychological separation, then decapitate the leadership, Kopassus, to remove it. Where you can find those people who are the underground through signals intelligence, try and target those people.'

The Australian government maintained a stony silence on the involvement of Kopassus and the Indonesian government with the 'militia' groups that were actively and viciously suppressing the East Timorese independence movement, but it was one of the most open secrets in Australian foreign policy. Then foreign minister Alexander Downer stuck steadfastly to the public line that only 'rogue elements' of the Indonesian military were involved. Keeping the Indonesian government onside was the key priority.

The East Timor experience gave Truscott the opportunity to use his guerrilla warfare skills, not in an offensive way but in a defensive way.

'We understood guerrilla warfare and were able to do anti-guerrilla warfare, if you like,' he says. 'While I've not been involved in the operations in Iraq and Afghanistan in the last five years, many of the guys there have been working with small indigenous forces not in a clandestine way, in an overt way, almost like the Australian training team in Vietnam, but using guerrilla-style approaches to war fighting. It's a kind of multiplier, just have one or two advisers in with some sort of local paramilitary force.'

Unconventional or guerrilla warfare training includes many of the unsavoury and unspoken aspects of war. While conventional warfare is largely rules based, in the unconventional mode there are no rules, but there is a large body of work for exponents of the dark art to draw upon.

'Australia has a substantial history in guerrilla warfare and while the capability has gone up and down in terms of how much effort has gone into maintaining it, we had quite a legacy and a lot of lessons pertinent to our region which has not changed,' he says.

In 1996 Truscott obtained a grant to 'go bush' for three months to interview 60 of Australia's special operations troops who worked in Borneo during World War II.

'Amazing stories, you know, of shooting prisoners, dare I say it, and summary justice and cutting heads off and stuff that wouldn't be tolerated under modern forms of warfare, but that's what happens in guerrilla warfare.'

Truscott now travels extensively showing corporations how to protect their businesses, utilising a network of former SAS comrades when he needs particular skill sets.

He sees the ability to establish rapport as the most vital of all the skills he learned in his military career when it comes to business.

'In a sales meeting it's all about personal relationships and knowing how far to go and keeping your head high when every day you lose a sales meeting,' he says.

As he left the army after the 2000 Sydney Olympics he was given some advice that has shaped his post-military life: 'Keep fit and never work for anyone else.'

The fitness part was not difficult, but it took some hard slog, self-doubt and several false starts and disappointments, including a redundancy from one job, before he managed part two.

'This was a really hard lesson for me and I started to learn about business combat and the mortality rate on the business battlefield compared with what you find in a peacetime army,' he says. 'It's brutal and there are casualties every day and fatalities every day.'

With four children and a mortgage it was a tough period and the lifelong soldier had to make a major adjustment to his values in order to succeed in the 'second battlefield'.

The first lesson was that in business, money is everything and loyalty is to your hip pocket. 'It took me a while to work out, when I was going to meetings, to say [to myself], "I'm not in the first battlefield anymore, I am in the second battlefield where I've got to think in terms of money, and money only. How the hell am I going to get money out of this?" I had to keep banging it into my head.'

The greatest professional change was learning how to sell. In the military there is plenty of lobbying but no hard sell. '"This will cost you $10,000, sign there!" It's not that sort of sales, which I do now.'

In just four years his business grew from zero to an annual turnover of $2.5 million, which he puts down to a simple formula: persistence, doggedness and determination. 'I know the formula to be a rich man.'

Truscott says a lot of people, when they leave the military, are still comfortable in employee mode and it is very scary to suddenly not know where your next dollar is going to come from.

'I now revel in that because my network's now big enough, but it's very scary until you are in that position to do it,' he says.

Before he left the army he had never even heard of crisis management. He fell into it without even realising that his ability to move, write and think quickly was exactly what was needed to help businesses that are under stress.

'We're there when things go terribly wrong; we work in the space of both commercial and operational problems. It could be insider trading in George Street, it could be a fertiliser ship runs aground on the Barrier Reef,' he says. 'I've just returned from Korea where we had an LNG ship collision in the Yellow Sea between Japan and Korea. Last week we had three guys in Irian Jaya working with [a US mining giant] on a major earthquake scenario, which is one of their prime business risks up there. The last four or five years have been almost like a Boy's Own adventure and blood on the boardroom floor, with all the things that go wrong in business.'

The firm conducts 'last resort risk management' for many top listed companies in Australia.

'Most business people are pretty good at crisis management when they get the hang of it, but because it's something that they don't practise every day it just takes a little bit of coaching and guidance,' he says.

He quickly discovered that, despite the so-called 'war on terror', business in general is not worried enough about the threat of terrorism to spend money on it. Governments spend the money on national security and business is happy to leave them to it.

'We focus on risks that really worry business. They are, dare I say it, inappropriate behaviour by senior management; ethical misconduct; white-collar crime; operational events; power failures; water supply; avian influenza,' he says. 'Business only worries about things that stop [it] making money.'

He now understands why a lot of business people made such good soldiers in World War I. 'The military makes you risk averse, but these blokes know how to take risks. In business when you miss that sale, second place ain't good enough.'

As he marched out the gates at the SAS base at Campbell Barracks, Jim Truscott could not have known that he would become a successful capitalist in such a short space of time. He is already thinking about the 'third battlefield'.

'I don't know what it will be, but I am sure it is going to happen. I'm going to do it in about five years' time. I'll be 55 by then, that'll give me another 10 years.'

Whatever it is, it will have to be commercially viable. 'I've learnt that. The concept of doing something without money is just bullshit, it doesn't happen,' he says.

Truscott admits to many mistakes in his business career. One involved a big American oil company and an aspect of military culture that absolutely did not translate into business.

'I was running a debrief after a simulation and I'm pretty blunt when I am on my feet talking to people. I smacked a bloke over the head a bit harder than I should have, but not in a violent way, more a training way. "Go and do that again", I told him. There was no malice, there wasn't any thought about it but I got the letter, "You are never to work for us again for the rest of your life, we reserve legal action —" from a valued client,' Truscott says. 'It was a dumb thing to do and you don't do it in business. Control your emotions, dickhead, and don't smack people over the head.'

He is philosophical about it. 'Even the best general loses, but as long as you win three out of five battles you will be okay.'

A world-class climber, Truscott admits that fear is the elixir of the sport. He climbs most weekends and finds it a great way to relieve the stress of business life. He has led some climbs known as 'grade 23s', which means just 1 per cent of the population could manage it.

'You come back on Monday and you were fearing for your life yesterday and business is just fucking easy, dead easy, a doddle,' he says.

'I've climbed ever since I was 15. I'll die climbing, I'm sure of it.'

chapter thirteen

AS THE CROW FLIES

After a year of uncertainty, the transition out of SAS was a simple matter for former Warrant Officer Steve. He left Campbell Barracks to go on long service leave on a Friday and on the Sunday was on a plane to Kabul to begin the next phase of his career.

A 20-year veteran of the SAS and one of its most experienced senior soldiers, Steve had pretty much done it all. He had fought at the battle of Anaconda in Afghanistan in March 2002 and was the Squadron Sergeant Major of 1 Squadron when it became one of the first coalition units to invade Iraq exactly one year later.

When they returned triumphant from Iraq having won the country's highest force military honour, the Unit Citation for Gallantry, 1 Squadron went on to counterterrorism duty. For Steve it was the end of the line in the SAS, at least until he could possibly line up for the coveted job of regimental sergeant major (RSM). He had received an offer to become RSM at 1 Commando Regiment in Sydney.

'I then had to decide whether I was going to drag my family over to Sydney. My daughter was accepted into private school that year; we'd been in Perth for 20 years,' he says. And besides, once a soldier leaves SAS for the conventional army he drops money and for most there is no going back.

He was coming up to 25 years' army service so rather than go to Sydney he opted to take long service leave to consider his options.

'I had a few mates over in Afghanistan in the United Nations, so I flicked my CV across there and I received a phone call from one of them saying, "There is a position here in security. You need to be here in three weeks' time."'

So he took the job as UN security standards and training officer for the 2005 elections and before he knew it he was in Kabul sharing a house with two other ex-SAS guys. He stayed there from February until July 2005 and was able to indulge in the odd trip down memory lane to places such as Gardez where he had lived in the local fort eating crow, lamb and chicken stew during the 2002 coalition offensive against an enemy stronghold in the nearby Shahi Khot valley close to the border with Pakistan.

'As we approached it there was still an American (special forces) presence at the fort. It was right next door to it, about 150 metres away, a regular American community. We went there for lunch,' he says.

The crows had all gone, so fortunately they were no longer on the menu.

He also remembered the five men killed and 33 wounded during the first night of the ill-fated Operation Anaconda.

Steve had spent the early part of the battle with a local Afghan force pushing along the western side of the whale feature, a large whale-shaped hill, when it was forced to withdraw under heavy Taliban mortar fire from what became known as 'the bowl of death'.

'I drove through Zormat, which was the town just outside of where Anaconda was, and looked at the whale feature and it was still there, hadn't been bombed flat — a bit of nostalgia.' he says. 'It was a little bit surreal, driving past the whale feature. I was tempted to chuck a left and go in and have a look, it was just a couple of kilometres, but obviously I couldn't.'

UN staff working in Afghanistan were not supposed to be armed, but there was no way these ex-SAS men were travelling around their old stomping ground not 'bombed up'. They carried handguns, an AK-47 under the back seat just in case and their own ballistic vests as they traversed the countryside in their standard-issue white UN Toyota Landcruiser.

'It was great, I got to go all over Afghanistan again,' Steve says.

During his five months in Kabul no major incidents occurred and he and his team did not get into any trouble.

'You present yourself as a hard target as in doing the right security, taking different routes on the way home, making sure you wear your body armour and if they say keep away from that area you keep away, and don't break curfew,' he says.

As the summer wore on and the snows melted from the surrounding mountains, Kabul underwent its annual transformation from a picturesque, if muddy, city to a sickly dust bowl.

Keeping fit was a challenge for the ex-soldiers who maintained their strict regime of early morning physical training.

'We had a UN guesthouse which was 300 metres away so we'd try to get up at 5 a.m. and walk across there to a small running track. It was 50 metres, so we'd run around it 100 times to do a 5-kilometre run, so that in itself made it difficult to live there.'

Steve was frustrated by the attitude of many younger UN staffers.

'Unfortunately when you start a project a lot of young 20-year-old kids want to save the world and go to places like Afghanistan and say, "It's such a lovely place." We would run a four-day package of what to do if you are kidnapped, techniques, defensive driving, those sorts of things,' he says. 'I remember one particular course I ran, there was a young Romanian girl and she just didn't give a fuck, didn't even care. As far as she was concerned Afghanistan was a lovely place and no one would hurt her, so I said to the Canadian guy I was working with, "You need to speak to this girl."

'So he pulled her aside and said, "We are really concerned about your whole attitude. You've only been in the country for three days, you are going to get yourself hurt." And as far as she was concerned, she said, "No. Afghanistan needs a chance and I work for the UN, no one is going to hurt me",' Steve says.

The girl left Kabul to work in one of the provinces and had a really difficult time.

'I think there was an attempted kidnap on her and she was out of the country. She really didn't understand what she was getting herself into.'

After five months Steve decided he had endured enough of the UN bureaucracy. The US$9000 a month could not compensate for the grief.

'It was a great transition opportunity as opposed to getting out cold,' he says now. 'I know guys who have gotten out and taken up a position working a nine-to-five job. They are climbing the walls; it is not in their blood.'

Steve had enrolled part time in a Bachelor of Science in security management in 2002, figuring that would be a useful tool in his post-regiment life. In June 2005 he was contacted by another ex-army mate about a job in Papua New Guinea. It was a month on, month off contract working on security for an oil and gas operation.

'I left the UN in July and came home for about 10 days after being there for four months straight and went to PNG as operations manager for a security company in the Southern Highlands,' he says.

He stuck it out until the end of 2005 but found the frustration of being outside the decision-making chain was too great. 'Although I had 200 Papuans working for me, in terms of making decisions for the oil and gas asset itself, it was a glorified guard command job.'

So in early 2006 he quit and placed himself on the consultant market. A busy year followed working for numerous international security companies. He spent two months in Pakistan as a security adviser to the Australian High Commission in Islamabad and then travelled the world working as a security consultant in a high-growth industry.

'I was running security awareness courses for [the Australian government] as a contractor, going to Africa, Japan, Taiwan, doing security surveys, threat assessments for the Queensland government, trade information in Los Angeles, London, Japan. As a career it was ballistic,' he says.

The pay wasn't too bad either, anything from $600 to $1000 a day.

'There are a lot of guys out there who call themselves security experts: they can do the personal security detail work, but very few can actually put pen to paper and be paid to go to a large blue-chip company, conduct a security survey and identify threats and risks and put it on paper, so that's what I did.'

He even went back to PNG to do a risk assessment on a gold mine and he also managed to fit in some army reserve time and help out with an SAS selection course.

The enduring thread in all of Steve's post-SAS experiences is that he has encountered the network wherever he has been in the world. There is no suggestion of unemployment. Just a single message on Skype and the job offers come flooding in.

'Whenever I go through Dubai airport I bump into one of the boys,' he says. 'There are so many offers out there. There is a company here in Perth that wants me as director of safety and security. They said if I joined as director of safety, I would be on 50 per cent of the gross plus a day rate of $800. That is for a nine-to-five job in my home town.'

The demand for ex-SAS soldiers has surprised him, but he recalls a conversation he had with another ex-regiment mate several years ago.

'He was working offshore and his name was Dave. I said, "Dave, I don't know if I'm ready to get out." He said, "Steve, I don't get out of bed for under $800 a day and you won't either", and I just couldn't comprehend that. It was just ridiculous, but that is what is happening. I'd hate to see what he's on now, double that. That is the problem. When you've got a guy with a mortgage who potentially is going to be posted [away from the regiment], going to lose $20,000 to $40,000 in allowances, he has to pull the children out of private school and refinance their affairs. So he says, "Hang on, I can get out, earn some money, do some reserve time and I don't have to turn my life upside down."'

chapter fourteen

BEYOND BLACK HAWK

When in 2005 Iraq held its first UN-supervised elections after the toppling of Saddam Hussein's regime, it was a former Australian SAS officer who won the lucrative contract to secure and deliver millions of ballot papers.

Over one weekend his expanding company devised a clever plan to deliver the ballot papers by helicopter to three central locations and from there out to 20 provinces.

The contract would cement their Middle East business operations.

Ironically, while helicopters were to bring him good fortune in his new life, Bob Hunter's military career had been cut short in the aftermath of the terrible 1996 Black Hawk helicopter tragedy.

After serving in the SAS for eight years, the then Major Hunter became embroiled in the most awful and stressful event in the regiment's history, which claimed the lives of 15 elite soldiers and three army aviators. It would mark the end of what should have been a long and distinguished military career and it left a bitter taste in the mouths of many SAS officers and soldiers who hold Hunter in high regard and believe that he was made a scapegoat.

He was officer in command of the counterterrorism squadron on that horrible night in June 1996. The episode had a massive impact on Hunter the soldier and the man. Despite assurances from the top brass that his career would not be affected, he knew that his record would always carry the dark stain of the tragedy. Like most high-achieving officers, he had ambitions to become commanding officer of the SASR.

'It's all about perceptions and how is that going to look when we are looking at two candidates for CO of SAS. One has no blemishes, the other is Bob Hunter. "He's the Black Hawk guy",' he says.

Hunter has managed to expand his security and risk management business while keeping his family together and based at home in Perth. Yet another ex–SAS officer with an MBA, Hunter regards 'leveraging off his SAS pedigree' as a valid business tool.

But for a colour perception problem, he might have been lost to the army and become a naval officer.

Born in Hobart in 1963, the doctor's son enrolled at the Royal Military College, Duntroon, after he graduated from Hutchins boys' school in Hobart where he had been in the army cadets. He was also a prefect, played First 11 cricket and First 15 and state-level rugby and had been in cubs and scouts, so the transition to military life was not such a big shock. At the end of his four-year officer course, he won the Sword of Honour as the top RMC cadet and graduated with an arts/geography degree before joining the infantry as a second lieutenant.

After serving in the Parachute Regiment at Holsworthy near Sydney, Hunter decided in 1988 to apply for selection to the SAS. As it happened, his selection cohort included an outstanding group of young men such as Peter 'Gus' Gilmore who would command the SASR and go on to higher things in the military; Angus Campbell, now a senior public servant working in the highest levels of national security policy; current West Australian Labor MP and former navy diver Paul Papalia; SAS executive officer Major Grant and others. Often just one or two officers make it through the demanding officer selection course, but these men all made it in the same cohort.

Hunter had had his first contact with the SAS via a senior instructor at Duntroon, Clem 'Sas' Dwyer, whom many young SAS men from that era cite as instrumental in their decision to attempt selection.

'He had those unnerving, focused blue eyes and he used to be the subject of some intrigue amongst cadets because in those sorts of circumstances, if you don't know facts, people make them up and it breeds its own . . . ethos,' Hunter says.

Like most military officers, money was not the driving force behind his decision to serve in the army.

'I was doing it for the challenge, I liked the organisation, I liked the culture and some of those things changed for me towards the end and I also had a public service . . . attitude to it,' he says. 'I'm not a rabid . . . nationalist, but to me it was part and parcel of doing something for the country, for the community.'

In addition to his belief that his military career was marred by the Black Hawk crash, the other key aspect of Hunter's decision to leave the army was his family. By that stage he was 35 and he and his wife Nicole had two young children.

'At 35 you've got energy. At 45, which would be post-command or something — well, yes, you might have energy and you'd have additional experience that you can perhaps [take] into bureaucracy but you are certainly not going to go off and say, "Right, I'll give something a go myself." These were all the thoughts.'

So by late 1998 the Hunters decided to pursue their own business.

Hunter says his wife often reminds him that he never does anything easily and this decision was no exception. Starting an international business with very limited capital, a young family on the go and a new house, while studying part time for an MBA, is not for the faint-hearted.

'So there we were, business without capital, two young kids. Early parts of businesses never go as you expect them to, so that first 12 months was very tough,' he says. 'You go away from a secure income, you go away from some reasonable support mechanisms, like rental assistance, medical, dental, all those sort of little aspects that are hard to quantify in a dollar term in your package, until you have to pay for them yourself.'

Hunter concedes that he thrives on pressure, but in the early days of the company, OAM, it was pressure the like of which he had never known.

'It was a fairly full-on kind of period. Again, Nicole absorbed a lot of that and she has got a wonderful capacity in that respect. I'd get up very early and do my studies, and work was work and I'd try and do as much as I could for the growing family.'

He was very focused at this time because of the magnitude of the decision to leave the military. He had debts to service and hungry mouths to feed.

'I probably worked too hard, getting up early and going through. It's a pretty hectic time for a young family no matter what is going on work or otherwise, just having babies coming.'

Staying in Perth at least meant that Hunter could maintain his old network while establishing a business culture that fed directly off his special forces pedigree. 'We weren't transiting into an alternative business that was established and trying to sell fairy floss or something. We were selling security risk management so we were trying to leverage off our pedigree and our knowledge base. It was trying to do a commercial version, but it was more focused on collecting risk management plans for businesses,' he says.

The term 'security risk management' includes a broad range of topics from physical security to weather forecasting. OAM targeted the resource sector, particularly operations in Indonesia where the post-Suharto turmoil was continuing.

'Security risk management covers a whole bunch of stuff. It covers an audit on a mine site's operations — they might be pulling gold out so it has issues around the digging zone of illegal miners who want to get in there before blasting or after blasting so you then have to . . . control that access so you don't end up with dead illegal miners,' Hunter says. 'You've also got loss prevention issues . . . large companies, big buildings, lots of attractive items, it attracts a lot of fraud or theft. It can be at the highest level — we are going to steal gold or we are just going to rip off fittings and fixtures and fuel and all those sorts of things — so you control systems.'

In military terms it is not unlike establishing and securing a base, only the troops are foreign and the motivation is profit. Once the plan is written, the firm provides trainers to implement it and to teach the local workers how it operates.

'You don't put in 100 expats to secure a mine,' Hunter says. 'You might have 150 locals so they've got to be trained, monitor the standards, so you've got to lead, manage, communicate and it also then gives management a sense of, "Right. I can talk to Jonesy my man here." And he is watching the watchers, if you like, keeping them on the straight and narrow so reducing acts of crime and theft whereby the active participants were security personnel.

'The corruption, collusion and nepotism, it's an in-bred cultural trait ... It's never perfect; there are lots of different challenges depending on location.'

Like many security and risk management firms, OAM underwent a fundamental shift following the invasion of Iraq.

'There was opportunity there, similar services but perhaps in a more aggressive posture, where you would need to have weapons and the like,' Hunter says. 'Dealing with all those variables is all a part of the pedigree that defence helps you with, particularly the SAS side of it.'

Working in Iraq or Afghanistan requires clear mission statements, strong operating procedures, weapons safety and liaison with local forces. OAM has been involved in a variety of projects in Iraq, ranging from vehicle delivery to personal protection for aid workers, supply to development projects and communications but their most important job was securing the ballot papers for the 2005 elections.

'It was all about timing and opportunity and we came up with a different flexible plan which won us the job,' says Hunter.

After the US military announced that it could not be involved, the United Nations put out a tender at very short notice. 'They put it out on Friday and wanted it on Monday, "This is for a multi-million dollar capability to take x tonnes of material from one central location to three locations and then out to 20 provinces." How the hell do you do that and secure it? Because the vulnerability was they would be a target of insurgents ... so we came up with a solution of choppers.

'Choppers were expensive in one respect, but not as expensive as 30 armoured cars and details to move it around. We had to ramp it up at short notice. So that is where the network of contacts, things like today's communication system of email [comes in]. One guy gets it, "I can't do it, but I've got 10 mates who might be interested", bang, so we had to pull that together pretty quickly. We didn't get all of our manpower and recruiting processes right, but again we couldn't have done it without the defence pedigree and knowing what skill sets we needed.'

The job went over five or six months.

'When it was all said and done when you wrap it up, you'd have to class it as a success because [there was] no loss of papers, people, assets or anything, it was done quickly and in an efficient manner. Now whether people were targeting it or didn't choose to target it, who knows? If it all fucked up there would be plenty of retrospect scopes out there, learned knowledge masters telling us why it all went wrong, but it didn't and in some respects [it was a case of] the clichéd adage of "Who Dares Wins". But it came from a slightly innovative plan, solid planning and then continual operational management.'

They managed strong levels of operational security so that information was kept on a strictly need-to-know basis.

'First thing people knew was a chopper arriving,' he says. 'The principles of military planning, the appreciation process, understanding the problem and working through it and developing it were very high in our businesses solution to that.'

He compares the private security environment in Iraq with the gold rush.

'Someone said there was gold and every man who could pick up a pick or a wheelbarrow [went], so people saw it as an opportunity. "Yes, I was there; yes I've got the skill sets." So you've got a lot of one, two, three-man bands operating there and then they develop a rapport with the client, clients are happy with that company, develop an opportunity, so a lot of businesses sprang up out of that, and a lot went by the wayside.'

OAM always targets the small to medium jobs simply because they have more control over the processes.

'You don't have the external investors and other parties trying to influence what you do; few of those have been grown into middle and larger players. Once you sign up for a five- or 10-million-dollar contract one way or another, there doesn't have to be a high percentage margin to make some money and go forward.'

Hunter says he seldom looks back with any hankering for life in the SAS, although during times of high operational tempo, such as East Timor, he did think it would have been nice to apply all that training directly.

'It's nice to see the skill sets are being used, it's good to see peers, mates are doing all those things, it's good to say, "I know I could do that", so that's how I sort of balanced it out in my own mind,' he says. 'I am one of those blokes that says, "The past is fine, we use it for lessons, but it's there, it's not for living in."'

COMMANDING OFFICERS

chapter fifteen

THE BRIDGE BUILDER

When Australia's most powerful security body, the National Security Committee of Cabinet, meets, Duncan Lewis sits close to the right hand of the prime minister.

As deputy secretary to the Department of the Prime Minister and Cabinet, he oversees the prime minister's policy advice on national security and international affairs.

Mr Lewis, as he is generally known in the department, is a civilian. But he has not been one for long.

After a 30-year career in the army, most of it in special forces including a stint as commanding officer of the SAS regiment, Lewis became a major general in December 2002, and was appointed the inaugural head of the upgraded Special Operations Command (SOC). Two years later when his posting was coming to an end he got a call from his superiors. This was as far up the military brass chain as the two-star Major General Lewis was going to get and at the age of 50 he contemplated life after the army.

He did not have to think for long. Canberra being a small, powerfully networked city, the then secretary of the department, Peter Shergold, got wind of it and could hardly believe his luck.

He promptly hired Lewis in early 2005 to run the national security division (at the civilian equivalent of his two-star rank of major general) and soon promoted him to be deputy secretary, the equivalent of a three-star rank, with responsibilities ranging from national security to international strategic policy.

'Essentially my central function is to provide advice to the prime minister on national security and international engagement issues and to coordinate between government departments and agencies on those matters,' Lewis explains. 'So they're the two verbs if you like — advise and coordinate.'

For the prime minister's department to have a former special operations commander, versed in unconventional and asymmetric warfare, in such a crucial role at the top of government was unprecedented. It was also a matter of pride for the SAS, an army unit that is often seen by other sections of the military as elitist and something of a law unto itself.

Sitting in his modest office inside the department's new building, a stone's throw down the hill from Parliament House in Canberra, Lewis says, 'I've loved the work, it's wonderfully engaging sort of stuff. You're always dealing with current issues and then some longer-term policy matters, so you've got a nice mix of both. There's managing the crisis on the day-to-day basis and then the longer term and more cerebral policy work that's required.'

With a new Labor government in power since 24 November 2007, and the prime minister, Kevin Rudd, being a former diplomat, it has been a hectic time. The days are long and with troops stationed in the Middle East and throughout the region the travel schedule can be punishing.

At Christmas, 2007, Lewis returned from Afghanistan and Iraq with the new prime minister on Christmas Eve, rushed around to do some last-minute shopping, had 25 December with his family and a few days in Tasmania with friends before returning to his desk.

Even when he is on leave he is on duty and as one of the government's principal national security advisers he can never be too far away from Canberra or switch off his mobile phone.

He describes his workload as 'different' as opposed to heavier than the one he carried as head of Special Operations Command.

'There's nobody in harm's way immediately in my area right now. I'm not being woken up at three o'clock in the morning with news of some catastrophe on the other side of the world where some young man's just been terribly injured or worse. So you don't have that sort of workload, but by the same token the hours are extraordinarily long,' he says. 'You're serving the prime minister of the day and so you're providing very large volumes of advice and then that advice needs to be timely, so if it's required at odd hours of the day then that's when it's provided. It's a different kind of work but it is very long hours, there's no doubt about that. It's pretty heavy going some days.'

Lewis describes his job as a 'grab bag' of responsibilities and has no regrets about his career change, even though he admits the decision to leave the military was for him, as it is for everyone, very complex.

'I had to think long and hard when I was made an offer to come to this department,' he says. 'You don't often get the invitation to come and join the prime minister's own department and it was clearly a very attractive offer to me at the time.'

The thing he misses the most is the soldiers.

'You do miss contact with the soldiers and I just had a visit a week or two before Christmas to Afghanistan and Iraq and it was fantastic to see the soldiers again, to be able to chat to them and catch up with quite a lot of old colleagues and comrades of mine who were working on the Special Forces Taskforce in Afghanistan, for example.

'It was great to see those guys again and it's at moments like that that the heart sort of tugs a little and you wonder what on earth you're doing. But no, I've been very fortunate, very lucky, blessed in a way to be able to make a transition from a career that I loved — I mean, I loved soldiering and always will — into something else that I find is extremely challenging and interesting and making what I think is, what I hope at any rate, is a contribution to this country.'

There is no doubt that he occupies a far more influential position now than he could ever have done if he had stayed in uniform.

'You can have some significant influence over some very big decisions where I'm working right now,' he admits. 'Quite obviously, you're providing advice directly to the prime minister on what he or she might contemplate doing and I think that clearly puts you in a position of significant influence. That's not to say, of course, that any senior officer in the military hasn't got significant influence within their area of responsibility . . . it's a different sort of influence.'

He is also able to bridge the gap between the rest of government and Defence. He understands from personal experience why such a large and self-contained organisation as Defence can become insular and appear to be extremely slow moving.

'It can become less aware of what is going on around it than perhaps it should,' he says. 'On the other side, the whole-of-government side where I'm working now, there is frequently a lack of understanding of what Defence does as well. A lot of Defence matters are quite arcane, you know, "Why would you want to do this, that, or the other thing with troop movements?" or "Why would it take you this long to move forces from here to there?" or "Why would certain capability requirements be needed? This seems unnecessary!"

'Well, they're the sort of discussions that you can get involved in and act almost as a translator and say, "This is why it takes x number of days" or "This is why you'd want a machine that does x or y." Because you're able to see both sides of the track.'

Many people in a small, fast-moving department such as Prime Minister and Cabinet with just 350 or so staff find it difficult to imagine the competing demands and the chain of command in Defence, with its 70,000 staff including more than 50,000 who have signed up to wear a uniform and to die for their country if necessary.

'People often say how long it takes for Defence to make decisions, you know, the big machine. And of course I understand that. I've been part of that machine for 30 years!'

During high-level meetings he is able to say to civilian colleagues, 'Look, it's not being perverse, it's just that it is a very large and complex machine and it takes a while for the wheel to turn over and if you start spinning it any faster than that then bits fly off and it comes unstuck.'

'Not that it can't move fast when it has to, but when it's handling routine administrative stuff it just takes a while for the machine to get through it,' he says.

Despite the obvious differences between the old and new governments, Lewis says the transition has been surprisingly seamless.

One area where some differences would be expected is in dealing with troops on the ground. John Howard was very popular with soldiers after he increased Defence spending and boosted the operational tempo for the forces around the world in support of his close mate George W. Bush in places such as Iraq. During his first tour to the Middle East Area of Operations, Rudd had to sell the policy of withdrawing the army battle group from southern Iraq and reassure the troops about Defence spending. But the prime minister is the prime minister.

'In terms of popularity, Prime Minister Rudd had a very successful tour, he was very well received I think by the troops, he spoke extensively to the troops both in Tallil in Iraq and across in Tarin Kowt in Afghanistan,' Lewis says. 'He had extensive contact with the diggers in both those places and they're always keen to hear from the prime minister about what's going on and what's happening to them and to Australia and he of course manages all those things very well.'

From day one Rudd was at pains to assure the military that Labor would not cut Defence operational spending and would maintain the emphasis on modernising the military, with special emphasis on the army.

Lewis regards this modernising process as vital to the future success of the army and particularly the special forces elements of it. He likes to compare the army's ground forces with a train. In the front carriage are the special forces, developing cutting-edge tactics and technologies. Gradually the capabilities are passed down from carriage to carriage.

He believes that the standard of the wider infantry forces, in the rear carriages, is much higher than it was 10 or 15 years ago.

'And most of the stuff they carry now is stuff that was at some stage in the hands of just the few special forces in the Australian Army. Mainly because it was technology that was being tested or there wasn't a lot of it around or it was very expensive whereas through time it becomes more accessible and so it gets passed back down through the carriages until the entire army from end to end is equipped with that particular piece of equipment,' he says. 'Night vision capability is one of the best examples of that — it's happened over the last 25 years where originally it was only in the hands of a few and now every soldier in the field has some form of night vision assistance, the ability to see at night.'

The nature of warfare has also changed dramatically as the information revolution has been applied to military forces. The flow of quality and immediate information allows commanders to apply far fewer troops to a particular task than was the case in previous years.

'The fact that if you are few in number but isolated, so long as you know what is going on around you then you are safe, because you know what is happening and you can respond accordingly,' he says. 'So [in] the jargon of "situational awareness", people are situationally aware now in a way that they weren't in the past.'

That enables small numbers of conventional soldiers to do the same job that only a small cell of special forces troops could have done just a few years ago.

He says both conventional and special forces soldiers are now capable of doing all sorts of things that they couldn't do not very long ago.

'Operations in Iraq and to a greater extent in Afghanistan have demonstrated to us how you need to maintain a real balance in your force. You've got to be able to turn your hand to whatever comes up next and that's the acme of success, being able to develop a force which is sufficiently balanced to be able to move left or right, depending on which way a conflict is going.'

That movement can sometimes take an unexpected twist and force soldiers to think and act outside the square.

'One of the proudest moments I ever had in uniform was halfway through the *Tampa* operation when I contacted the ship and asked this young bloke what was happening and he said, "Oh, what we're doing, we're cooking", and they were cooking for the refugees on board,' he says.

'I was just astonished. This steely-eyed trooper who had gone on board in order to conduct a security operation had, along with his colleagues, very quickly realised that the situation had changed in a moment and what we had was a sea of human misery on board the ship that needed looking after.

'I'm not saying that every SAS soldier needs to be trained as a cook, but that's the kind of flexibility of mind, that function you need to have in my view in the special forces. You need it right through the force, of course, but it is particularly so in SF.'

Such flexibility is also vital in the ongoing campaign against terrorism. Lewis says the 'war against terrorism' might be a contested expression, but for the digger risking his neck on a hillside in Afghanistan it is most definitely a 'war'.

It is one which is based increasingly on intelligence and there are no better intelligence gatherers than SAS troops.

'We have always known that countering terror would require high levels of intelligence feed and situational awareness. It's like hunting for a needle in a haystack,' he says. 'You see this confluence between counterterrorism operations and counterinsurgency and you hear lots of military theologians speaking currently about counterinsurgency. And all of that implies that you've got a terrorist who is operating in his or her comfort zone. They're in a community where they are comfortable, they can move around relatively freely.

'Our problem is to identify that person and to make sure that they can't go about their nefarious work. That requires high levels of intelligence and that's where of course special forces come into their own, because they're very good at looking, watching and reporting.'

Although science and technology have made huge leaps in recent years, the 'mark one eyeball' remains the most reliable intelligence-gathering tool.

'We're now able to see things that we couldn't see before in an electronic sense. But if you're actually going to start doing something about that, that is bring fire to bear, then you need to ensure that it is exactly what you think it is,' he says. 'I mean, history's replete with all sorts of fires that have gone wrong and every war has its stories about fire that was incorrectly placed. The best way to ensure — and there's still no guarantee — is to make sure that it's the "mark one eyeball" that has actually identified what it is that you're going to fire on and then have absolute control over the fire that's going onto it.'

One of the biggest advances in military technology is a commander's ability to see, either via camera-equipped unmanned aerial drones or satellite imagery, precisely what is over the next hill and to deliver fire remotely.

'Over the hill might be 50 kilometres, it might be 100 kilometres, it might be 1000 kilometres, but you can actually see over the hill electronically. You can then deliver fire onto something which you're not in physical contact with. You don't have to actually carry it to the point of delivery, it can be delivered by aircraft or a long-range gun or a ship or some other free rocket over ground.'

The fact that people can view military operations in their lounge rooms almost in real time adds another dimension to the challenges.

As 2008 wears on and the memories of 9/11 and Bali 2002 begin to fade, it falls to men such as Duncan Lewis to be vigilant in the sure knowledge that another terrorist attack is inevitable. They don't know where and they don't know when but they do know it is not a question of 'if'.

He says the world is definitely not becoming safer but is unsure whether it is becoming more dangerous. 'I think it's just a case of it being a dangerous place. Terrorism won't go away, there's no doubt about that,' he says. 'We can be fanciful and glass half-full and say, "Oh, you know, it's getting better", but the bottom line is that the root causes are still there; they haven't been addressed. The assault on our way of life remains as a result of those root-cause tensions and so long as we are prepared to defend our values and our way of life then we need to stand up and be counted.'

While the west is becoming more adept at counter-radicalisation strategies, there is a long, long way to go. The challenge is getting to understand what drives a young man or woman to cross that Rubicon between lawful and extraordinarily unlawful behaviour.

'What would cause a person to cross that line is often unclear. It's certainly a path to radicalisation that we don't fully understand and we need to do some more work there.'

Lewis regards the physical security measures that have been put in place since 9/11, at a cost of billions of dollars, as adequate at this stage. 'There are some issues quite clearly still to be resolved with regard to legislation and with regard to some of the infrastructure security requirements,' he says. 'Generally speaking, we've done a huge amount and I'm reasonably comfortable that we're in a maintenance phase. We need to maintain what we've got.

'Terrorism is like a malarial strain that changes through time and you need to be like a malarial prophylaxis to fight it. You need to be moving not only with the strain, but in front of it so that it's not getting away from you. We need to be sufficiently agile, like the malarial prophylaxis, to be in front and in a blocking position each time terrorism appears in whatever manifestation.'

Lewis is certain that terrorists will not become less inventive in the way that they go about their business. 'Their levels of inventiveness have always astonished me and they will continue to astonish me.'

But vigilance is the key and vigilance is difficult to sustain six years after the Bali bombings. 'It comes and goes . . . the trick is to keep the issue sufficiently in front of the population that they are aware of the need for security, but not so much that they are frightened out of their minds.'

chapter sixteen

THE RELUCTANT EXECUTIVE

The first time that he walked into an executive meeting at his brother John's company, Multiplex, Chris Roberts could barely understand a word that was said.

'We had this big meeting on day two and the only words I could recognise were, "Chris Roberts'll do that." It was like being in a meeting of the Gaelic Debating Society,' the former SAS commander recalls.

Roberts, known to his peers as 'CAM' because they are his initials, had been unsure about what he would do once he left the army. But he did know what he would not do.

When, as a brigadier, he retired in 1998 as Commanding Officer of Northern Command in Darwin after a distinguished 32-year career, he was canvassed for several jobs, including in the defence industry and the Northern Territory government.

'There were a couple of things I said I'd never do,' he explains. 'I said I'd never be a gun-runner and I would never snipe from the sidelines, be a consultant or that sort of thing. What I wanted to do was make a complete break from the army. My view is, "The king is dead, long live the king." It's a young man's game and what they don't need is lots of old retired army officers telling young people how they should do their business.'

Regarded as one of the most uncompromising special forces officers to have served in the Australian Army, Roberts, who was also known by the nickname 'Sniffy', was a tough nut, a stubborn man who said what he thought and refused to play politics. As a result his career did not scale the heights that some of his early mentors might have expected, but it is with considerable pride that Roberts reflects on what he did achieve.

Born in Albany in Western Australia in 1945, he graduated from Duntroon in 1967 and went straight into the SAS after completing the officer selection course.

'I just put down SAS as my first choice and then two infantry battalions as my second choice and I was quite surprised when SAS came up,' he says.

The Vietnam War was at its zenith and Roberts became only the second young army officer to be accorded the privilege of direct entry from Duntroon to the regiment, the first being Gordon 'Sam' Simpson. Most officers and soldiers must serve in a battalion or another corps before they become eligible for SAS selection.

He served as a troop and patrol commander under Major Reg 'the Beast' Beesley and led numerous patrols against Viet Cong strongholds in the May Tao mountains in the north-east and the Long Hai hills in southern Phuoc Tuy province.

From there, Roberts was posted to the 5th Battalion as adjutant and then to the Portsea Officer Cadet School as an instructor. He then went back to university at the University of Western Australia to complete an honour's degree in Arts. His circle back to SAS was closed in 1975 when he returned to the regiment as a squadron commander, first under Neville Smethurst and then Mike Jeffery.

This was a period of soul-searching for the SAS and Jeffery was desperately seeking a role for the regiment in the post-Vietnam era when Defence spending was cut by the Whitlam Labor government and the future of the SAS was in some doubt.

In addition to the counterterrorism function, which would provide the bread and butter to keep the place running, Jeffery asked Roberts to write a concept of operations for regional force surveillance.

'We put all that together, culminating in a couple of exercises and it's now the concept for the regional force surveillance units. They use the same concept to this day,' Roberts says.

He also took a water operations troop across to San Diego to train on exchange with the United States Navy SEAL team. The exchange brought home to him just how good the SAS was at its job compared with other forces.

After another couple of postings he went to the directorate of Special Action Forces in Canberra, again under Jeffery. His job was to establish the new counterterrorism training facilities at Campbell Barracks in Perth and to help write a submission to government for the Special Action Forces Allowance (SAFA) that is paid to SAS soldiers in recognition of their hazardous duty.

He became commanding officer of SASR in December 1982 and immediately set about rebalancing the regiment for a war-fighting role.

'When I got there I found that we had no war roles capability left,' he says. 'Everything had been diverted into the counterterrorist function and I made the assessment that counterterrorism was not necessarily the next operation that we were going to tackle. If it wasn't, we were not in good shape to do it.'

He ordered his squadron commanders to establish a strategic war roles capability and to take steps to have SAS trainers operating in South-east Asia.

'I was disappointed that we were not training overseas people in our region — it was being left to the Germans, the British and the Americans,' he says. 'This was 1983 and I said, "In seven years we will have a strategic war roles capability and we will have training instructors into South-east Asia."'

The first instructors went in during 1988 and a strategic war-fighting role was demonstrated at the Kangaroo '89 and Kangaroo '92 war games.

He had some brilliant squadron commanders, including Majors Jim Wallace, Duncan Lewis and Mike Silverstone, who would all rise to command the SAS.

Roberts's other major reform as CO was to modernise the SAS selection course. He assigned the brilliant Silverstone to the job and told him to focus on a soldier's intellect, character, moral courage and mental and physical endurance.

'My point was I could train a man to run nine miles in 90 minutes, but I couldn't train him to have physical and mental endurance,' Roberts says. 'In those days if you failed the two-mile run and you failed the nine-mile run you failed the course. So I stopped that.'

Having killed off one sacred cow he tackled another, eliminating the concept of negative feedback or denigration of soldiers. 'I said, "If you can't say anything positive, say nothing at all."'

He assigned the regiment's best sergeants to Silverstone's team and they produced what Roberts regarded as a very good new selection course.

'My reason for this is that reinforcements are our lifeblood. If we don't get them right and we get the wrong people into the regiment then the regiment can go bad and it can become a bunch of cowboys, which is something I really didn't want it to be.'

Roberts says that course still runs pretty much the same way today, 'Which means it needs to be bloody looked at with a fine-tooth comb and re-jigged, because that was 25 years ago. You've got to keep looking at things and improving and saying, "Is this relevant to what we need now?"'

During his stint as CO from December 1982 until June 1985, Roberts had become disillusioned about the way the wider army viewed the SAS and how nobody on the east coast appeared to know how to use the regiment. So when he became Director, Special Action Forces he set out to fix that. He wrote a paper that recommended bringing all special forces together under the one command. He encountered fierce opposition from the top end of the army, but eventually won the day and Headquarters Special Forces, the forerunner to today's Special Operations Command, was born.

After a year bedding it down, Roberts moved into the Canberra bureaucrat stream before his final active posting as CO of Northern Command.

During the Gulf War in 1991 Roberts lobbied hard to get an SAS squadron onto the ground in Iraq. But the then CDF General Peter

Gration told him that the Hawke Labor government would not allow ground forces into Iraq under any circumstances.

'It broke my heart,' he says. 'I knew we had the soldiers who could do the job. I remember sitting in his office saying, "Sir, we can offer a squadron, we can get the guys a sense of purpose", and he said, "I'd love to, Chris, but the Prime Minister has said no ground combat troops."'

After retiring and taking an overseas holiday with his wife, Judy, Roberts found himself in the job market. Offers included a public service position in the Northern Territory and a job with a major defence supplier.

At the same time he received the first of several phone calls from his older brother John, the billionaire chairman and founder of the construction giant Multiplex. He hadn't seen much of his brother, who was 11 years his senior, during his time in the army, but he was interested in hearing him out. Multiplex was building on several continents and his brother was listed by BRW as being worth in excess of $1 billion.

'I said to him, "Jesus, I know nothing about construction, why do you want me to come and work with you?"

'He said, "You're family! Come and work for me."'

John Roberts hadn't reached the top of the dog-eat-dog construction game by taking 'no' for an answer. After more persuasion, Brigadier Roberts joined Multiplex.

Apart from John saying he wanted him to start an engineering division and be the office manager in Perth to 'coordinate stuff', his role was not clear. But soon his nephew Andrew Roberts, who was deputy CEO of Multiplex, asked him to examine how the company could get a leg up in East Timor.

After travelling to Dili to meet with senior Timorese officials, he recommended that Multiplex stay out of East Timor, because it offered only small-scale construction opportunities — really just 'beer money' for the likes of Multiplex. He was overruled and the firm won a contract to rebuild the Portuguese embassy. It emerged 18 months later with a small loss and the boss saying, 'We should have listened to you.'

Roberts soon found that his office manager duties were not keeping him busy enough so he started travelling, arranging meetings for Multiplex with the likes of Defence and the Northern Territory government. Company executives were surprised that so many people knew him.

'We were working hard, but I had plenty of people and by about three o'clock in the afternoon there wasn't much to do, unless of course you were a micro-manager and that's not my style,' he says. 'I believe in supervising lightly those who you trust and are competent and only supervising closely those who need the supervision or that you don't have any confidence in.'

By the end of 1999 he had had enough of being away from Judy at home in Canberra. So the company asked him to establish operations in the national capital.

'I thought I'd have a guy to work to, a general manager, and I'd help him out,' he says. 'So I arrived in Canberra with a laptop and a mobile phone and no office and by myself and [I was] told to start a construction company! We won our first contract about nine months later.'

He applied his military management skills at almost every turn. He wrote a major paper on restructuring the company's finances and ran strategic workshops and then they asked him to run Multiplex Facilities Management.

'It was a fairly new company but it just was losing money,' he says. 'So I got the team together, the managing director and his key people and I took them down to Bowral and we said, "Right, let's just talk this issue through."'

They came up with a strategic plan. It was accepted, Roberts was appointed chairman and a year later the division recorded a profit. His business career was booming and before long he was sent to Melbourne as group general manager corporate planning and human resources.

He almost killed himself with 15-hour days. 'I remember walking down Elizabeth Street in Melbourne on the mobile phone to London and it was 1.30 in the morning and I said, "What the fuck am I doing?" I was absolutely stuffed!'

By this stage his health was suffering and he tried to resign. 'I was told I couldn't resign, that it wasn't in the lexicon but I said, "Sorry, I'm not going to work in these conditions."'

Instead, he was asked to do a major cost-cutting activity. Like much of corporate Australia, the Multiplex cost-cutting strategy focused heavily on sacking people. Roberts said, 'I'll do the cost-cutting but I won't touch the people. There are a hell of a lot of areas where we could save money.'

So he hired an old army mate and between them they identified $15.5 million in savings from the company's $56-million direct cost budget.

That was his last hurrah with Multiplex. In June 2006 his brother John died, aged 72, after a long battle with diabetes. Chris Roberts decided he didn't want to go out in a box, so he retired. He has taken on some minor projects, including producing a film on Long Tan for the Australian War Memorial, and is painting. 'I'm about to start my intermediate watercolour course, I do a bit of writing, I'm on a couple of boards and my health's improving.'

Overall, he says he enjoyed his time in the corporate world and when he does guest lecturing spots at the Australian Defence College he compares it favourably with life in the SAS.

'I found participative leadership,' he says. 'In fact, I found the corporate world very similar to SAS — people ready to take risks, people ready to try new ideas, people ready to make decisions and so in that sense it was quite a natural slip from the SAS world to the corporate world.'

He doubts whether the fit would have been as good had he been in the conventional army, where the further up the chain people go the more risk-averse they tend to become.

'It doesn't surprise me that a lot of SAS people slip quite easily into the corporate world because they've got something the corporate world hasn't got and that's discipline. And they've got one other thing the corporate world doesn't have. When you ask an SAS soldier to do something, you know it will be done.'

What he liked about Multiplex was that the leaders would help with problems, help come up with decisions and talk to people.

'That's very much an SAS approach to doing things, whereas in the higher ranks of the conventional military you have your own personal staff around you and then you have a bigger staff around you who do the thinking. You get the papers presented to you and you make your decisions on that.'

One aspect of business that he found particularly challenging was finance. In the military you are allocated a budget and you spend it.

He also found that in the commercial world, former high-ranking military officers are often regarded as too expensive to hire because they expect a huge staff to support them. 'That's where I think SAS people have no difficulty with making the transition. You know we're not big on rank in terms of wearing your rank, we're not big on pomp and ceremony. In fact I loathe pomp and ceremony. Each one of the class reunions, I'm one of the few that don't go to the parade at Duntroon because I think it's a waste of soldiers' time.'

Roberts has mellowed somewhat in retirement but he makes no apologies for his no-nonsense approach during his time in uniform.

That approach was forged in the jungles of Vietnam where he discovered how unforgiving war really was. As a troop commander with 3 Squadron he didn't lose any men, but the Kiwi troop attached to the squadron lost one of its finest patrol commanders, Sergeant Graham Campbell, who was killed in action in January 1970.

'There are no beg pardons,' he says. 'Once the bullet goes through you, you're dead.'

Roberts was chuffed to receive a Christmas card recently from one of his former corporals who lives in Deniliquin in rural New South Wales.

It read in part, 'You're a tough bastard but we knew where we stood.'

That will do CAM Roberts for an epitaph because, he says, 'Soldiers need to know.'

chapter seventeen

THE WINDSURFER

The head of the Corruption and Crime Commission of Western Australia, Mike Silverstone, has been in a political hot seat on more than one occasion.

The commission was in the news for most of 2007 because of a new investigation into disgraced former Labor premier-turned-lobbyist Brian Burke in relation to a breach of cabinet confidentiality which spread its tentacles eastwards, unexpectedly claiming the scalp of one federal coalition government minister, Senator Ian Campbell.

But Silverstone has faced far tougher challenges.

When he was commanding officer of the SAS in 1996 he took a great deal of political heat for the Black Hawk helicopter tragedy. And in 2001 Brigadier Silverstone, by then the commanding officer of Northern Command in Darwin, became embroiled in what would become known as the 'children overboard affair' just before the federal election.

Silverstone, believing that the captain of the frigate HMAS *Adelaide*, Commander Norman Banks, had told him by telephone that a child had been thrown overboard from an intercepted refugee boat, properly passed the information along the chain of command. Banks, however, believed he had said a young child had been held over the side, not thrown overboard. It was a classic case of the 'fog of war' and miscommunication, but when then Attorney-General Phillip Ruddock announced the untested information as fact, it blew up into one of the biggest political scandals of the Howard government's 11-year administration.

In the end, the Senate committee that spent months examining the complex chain of events strongly supported the integrity of both Silverstone and Banks, but both men sustained collateral damage.

Despite wounds inflicted by both of these episodes, Silverstone was set for his second star and a promotion to major general when, in March 2004, he suddenly resigned from the army.

'Driving across Kings Avenue bridge [in Canberra], I looked up at Russell [Defence HQ] and thought, "I don't really want to do this anymore."'

The 48-year-old Canberra-born son of an Artillery Corps brigadier had simply had enough and was not willing to jump through the political and bureaucratic hoops that he knew would lie ahead in the 'generals' club'.

He didn't really expect to get the WA Crime Commission job. He thought it would go to a lawyer or a policeman, but when it was offered to him he jumped at the chance to return to Perth.

'I'm a great believer in the Lotto test: what you would do if you won Lotto? One of the things I thought I'd do is come back to Perth and go windsurfing,' he says. 'I never really thought we'd come back to Perth but here we are because of this job.'

As he looked around at his army comrades he saw that they had less freedom to do things and were under pressure from a number of fronts. 'The expectation to perform to a range of bureaucratic expectations was becoming increasingly highly pressured and perhaps not as attractive as doing other things, but all jobs were carrying those pressures,' he says.

Silverstone had also found himself at odds with the concept of the government as 'customer'. The top management regime in Defence at the time, Admiral Chris Barrie and Secretary Dr Allan Hawke, had introduced a managerialist approach that grated with many senior officers and Silverstone was one of them.

'I'd taken issue with that and written to the secretary saying [that] when you move to a situation with the government as the customer and the owner, you do get to a situation when the customer is never wrong and that can actually distort the process of quality advice to government. It is just the way it is,' he says.

His own doubts about his long-term prospects had first surfaced in the wake of the Black Hawk tragedy.

After the accident he suffered the onset of depression.

'I had depression, I was diagnosed with depression and you talk to my wife, she talks about walking on eggshells around me,' he says. 'I went to the doctor and had a number of aches and pains and the doctor said, "Read this list, you have depression."

'Now I was very fortunate in the sense that having had that explained to me, and I read a whole bunch of books and talked to lots of people, it was a very transient process and I don't have depression now. But I know what it looks like and it really sneaks up on you if you are not conscious of these things.'

His condition was probably exacerbated by having to sit by and watch the treatment meted out to the two junior SAS officers in charge of the fatal exercise near Townsville.

'My view has always been the accident occurred because of pilot error. My view was the board of inquiry failed to sufficiently focus on that and I think I'm on the record in a number of places that Bob Hunter and Sean Bellis had not been fairly treated,' Silverstone says. 'It's deeply sad the soldiers died but that is part of our operating and training environment. It is an enormous cost to the family, but to then have to defend the regiment and two very capable officers, I found the sort of criticism I was subject to an unpleasant experience and that weighed heavily at the time.'

It was following the board of inquiry and the eventual decision not to censure any individual officer that Silverstone consulted his doctor.

'I had a meeting with a friend of mine who is a military doctor but not in Canberra. Then I went to meetings down in Sydney and I flew back late one afternoon and it had been raining and the sun was shining off the dams and I thought, "Yeah, you have a reason to be depressed, but it is not in your nature." So for me at that moment it was an . . . [epiphany]. I was lucky that I could step away from it. I was still bloody angry with things for a while, but that for me was the moment that required recognising what had happened and having the opportunity to think about it and deal with it. But not everybody is that lucky and they need support to deal with these things.'

He says there is now an acceptance that depression does occur and that it is a natural process. 'You live off adrenaline for months and months, if not years and at the end you are in debt. You have to pay a cost for that.'

He had also formed a view that command opportunities would be limited because of the accident and perhaps he should look elsewhere while he was still young enough.

Silverstone tends not to dwell too much on the past or worry too much about the future. He has a busy job and a great and happy life in Perth.

'I enjoy my current job, I have a couple of years' contract here, I windsurf, I will probably work doing some type of job like this for another four or five years and then I'll probably transition into something else,' he says. 'I'll write, I'll study, work part time, consult and remain intellectually engaged, and be as physical as I possibly can and enjoy myself.'

chapter eighteen

BREAKING THE CHAIN

James McMahon, a recent commanding officer of the SAS, was one of those bright young army officers who had 'General' stamped all over him.

In early 2007 McMahon was at the top of his game and, according to some senior officers, could have the military world at his feet.

As he approached the end of his command of the regiment he had joined in the late 1980s, he came to a crossroads. His eight predecessors as CO SAS had gone further up the military ladder. Several had risen to the top of Special Operations Command or its precursors, but McMahon was on the verge of breaking the chain.

After winning both the Distinguished Service Cross for exemplary command in Afghanistan and Iraq in 2005 and 2006 and the Distinguished Service Medal for his work in East Timor in 1999, McMahon had already seen more action than many army officers experience in an entire career.

He had also worked on high-level war plans in the United States Central Command directly under American supremo General Tommy Franks in the lead-up to the so-called 'war against terror' in Afghanistan, following the attack on the World Trade Center in 2001 and he was also involved in the 2003 Iraq conflict.

Eight years after first seeing action in East Timor, McMahon, a modest, open-faced man with a broad, infectious smile, was wrestling with the perennial dilemma faced by many people who choose to serve their country in a uniform: when is a good time to leave?

It was not about cutting ties because the army reserve could ensure that he never did that. It was about one thing only — his family.

After serving as CO SASR, his appointment complete, there were no more jobs for him in the regiment.

'If Canberra was here [in Perth] I wouldn't be leaving, but it ain't,' he says simply.

After 22 years of devoted service to the military and with his wife and two children aged under eight firmly settled in his home town of Perth, he felt it was time to place them ahead of personal ambition.

They wanted to raise their two children in the west, close to both extended families, but if he stayed in the army the family would inevitably have to move to the nation's capital or continue to be moved around and be unsettled.

'For me it wasn't so much that I was moving because of the circumstances of my work, in fact it is quite the opposite. From a personal level I really enjoyed everything about what I've done over the last 22 years. The issue for me was about family stability and choosing a place where I wanted to raise my family,' he says.

But he readily admits that he is torn. 'My heart is in [the army] but I've got to balance the ledger with the family. You make life choices.'

For the past 22 years his primary commitment has been to the army and the SAS. 'I was away for both pregnancies, the system was good enough to get me back for both births, but soon after I left again. I was away from my family for at least 80 percent of my time as CO when you add it all up, so the lack of balance was pretty undeniable at that point; however, the job requires and deserves that commitment.'

Consequently, McMahon spent a large chunk of 2007 on leave as he contemplated his next step. A former athlete and student of commerce, he set about drawing on both these fields of endeavour as well as his military training to carve out a new life. He enrolled in an MBA and company director's course and completed both in 2007. He was also invited to become a director of the West Coast Eagles AFL club, to help instil a set of values in the club at a time when it was in turmoil over the drug habits of its star player, Ben Cousins.

Later in the year McMahon joined the world of high finance in a boutique investment bank as he still contemplated severing his full-time ties with the military.

The most difficult aspect, and the cause of most of his separation anxiety, was the strong feeling that he could be letting the side down. As an SAS officer that is probably the worst thing he could contemplate.

'But in my mind, post command was the right time to do it, because [in] everything you have done as an officer, you have trained to be the CO. From troop commander you train to be squadron commander, squadron commander you train to be the CO. I've been trained extremely well, I've had great opportunities — and then I think to myself, "Actually, I've given the system as good as I've got." So I don't feel that it's uneven in any way,' he says, debating the point with himself.

His personal dilemma is one that he has seen played out many times with soldiers and officers of the SAS Regiment. Due to the close-knit nature of the unit, leaving is never an easy decision. It is especially difficult for the modern-day special forces soldier, when the SAS and Commando regiments are the busiest they have been since the Vietnam War.

It becomes a question of balancing opportunities: travelling to unusual places as a special forces soldier to fight wars and be paid a good tax-free salary, taking a highly paid private sector security job in Iraq or Afghanistan or joining the corporate or public sectors with the chance to be with your children as they grow.

When he started as CO it was a time of high turnover, when private security companies were plundering special forces outfits around the globe.

McMahon believes that to stay in the regiment, men need to be at least 100 per cent motivated, both for their own sakes and for the sakes of those around them.

'You didn't come here with 95 per cent commitment, you most probably came with 110 per cent commitment and you need that to be in the regiment.'

He also believes the army pays SAS men a fair wage for the job they do. 'There are not many occupations in this world offering the excitement and exhilaration of actually being involved in a conflict and for the right reasons. In a lot of other jobs you just don't get that.'

Putting a price on such a unique job and its many and varied opportunities is virtually impossible. How much money can compensate for the camaraderie and the variety of tasks? Because no one could tell him what answer to give his men who were contemplating leaving, James McMahon, the numbers man, did some figures.

Whenever one of his troopers or officers came into his office and announced he was leaving to pursue the big dollars, he would sit them down for a frank discussion.

He believes that the vocational aspects of the job are often undervalued when a soldier decides to quit. 'I've been out seeing civilian salaries and there are a lot that are higher, but they just don't offer the same dynamic environment that service in the SAS or ADF does,' he says.

He believes that many military jobs offer a level of technical expertise and job satisfaction that is impossible to achieve elsewhere. 'I would argue that the vocational aspect of what the defence force has is the key to the motivation. The money satisfies the need to eat and live and educate your children.'

As each departing soldier came to see him he would go to the whiteboard and say, 'Tell me what you are going to earn.'

They would mention figures in the region of $250,000 or $300,000 tax free.

'Then I worked out where they were, their superannuation, expenses of their families and when you boiled it down, the premium that someone gets on their getting out, as in big money, is most probably about 30 or 40 per cent.

'You can say, "I can earn more money", but when you start looking at longevity, risk of job . . . We do risky things but we do them with trusted teams, with a motivated bunch of blokes, blokes you can trust who will pull you out of the line of fire. On the other side [it is] not so sure, and when I explained that analysis, I think a number of guys realised that 30 or 40 per cent is quite small,' he says.

Many SAS soldiers who have resigned have then found that the money for security jobs, which has declined substantially since the heady days of 2003, is not enough. Some are returning to the regiment for the very reasons that McMahon outlines.

'I think for that 30 or 40 per cent premium, it doesn't cater for the risk, lack of mates, lack of why you are doing it, motivation. This is about vocation, fighting for your country and your mates, it's about servicing your community and service before self,' he says. 'In some of the more risky areas of the security industry, it's about money and fighting for money, without the backup and being surrounded by your mates. It just doesn't add up.'

He has been offered lucrative contracts in the security industry but says that if it were a choice between that or the military, he would stay in the military. 'If you are being shot at just for money, how much value is that on your whole life?'

To those who wanted to leave, McMahon would say, 'I'd rather you go and take long service leave and think about it because you are moving from a vocational area into a commercial area and the two motivations are very different.'

He acknowledges that the growing global network of former special forces soldiers working in a variety of fields, of which the security industry is just one, is very strong. He thinks the reason is quite simple.

'It is about the length of time served with people and the basis for serving with people,' he says. 'The ability to serve in that [SF] environment is that you go through a series of checks and balances.'

Integrity, looking after mates and trust are paramount.

'I think that is why the network is strong,' he says.

Employers who call up 'the network' offering a position know that what they are told they are getting is exactly what they will get.

'It is a very easy way to do business . . . it takes away the bullshit,' he says. 'I think integrity is paramount in business. When you are giving people a look in the eye, they realise your background and I think people trust that. Dare I say it; they look at the brand and say, "That's a good brand to deal with.""

In entering the world of consultancy he has found that integrity, creativity, speed of thought, judgement, commitment, communication and character are high-value currency with employers and they are precisely what many military personnel have to offer.

SAS soldiers have an extra string to their bows by offering an acute ability to operate within complex and rapidly changing environments and to produce results.

The bottom line is 'sustained competitive advantage'. Whether planning to attack a Taliban stronghold, respond to a militia atrocity in Timor or managing a corporate project, the outcome hinges on a sustained competitive advantage.

'The few consultancies I've done all indicate there is really no difference, because at unit level, organisational level, senior levels of management and leadership, it is about the competitive advantage,' he says.

Because of the high tempo of special forces operations during the past decade, an SAS officer and soldier has dealt with many complex situations. 'The difference over the last five or ten years is that we have been able to implement our training and learn valuable lessons. Along the way you are changing things to make yourself and your organisation more competitive. My greatest experience was fitting the strategic requirements to what was happening tactically.'

This 'X-factor' comes from operating in a dynamic environment with vastly more stakeholders than the traditional mix. In commercial terms, that should translate into a higher position on the list of applicants for private sector jobs and a better salary.

McMahon has great respect for men who have taken senior positions in the security forces of some Middle Eastern countries because of the responsibility and influence these roles demand and the great example of being Australian they promote.

'Their loyalties and their allegiances are Australian and they have served our regiment with distinction and I can say that having known most of them.'

McMahon says it was a mistake for the army and the SAS to allow some of these men to leave and work overseas.

'I've seen the right moves in recent times in terms of HR flexibility. I would argue that we were still behind when some of the more experienced personnel were leaving,' he says. 'If circumstances were the same now we would have created a job to accommodate their requirements and I think there would be people in our system now who would have stayed in and seen the benefits of it. Flexibility in human resources is almost the same as having the best combat system; in fact, I'd argue it's more important.'

Even working with the West Coast Eagles, he picks up concepts that could be of use to unit commanders.

In the background to all of this is the fundamental need to keep something in reserve.

'It is a cliché, but be prepared for the unexpected. It is that ability of constant monitoring, always having a reserve, a strategic capability, always having some type of thing to react to something,' he says.

In Timor, Afghanistan and Iraq, he says, that has been a central theme of command. 'You've got guys that want to go and fight at 100 miles an hour, but the trick is always be prepared, having a reserve contingency. The analogy I draw is the capital structure of the company. You want to have a balanced capital structure that allows you some flexibility to operate. In my mind it equals having a balanced force structure and contingency reserve.'

Fundamental to this approach is relying on the team and the concept that 10 minds are better than one.

'Empowering those 10 people is the key and allowing a trooper to say to a CO, "What about this?" In my experience a lot of organisations talk it, but they don't actually do it,' he says.

★ ★ ★

A few months into 2008 McMahon was still agonising over his future, but it was beginning to look likely that he would balance a corporate and family life on the one hand and a commitment to the army reserve on the other.

Who knows, James McMahon might yet become a general.

ANZAC SPIRIT

chapter nineteen

BLOOD BROTHERS

Pete Bradford struggled to hold back the tears.

Standing in the shadow of snow-capped Mount Ruapehu on a cool summer's day, the former Australian air force chopper pilot steeled himself to speak.

Then, quietly but clearly, he took his audience back 38 years to an ill-fated New Zealand SAS patrol in the jungles of Vietnam and the mission to rescue Sergeant Graham Campbell and his men.

Bradford had waited a long time for this day of absolution as he recounted the story of his role in trying to save the life of the man who, on 14 January 1970, became the second of only two Kiwi SAS soldiers to have died on operations in the regiment's 53-year history.

The handsome, greying retired Aussie pilot with a cheeky smile had been invited with his wife Wendy to the New Zealand Army training camp at Waiouru in the North Island in January 2008, to attend a special Maori dedication ceremony in memory of Graham 'Grumpy' Campbell.

The ceremony took place at the army's *marae*, or sacred meeting place.

After a traditional Maori welcome, led by an army sergeant, tribal elders and three ex-SAS soldiers who are now ministers of religion, Bradford stood before three of the survivors of Campbell's six-man patrol, his widow Ellen and another 100 or so veterans and guests.

The years dissolved, back to a typical day in the life of the RAAF's 9 Squadron and their 'Huey' choppers. The deep, throaty 'thump, thump, thump' of an incoming Huey became an anthem for the war and a sound to savour for countless soldiers who were rescued by the machines and their brave crews.

The New Zealand SAS had a troop attached to Australia's 3 SAS Squadron and several Kiwi pilots also flew with 9 Squadron, so the Anzac spirit was alive and well.

The chopper squadron was based at the Australian support base at Vung Tau down on the coast and their Iroquois UH1H 'Huey' machines flew into the task force base in the inland rubber country at Nui Dat each day to conduct operations.

The squadron had 16 Hueys on the flight line, including three specially modified heavily armed 'gun ships' known as Bushrangers for attacking enemy positions or laying down suppressive fire during 'hot' extractions when soldiers were airlifted under enemy fire.

The aircraft supported the army's day-to-day activities including troop movements, resupply, medical evacuations and troop extractions or 'dust-offs'. Many of their missions were in support of SAS patrols that operated behind enemy lines and who were often inserted and extracted by chopper, regularly in highly dangerous situations. The Viet Cong called the SAS troops Ma Rung, which means 'phantoms of the jungle'.

On most days the squadron would move six Hueys, four transports designated Albatross 1, 2, 3 and 4 and two gun ships to Nui Dat early in the morning to be on standby for operations. They usually returned to Vung Tau before last light.

'We got word that a Kiwi SAS patrol was in trouble. We knew someone was wounded but we didn't know how badly,' Bradford recalled.

This day just five choppers set off, including the two gun ships, Bushranger 1 and 2. Bradford and his co-pilot Stuart Dalgleish and crewman gunner 'Pinky' Pinkerton in Albatross 02 were assigned the job of extracting the soldiers.

With the command chopper, Albatross 01, calling the shots and talking to the patrol, they departed for the hot extraction to the east of Nui Dat on the edge of the May Tao mountains and the eastern edge of the Anzac area of operations in Phuoc Tuy province.

'In fact it was just outside the province not far from a village called Ham Tan,' Bradford recalls.

The command chopper flew at about 2000 feet (610 metres) high to stay in radio contact with the six-man Kiwi patrol and direct operations, while Bradford and his crew took Albatross 02 in at tree-top height.

The patrol used coloured smoke to guide Bradford's chopper to their location under the thick jungle canopy. There was nowhere for it to land so the crew would have to winch the soldiers out.

The patrol was invisible to the helicopter crew who would drop a winch line attached to a heavy jungle penetrator that hopefully would force it through the canopy and to the ground. Attached to the penetrator were two small seats for the men to perch on as they were winched up through the trees.

With his skids literally touching the tree tops, Bradford hovered above the patrol as the penetrator, which resembles a ship's anchor with the prongs folded inwards, was deployed and the gun ships began laying down heavy suppressing fire.

'I couldn't hear the firing, but there was still firing going on beneath us,' he says. 'The patrol was still desperately trying to break contact with the enemy, after about a two-hour run. While I'm in the hover, Bushrangers 1 and 2 started to make their firing passes either side of me, as close as they could get, with their mini-guns and rockets to put in suppressive fire to help the blokes on the ground.'

It would be 38 years before patrol scout Bill Taare would tell Bradford that the noise from the mini-gun fire on the jungle floor was like a gigantic hailstorm belting a tin roof.

The gunner on Albatross 02 was also firing into the jungle and in between winching duties, Pinkerton, who was attached to a long line, joined the fray with his M16 carbine.

'The first Kiwis onto the jungle penetrator were the wounded man, who was Graham Campbell, who, we learned later on, was at this stage deceased with one of his patrol members supporting him on the winch. The crewman brought them up, and I can remember we had difficulty swinging them in, because Graham was a heavy weight on the winch ... [Even] with the help of his supporting Kiwi SAS man and the crewman, there was quite a delay in swinging him on board. Once we got them on board the winch had to go down again to get the next two.

'In the meantime, Graham was propped up against the bulkhead in the back of the chopper and his mate was leaning over the side lying on the floor of the chopper, assisting with the suppressive fire into the ground. The winch seemed to take forever and a day to go down in each of its cycles — it was a fair height — the next two got themselves on the jungle penetrator and then came the process of the up-winch, which once again seemed to take an interminable amount of time,' Bradford recalls.

'Getting those two on board was a lot easier because they were both able-bodied. And then finally it had to go down the third time to pick up the last two. I might add, the thought that goes through every pilot and crewman's mind in this sort of operation is, "What are we going to do if the winch burns out, or suddenly fails, or gets entangled?" But, God willing, it didn't — it went down the third time and the last two patrol members got on board and we winched them up, got them on board and the moment they swung on board we were off to that beach, the army hospital.'

It was 10.40 a.m.

The hospital at Vung Tau was located at the back beach and Bradford said he had never flown a Huey faster than he did that day. From the cockpit he had been unable even to see Campbell properly, let alone assess his condition.

Campbell had been hit between the eyes by an AK-47 round, but his comrades believed that despite the severity of his head wound he might still have been breathing and that was good enough for the aircrew.

The Kiwi patrol had been inserted on the afternoon of 13 January and early on the fourteenth moved towards a track they had observed the previous day.

As Campbell and his scout, Bill Taare, moved forward, Campbell trod on a stick that broke with a loud crack. They did not move for 45 minutes, but as soon as they did they were fired upon by an enemy force not more than 10 metres away.

Campbell was hit almost immediately and Taare called on the rest of the patrol to close up.

One trooper, Mac McCallion, a very tall man who would later coach the Maori national rugby team, moved up and retrieved Campbell and the secret codes from his pack. He carried his boss back to the patrol under heavy fire.

The survivors told Bradford at the 2008 ceremony that they had made a pact in the Vietnamese jungle that day in 1970, that they would not leave Sergeant Campbell behind. Even though McCallion believed he was dead, one patrol member worked on him for two hours to try and keep him alive as they carried his body through the jungle, evading and fighting the enemy force.

'They made an instant pact, the five of them, that it was all out or none out. They weren't leaving without Graham,' Bradford says with moist eyes. 'Amazing characters, and probably no different from any of the other SAS, but it gives you an indication of what sort of people we're dealing with here.'

When the chopper arrived back at Vung Tau in record time, a triage team was waiting to quickly transfer Campbell into the hospital. It was only then that the exhausted soldiers and the aircrew could relax, light up a smoke and reflect on the morning's dramatic events.

The rattling thump of an approaching Huey was music to the ears of most SAS and infantry troops who served in Vietnam. It usually meant salvation was at hand and the pilots from 9 Squadron flew some incredibly courageous missions to extract and support the SAS and infantry throughout the war.

Former SAS commander Chris Roberts, who served as a troop commander in Vietnam, says that he owes his own life to Pete Bradford and the 9 Squadron crews who pulled him twice from 'very hot' situations.

Roberts knew Graham Campbell well and he sheds a quiet tear as he recalls the day he died and seeing the Kiwi patrol just before they were inserted.

'I saw Graham on his way out and I said to him, "Keep your head down." I never said those words to anyone ever again,' Roberts says.

According to Campbell's SAS mate Sonny Taniora, who handed his bunk and his M16 carbine over to him as he departed from Nui Dat, Campbell was a top bloke and a fine soldier. He was head boy at the Maori boarding school St Stephen's College in South Auckland and he studied at university. He was a very good rugby player and had represented counties and the armed forces.

'I said to him, "Here, mate, it's yours, it's got ten kills on it. Keep your head down." He had a future, he would have gone a long way,' Taniora says.

For Bradford and his comrades the job of flying Hueys in Vietnam was a tremendous adventure. 'We all had this feeling of invincibility and that we were bullet-proof any time we were working with the SAS,' Bradford says.

'Certainly in this case the boys said that once they saw me hovering over the top of them they figured that they were going to get out, and particularly with the gun ships laying down this suppressive fire, which is awesome, apparently, when you're on the ground.'

That fire meant that Bradford's machine was not struck by a single enemy round while it loitered over the site for what seemed like an age.

After he shut down the chopper on the Vung Tau helipad, Bradford and his crew sat and talked with the survivors about their ordeal.

'I could see by the looks on the faces of the five SAS guys, that they were as shattered as a human being could be — both physically and mentally. The mind boggles at how they managed to escape and evade for two hours with Graham's body, having made this pact that none of them would be coming home if Graham couldn't be brought out,' he says. 'I decided to sit on the pad with the chopper shut down until such time as we got advice on Graham's welfare, which strangely enough seemed to take forever and a day.'

Eventually a medico walked up to the exhausted group and glibly announced that he didn't know what they were hanging around for because Graham was dead when he arrived.

'To this day he [the doctor] probably doesn't know how close he came to being almost killed by a Kiwi SAS soldier. At that moment I remember putting my arm around this SAS guy who was going to take offence at this comment and I said, "C'mon, let's go home."'

'We just climbed on board the chopper, fired it up and flew the guys back to Nui Dat, back to what was known as SAS hill. 'There was a little feature on the Nui Dat army bases — the highest ground — that the SAS occupied, that was commonly called SAS hill. And unfortunately, or fortunately for me I suppose, I came home within a few weeks of that — in fact, just over a fortnight — and had absolutely no contact with those guys until Waiouru on 12 January 2008.'

The Bradfords' younger daughter, Gillian, is a journalist with the ABC and she was posted to Auckland as the Corporation's New Zealand correspondent.

During a visit in 2005, she suggested that her father spend some time at the War Memorial in Auckland.

'I saw Graham's name written on a rather large plaque: "Graham Campbell, Killed in Action, 14th January 1970". At that point I decided that I wouldn't rest until I could say hello to his family if that were possible, as well as make contact with the surviving members of the patrol.'

As luck would have it, he found Campbell's old SAS boss, Terry Culley, who had married Campbell's widow Ellen some years later.

'We caught up in Auckland six or twelve months after me seeing Graham's name on that plaque and the experience of meeting Ellen and the hug that I got from her was worth a million dollars,' Bradford says.

He was able to fill in some blanks for the widow who, in typical military fashion, had been left in the dark about aspects of her husband's demise. The Bradfords are now good friends with the Culleys and they have met and befriended Graham's three children, James, Anna-Marie and Jacqueline as well.

So in January 2008, exactly 38 years after the fateful hot extraction of a Kiwi patrol, Pete Bradford stood outside the marae at Waiouru army camp and with three of the survivors, Mac McCallion, Sid Puia and Bill Taare, broke into a scratchy verse of 'Waltzing Matilda'.

When Bradford returned to Australia a fortnight after the Campbell extraction he found that flying helicopters at home was somewhat boring after Vietnam. So he transferred back to fixed-wing aircraft where he had started his career several years earlier.

A Queenslander, Bradford started flying light aircraft privately at Archerfield in Brisbane in 1962 when he was working in the Commonwealth Bank. He joined the RAAF in 1966 when he enrolled in the pilot training course at Point Cook near Melbourne.

After leaving 9 Squadron he was posted to 37 Squadron at Richmond RAAF base near Sydney to fly C-130 Hercules heavy transport aircraft.

He became an instructor on the workhorse of the air force fleet before moving to Canberra to see out his air force career on VIP duty with 34 Squadron based at RAAF base Fairbairn. He mainly flew the BAC-111 aircraft, ferrying around dignitaries.

'It was most interesting and very rewarding to meet and see people you'd never otherwise meet in your wildest dreams,' he says. 'The Governor-General was Sir Zelman Cowan who was just an outstanding character to get to know — he and his wife. People that I carried included the Duke of Edinburgh, I had a couple of days with — in fact, because I was a qualified flight instructor and he also could fly the BAC-111, I was briefed that if he wished to have a fly I was to enquire, and was authorised to do so. But he was quite happy to sit back and enjoy the trip and relax. The PM of India, Indira Gandhi, was out here for CHOGM [Commonwealth Heads of Government Meeting] during those years. I hate to say it, but I flew Comrade Mugabe [Zimbabwean strongman

Robert Mugabe] around for quite a few days in Australia. Tragic to see the outcome of what's happened to his beautiful country.'

After being transferred to a desk job at air office in 1982 he resigned and took a job with Qantas, which has poached hundreds of RAAF pilots over the years.

He started in the training department, instructing on the 747-300 jumbo jet, before moving onto the flying line and flying the big birds all around the world for six years.

By 1996 the gloss had worn off commercial aviation and hotel rooms and he was offered a job as personal pilot to Australian magnate Kerry Packer, flying him around on his private DC-8 intercontinental jetliner.

The Packer job was one of the most interesting flying roles that Bradford had and he remembers the billionaire and their overseas trips with great fondness.

The DC-8 was an old aircraft and a lot of money was spent to maintain it in an airworthy state for the exclusive use of 'KP' and 'KP' only. Its main feature was the extra long-range fuel tanks that meant it could fly anywhere on earth with just one refuelling stop.

'He was the only person who ever used the aeroplane,' Bradford says. 'We never flew his family or anybody else on that aeroplane without him being on board, so therefore we weren't at the beck and call of any other users of the aeroplane and that made it a fairly enjoyable job.'

Bradford flew his boss all around the world from regular stops in Las Vegas to gamble, Ohio to play golf with Jack Nicklaus, to Europe, Alaska, London and South America for the polo.

'Las Vegas was high on the agenda,' he says. 'When he was in reasonably good health I think the best we had was six trips to Las Vegas in one year.'

There was also one memorable trip back home to Sydney from a polo trip in South America via the South Pole.

After taking off from Rio Gallegos in southern Argentina their track was 140 degrees or almost due south under the globe to Antarctica, over the Pole and then back up to Hobart and on to Sydney.

He describes the 13- to 14-hour adventure as 'terrifying', because of the extreme cold they encountered flying over what was essentially a black void on the underside of the planet. At such extremes fuel could actually freeze in the wings.

'And all of the communications were shut down over winter — no one to talk to for many hours,' he recalls with a chill.

Flexibility was crucial during the six years he flew for KP, and his air force training proved to be ideal.

The aircraft was based at the Qantas base at Mascot and he remembers one night preparing to fly to London via Honolulu and Los Angeles to pick up a Packer mate, just before that evening's airport curfew kicked in.

They had three pilots and two flight engineers on board and had just started the first engine when KP's secretary came up to the cockpit and announced that the boss wanted to go the other way.

'We looked to each other, and put two and two together and thought, "Ah, he wants to fly direct Sydney–LA if we can."

'So the answer was, "No, sorry, we can't do it, the winds are no good. We'll have to go via Honolulu."'

'She disappeared and a couple of seconds later, she's back, "No, he means via the Indian Ocean." He wanted to go to London via the Indian Ocean.'

After a mild panic and with the curfew fast approaching, they revised their flight plan and left Sydney to fly to London via the Maldives. Diplomatic clearances were obtained in-flight and the flight proceeded without a hitch.

Another flight via the Middle East was not so fortunate and when the aircraft's transponder (identifying radar) broke down they were grounded in Bahrain.

'We knew we had a problem in Australia but it seemed to be working intermittently and of course we happily departed Sydney,' he says. 'Coming up to the Middle East into radar contact at Muscat they said for us to check our transponder. And of course we knew there was a problem and were asked the question, "What are your intentions?"

'We said, "To continue on through the Middle East to London."' We were informed that we had five minutes to make a decision on where we were landing, because our transponder had failed. So we landed in Bahrain, and discovered we couldn't fix the transponder — there was a major technical problem with it.'

The boss was desperate to get to London to see his favourite polo pony in action the next day so they had to charter a plane for him. The on-board safe didn't have enough cash so they were forced to phone Sydney to get the butler's credit card limit upgraded to cover the $100,000 aircraft charter bill.

After that all the crew had their credit card limits extended, just in case.

The flight crew always kept a bag half packed in case the boss wanted to go somewhere at short notice, but generally the schedule was known in advance.

Sometimes Wendy and other wives would travel on commercial flights to meet up with their husbands in places such as Las Vegas or London for a brief holiday.

'It was a bit of a chance, a bit of Russian roulette, because you never quite knew if he was going to spend 24 hours in Vegas and then decide he wanted to go to London or something. But you'd take a punt and the hotels where we stayed would graciously look after the wives and if we did leave a bit earlier they'd then find their way home. But most of these trips where Wendy and the other wives followed us along worked out pretty well.'

Bradford got to witness Kerry Packer's generosity on more than one occasion and he recalls the time when a general hand at Mascot who used to load and unload baggage was suffering from terminal cancer.

Word of his situation reached KP and a message came up to the cockpit to put whatever cash was in the safe in an envelope and to hand it over to the man with the boss's best wishes.

'That was a fair wad of US dollars,' he recalls.

After Packer's kidney transplants his overseas trips were limited and in 2002 the DC-8 was sold and Bradford went back to Qantas as a 747 instructor.

He finally retired from commercial flying in August 2007.

Some weeks after the memorial service for Graham Campbell in New Zealand, Bradford reflected on it at his home in a lovely bush setting at Kurrajong, west of Sydney.

As bellbirds tolled in the background, Bradford explained the Campbell extraction in some detail and spoke about how honoured he was to have been invited to share the ceremony.

'That, to me, was just a phenomenal feeling — that they wanted to involve me and each of us could get together after such a long time. The guys in the patrol — I know a couple of them were fairly excited about it — just wanting to say thanks for something that was just our job.'

chapter twenty

THE FAMILY

Terry Culley was never really a close mate of Graham Campbell's, but the pair had served in the same platoon and played rugby together.

They also served in the New Zealand SAS and when Campbell was killed in action in Vietnam in January 1970, Culley was the regiment's acting commanding officer and training officer. As such he became the welfare officer in charge of the Campbell case. He was also flat on his back in hospital suffering from the malaria he had contracted as he departed from South Vietnam just days earlier.

'I remember Ellen [Campbell's widow] coming to visit me in hospital,' he says. 'I'm saying, "Hey! I've just heard that Graham's been shot, I should be coming to visit you." I was lying there like a gibbering bloody mess.'

In those days the New Zealand SAS was a tight-knit unit of about 80 men and fewer than half of them were married. Culley himself was a bachelor, but Sergeant Campbell was married with three young children, James and Anna-Marie at school and little Jacqueline at pre-school.

As the case officer, Culley spent a lot of time with Ellen Campbell and her kids, making sure things were taken care of and relocating them from their army house and so on.

'I found myself spending more and more time in their company making sure that things were okay,' he says. 'I was a bachelor, one of the bloody disposable people, but we had no training as welfare people. I suppose it's a common story — someone gets close to someone and the closeness becomes something else. Before you know it we were married.'

Two years later the couple produced a fourth child, Terence, who is serving in the RAAF at Edinburgh in South Australia.

'They were all brought up the same,' Culley says. 'We raised a family.'

It is not uncommon for army widows to marry another soldier, but in the intimate world of the SAS, Ellen had to endure quite a deal of ribbing.

'Ellen got heaps for marrying me,' he recalls. 'They said, "How could you marry another one of those SAS buggers or anyone in the army, let alone the SAS?"'

The pair have developed a very successful partnership and he describes her as his 'right-hand man'.

She guides and encourages him in his work with Vietnam veterans and is as determined as him to look after the men who served alongside both of her husbands.

'We've achieved so much it'd be ridiculous to just cash it all in and go back and play grandparents.'

Like many Vietnam veterans, Terry Culley now regards the war as a waste of time, but he has very few regrets about his own service.

'If we'd been told it was all going to go tits up at the end and basically hand everything back to the North Vietnamese — capitulation — my first reaction would have been not to have bothered even going,' he says. 'In fact it was the opportunity of a lifetime to go there and use the skills that we were trained for.

'The key thing about Vietnam was that we went there at the request of our government, did a job to the best of our ability and we brought back all that experience that we were able to pass on to others.'

Culley was born in 1943 in a quiet far-northern corner of New Zealand at a town called Kaitaia.

He joined the army after a stint with the post and telegraph department, undertaking officer training at the Australian Army officer cadet training school at Portsea near Melbourne. He returned to New Zealand to attend the officer training course at Waiouru to learn New Zealand-specific military laws and procedures.

His first contact with the SAS came when he was posted to its home base at the Papakura camp near Auckland as a signal troop commander.

The SAS troops based there were working up for a six-month deployment to Borneo with the British 22 SAS Regiment and an old mate who was preparing to deploy asked Culley to help him get fit. That meant long runs at 5 a.m. every day and after three months both men were bouncing out of their skins and his mate suggested Culley should join the regiment as well.

He passed selection and was due to go to Borneo at the end of 1967, but the troubles ended and the unit returned home.

It was mid-1968 before the NZSAS finally got word that it would be going to Vietnam. Culley was on a training mission about to jump out of a C-130 Hercules transport aircraft.

'At the time I was in an aircraft doing some parachute training over Lake Taupo,' he says. 'We were camped on the side of the current Taupo airport and had gone up for our first descent of the day. Lovely clear morning and there was I trying to fight my way out of the aircraft. The light went from red to green and I didn't notice it had gone back to red again.'

The message came through that something was up and the aircraft diverted back to Papakura.

Beside the camp was a civilian airstrip used mainly for training and light aircraft, not for Hercs but they landed on the strip anyway, and there waiting for them was a shiny bus.

'Another sign that something's up, getting special treatment. We travel in the back of trucks normally, but there was this nice bus waiting to take us back to camp,' he says. 'So all these sort of doubts — "What's going on?" So we got into camp and no one would say a thing. We were ushered into the briefing room and the boss stood up there and said, "Well, we're off!" and he read out the 26 names and I was on it and there was a huge cheer from those who'd been called out and a big boo from those who'd missed out.'

After a month of jungle training near Rotorua the troop left New Zealand under the guise of a visit to the Commonwealth Brigade in

Malaya to work with the battalion. The government had not announced that it was committing SAS to the war, so they had to sneak out of the country. They stowed their SAS badges and gear and wore plain infantry uniforms until they boarded the plane from Singapore into Saigon, then the red Rangers berets, which they wore in those days, came out of their bags.

'We went into Saigon first and had our night with the Ambassador and everybody else — our last taste of New Zealand vittles and whatever and then we caught a Caribou up the next morning,' he says.

Of the 26 men in the troop only three, including Culley, had not seen active service in Borneo.

'They were a pretty experienced lot, and the average age, even with us young ones built in — the youngest was 21 and the oldest was about 38 — was high twenties. They had their heads on, and it didn't take them too long to work out, going out on patrol with the Australians, how to fit in and adapt. We actually learned a lot of the standard operating procedure drills anyway in New Zealand and we did practise in Malaya while we were flying up there. But everyone went out as part of an Australian patrol prior to going out and mounting our own patrols.'

Their main tasks were pure SAS intelligence-gathering, sniffing about the jungle in small groups of four or five at a time.

'A sneaky peek, not letting them know you were there and then reporting back information to allow the task force commander to make his decisions on where to commit his major troops,' Culley says.

After returning to New Zealand in early 1970, Culley did the usual round of postings to various units and in 1979 he and Ellen decided to make a clean break and move to Australia.

He worked for a courier company based at Mascot in Sydney and was soon to get his first lesson about civilian life.

'I only caused two strikes by ordering people to do things that I shouldn't have been doing,' he says. 'The unions quickly bloody trained me after they were out on the streets a couple of times. They said, "Now look, if you want to talk to us, why don't you come and see me, the delegate, and we'll have a cup of coffee or a beer and then we'll come back and tell the boys what's going to happen, after we've agreed what's possible. But for you to stand up like a big ponce and give orders, it doesn't work."

'The TWU of Australia didn't want to know. So I learned those lessons the hard way, but enjoyed it.'

He survived and his next job was manager for the whole of New South Wales except Sydney.

'I spent three weeks of the month out on the road. I'd fly to Moree, jump into a rental car to Grafton, down to Coffs Harbour, get on another plane and fly home, or go down to Griffith. It was a hell of a good job for a Kiwi to have.'

Once he overcame the initial shock of dealing with a union shop, Culley found that the consensus style of management taught by the SAS fitted in very nicely in the corporate world.

'I've found in commercial life I'm more lenient and more consultative rather than planning things in detail and saying, "That's it", without getting someone else to check it,' he says.

'It all goes back to SAS training: it taught you to focus on the important things, to discard all the stuff that's not required, get right and focus on the urgent things.

'You can sit there and make a ten-page appreciation, but if the Viet Cong are coming over the hill shooting shit at you, you have to make a decision. Either stand there and get killed or get the hell out of there. Those are the things that a lot of civilians don't understand.'

After a happy and successful 17 years in Sydney, Culley and Ellen returned to Auckland to nurse his dying brother. Once again the network provided him with a job opportunity, which he grabbed with both hands.

The job was called 'industry training' but in actual fact they were setting up almost a duplicate of the Australian National Training Authority, the New Zealand Qualifications Authority.

Industry groups were formed as part of it and Culley slotted in to the electro-technology side of the business.

'It was a reasonable job, paid good money and they wanted me, so I said I'd have a go and that's 13 years ago and I am still doing it,' he says. 'It's been a labour of love because you see young people coming through in at this end as Neville Nobody, and out the other end as Mr Somebody with a qualification, getting a job, helping themselves and their family progress.'

Once the network was activated Culley was soon in touch with old SAS mates up and down the country.

His new colleagues in the authority couldn't believe the extent of his reach.

'Within days and weeks of starting my civilian job in Auckland I was getting phone calls and making phone calls to people around the country that I'd known 20-odd years earlier,' he recalls. 'My colleagues would say, "How do you know all these people?" My response was, "I belong to a very big family."'

A lot of them had left the army and were into all sorts of jobs.

'Every week and sometimes every day, someone would pass me on to someone else, who would probably help with what I was trying to do,' he says. 'Maybe I'd have something to pass back their way that'd help them as well.'

This networking allowed Culley to put some early runs on the board. Once back in his familiar surroundings it was simply a matter of picking up the phone and asking, 'Whom do you know?'

His workmates wanted to know the secret to his speedy success.

'I told them, you just ask one and you get seven names.'

The thing that would keep the couple in New Zealand and away from three kids and seven grandkids back in Australia was really their other family — the SAS and Vietnam War veterans.

'I've spent some time on the executive of the Special Air Services Association and more recently on the Executive of the Ex-Vietnam Services Association,' he says. 'When I came home I found that the associations were basically social enterprises — there to organise reunions, piss-ups, parties and making sure everyone could get a newsletter — there was a newsletter involved. At the same time though, when you had a piss-up, you found people coming to them — some of them were in terrible states of mental and physical health.'

The plight of New Zealand's Vietnam veterans is most graphically displayed when a comparison is done between them and veterans of World War II. It shows that most Vietnam vets die aged in their fifties while the WWII veterans live on into their late seventies.

Of the 3500 New Zealanders who served in Vietnam, only about 2600 are still alive and according to Culley they are dying at an alarming rate.

'Sometimes you get 20 a month,' he says.

Little was being done about it so he took matters into his own hands. He buttonholed prime minister Helen Clark at a function and did some direct lobbying.

'I was introduced to the PM by this politician and I grabbed her hand, introduced myself, and said, "Prime Minister, we have some real issues with our Vietnam vets not getting good support from your government agencies." She was trying to pull her hand out of mine, and I was trying to pull her towards me and in the end she gave up and said, "Why don't you drop me a line with these issues you're talking about and you and I can have a cup of coffee and talk them over."'

The prime minister gave them a very good hearing and at the end of the meeting numerous initiatives were under way including a commitment to a Welcome Home parade during 2008.

Many of the tricky issues concerning the effects of the herbicide Agent Orange remain unresolved and Culley just hopes that Ms Clark stays around long enough to get them resolved.

The government has conceded that the men were sprayed and it has accepted the science from American and Australian studies.

'We wanted to know why the NZ government would not accept the results of the US and Australian studies,' he says. 'She said, "Actually, I've just come back from a cabinet meeting and we're willing to do that if that's what you want. But if you want us to set up our own NZ study, we'll endorse that, too, and we'll start tomorrow."

'I said, "Prime Minister, we've been studied to hell. Please just tell your cabinet we want you to accept the studies done by the other countries and get on with it."

'And she said, "Okay, you're on."'

A joint implementation group was established to get the wheels turning and both Culley and Ms Clark sit off to one side and keep a weather eye on the process.

Terry Culley says that if his SAS training and the unit motto 'Who Dares Wins' has taught him anything, it is the value of getting on with things.

'I am braver now than I would ever have been,' he says.

'I've been taught resilience and decision making and getting on with life. I have a favourite saying now: "You don't sit around and plan for something, just do it." If you see the answer, just do it, rather than look for higher approvals and 10 months of budgeting and submissions and all this sort of stuff. Find out what it is, how much it costs, can we do it and then just do it.'

That has become the guiding principle of his life.

It also helps to sustain him and Ellen as they travel around their beautiful country visiting veterans and their families.

He has his Australian citizenship in the bag and who knows, one day this Anzac might cross the ditch again and settle with the Aussie branch of the family.

'We still call Australia home.'

chapter twenty-one

FRED AND SONNY

Fred Barclay and Sonny Taniora have been mates for more than 40 years.

The two New Zealand SAS veterans first served together in Borneo in the mid-1960s as fresh-faced 20-something troopers.

They were involved in top-secret cross-border incursions and surveillance operations against Indonesian forces from Sarawak into Kalimantan and even managed the occasional ambush targeting Indonesian troops. According to Taniora they had a reasonably quiet time, but the deep jungle reconnaissance patrols were of great benefit for their later deployment to Vietnam.

'Nobody knew we'd been across the border into Kalimantan,' he says. 'I was with Fred Barclay and we had a pretty quiet time. Some of the other patrols had some good moments. I went over with the third troop to Borneo. The first one was in quite a lot of action, the second one had a few skirmishes, but we went over and it was sort of quietening down a bit. We were still seeing the same stuff, gathering information, seeing if the camps were occupied.'

The men undertook a six-month rotation before returning home to New Zealand.

Fast-forward 41 years and Taniora sits on the back veranda of his house in the port city of Tauranga in the Bay of Plenty south-east of Auckland, on a cool summer's afternoon in January 2008.

With a gentle sea breeze blowing in from Mount Maunganui, or 'the Mount', as the locals call one of the country's most popular summer holiday destinations, Taniora recalls his army days with a mixture of pride and nostalgia.

He was born in the town of Taumarunui in the North Island's King Country in 1942 and joined the army as a regular force cadet straight from school at 16 years of age.

Fred Barclay's journey into the army took a little longer. He was born at Carterton in the Wairarapa region in the south-east corner of the North Island and went to work at 15 as a dairy hand and then on a sheep and cattle property. Barclay wanted to join the army, but his grandmother, who was his legal guardian, refused to sign the papers. Her husband had been wounded in World War I and her three sons had all served and been wounded in the Second World War.

'So she'd had a gutful,' he says.

Despite her misgivings he joined up when he turned 21 after undergoing compulsory military training at eighteen.

'I was working on a sheep and cattle farm in quite a rural area of NZ and I was the sole permanent employee,' he says. 'I came back very late one night from trying to shift some cattle through a road/river valley and turned on the radio news while I was cooking my dinner. This voice said he was General Sir Stephen Weir and he was announcing that tomorrow morning the recruitment of a battalion of soldiers to go to Malaya was to take place.'

He had spent all day trying to shift a mob of cattle through a single gate.

'They just wouldn't go out this gate . . . and very mountainous country. They'd shoot out into the bush and then I'd have to get them out of the bush, which is different from Australia — you can only see for 20 feet.

'So I joined up with 800 other guys and did my six months initial training.'

Both Taniora and Barclay undertook SAS selection after returning from tours of duty to Camp Terendak and the Commonwealth Brigade in Malaya. Barclay took leave without pay and after working as a farm contractor, he realised he would never have enough money to own a farm so he made the army his career.

'I didn't come from a family that had money, so I eventually went back,' Barclay says. 'I thought, well, if I go back in the army, I will make a career of it. I'd buggered about a bit in the first few years. I'd enjoyed myself when I was in town, been locked up a few times for being a couple of minutes late because there was a midnight-to-six curfew for the whole of Malaya, but like most young soldiers you'd imbibe a few and then you'd arrive back three or four minutes late, and bang! You're inside until you go back out in the jungle again. So I thought, "If I'm going to join up again I need to treat it as a career, instead of a bit of a holiday."'

After a second tour to Malaya he returned to undertake selection, going straight from the tropics to a New Zealand winter. Despite the cold, Barclay, who had been a bushman all of his life, passed the course easily and actually quite enjoyed it.

'I just didn't have a big amount of difficulty doing it, but I had problems with blisters because I'd been wearing jungle boots.'

Taniora and Barclay were both posted to 4 SAS Troop of the New Zealand Rangers and deployed to Vietnam early in 1968.

Taniora remembers the day he got the news about Vietnam as if it were yesterday.

'We were having a big parachute exercise down in Waiouru and I was safety officer on the drop zone,' he recalls.

At one stage he popped a smoke canister and set the entire landing area alight. Waiouru is in the centre of the New Zealand desert country and is extremely dry, tussocky countryside.

'The old Herc came in at 500 feet, popped up to 1000, opened the doors, and the guys couldn't see the ground. They had to drop them over in Napier, because they couldn't drop them there.'

Taniora thought his army days were finished as a helicopter came buzzing in and the crew wanted to know who was in charge. Eventually he got the message that the chopper was there to transport him back to base.

'I thought, "Oh, yeah, I'm going back to get court-martialled."'

But the reason he had to go back was to get ready to deploy to Vietnam with 4 Troop.

'I couldn't get on the chopper quick enough.'

As he flew over he saw the smouldering ruins of the drop zone and the biggest smoke show any paratrooper had ever seen.

For Fred Barclay, the Vietnam deployment was the ideal job. With his background as a hunter and deer-stalker as well as two tours of Malaya and one of Borneo, he was already an experienced jungle fighter.

And it didn't take long before he was in the thick of the action.

According to David Horner's excellent official history of the Australian SAS, *SAS: Phantoms of War*, Barclay picked up the nickname 'Bad News' Barclay very early in his tour due to his uncanny knack of serving on patrols that encountered fierce contacts with the enemy.

The first of those took place on 30 December 1968 when an all New Zealand patrol was inserted by helicopters. On New Year's Day 1969, the patrol found a large, unoccupied enemy camp. Sergeant Barclay was the scout and as the patrol moved to the eastern edge of the camp he stopped to inspect a track. Two enemy fighters were on the track and were killed by his comrades before another four appeared and assaulted the patrol. Barclay managed to kill one and a second was downed before they made their retreat. The patrol later encountered a larger enemy force and Barclay received the first of several shrapnel wounds that he would sustain during his 12-month tour.

Barclay says the New Zealand troop was a close-knit unit. Most had done selection together and all but a few were experienced in the art of jungle warfare.

Their Australian boss, Major Reg Beesley, told Horner that he was 'most impressed with the Kiwis' sense of purpose, their dedication and professionalism'.

'We'd all done the parachute course, which I didn't think had any tactical information, but is brilliant training, because no one in their right mind likes jumping out of a bloody plane,' Barclay says. 'If you can get guys to do those sort of things, then you know exactly who you've got, and you know the guy can control his fear.'

Apart from the death of his mate Graham Campbell a few days earlier, one of the saddest moments for Taniora occurred on 17 January 1970, just before he was due to return home.

He was a member of a patrol led by Warrant Officer Ray 'Ginger' Scutts. Also on the patrol was the only Aboriginal member of the Australian SAS, Corporal Ronald Harris.

'He was a great guy because he would go walkabout, have a look around,' he says. 'He was a good soldier too, but this time he came back in from a different direction and old Ginger's sitting there with the radio off and out of the corner of his eye he sees a guy coming through the scrub. He looks like a Viet Cong because he's dark, short, and he let him have it. Bloody unfortunate and a sad moment, that one.'

Harris was moving to Scutts to report enemy activity when he was shot dead.

An investigation cleared Scutts of any wrongdoing.

Taniora and Barclay both participated in what is regarded as one of the shortest SAS patrols in history. It was inserted by helicopter about an hour before last light. Almost as soon as they hit the ground Taniora, who was the scout, saw the top of an enemy fighter's head duck down behind a tree stump.

He opened up with buckshot and then all hell broke loose. Fortunately after inserting a patrol, choppers remained in the vicinity for about 20 minutes.

'They were miles away, but when we hit the old bleeper, the panic button, they know to come back in again,' he says.

The Bushranger Huey gun ships opened up with rockets to cover the extraction and a patrol that was scheduled to last for 14 days came to an abrupt end after just 12 minutes. And seven minutes of that was the fire-fight.

Barclay saved Taniora's life on another patrol when they stumbled upon a complex of tunnels and underground bunkers.

'Fred and I were going up there and we spotted a sentry on top of this huge bloody rock,' Taniora says. 'Fred was yelling at me and I didn't hear him and he was shooting a guy standing right in front of me. That's how close it was.'

As they withdrew Barclay said to him, 'Didn't you see the guy right in front of you?'

'I said, "What guy? I was shooting the one on the top." 'He said, "The one standing right in front of you, he just popped up."

'I said, "Oh, I left that one up to you, mate." I didn't want to tell him I didn't see him.'

Two-thirds of the way through his tour Barclay took some recreation leave and flew down to Malaya to take care of some very important business. He had met his bride to be, Rae, before he deployed to Vietnam and they had planned to marry in September of 1969.

'I began to believe that I just might not get out the other end,' he says. 'The NZ army was still at Terendak camp in Malaya and I had a number of very good friends there, so I was able to communicate with them very quickly, but not with Rae.'

The marriage proposal reached her second-hand, via one of the mates at Terendak and she accepted immediately and flew to Singapore where they met and travelled to the camp for the wedding.

'I had my five nights, and I went back to Vietnam and Rae came back here.'

When he returned from his tour, Barclay spent time at the parachute training school and eventually re-joined the battalion as a staff sergeant. He was posted to Singapore where their daughter Rachel was born.

By 1986 after postings as a company sergeant major and then regimental sergeant major, Barclay had reached the end and after a brief posting to Tonga as a weapons instructor, he resigned from the army.

Just before he left, a mate called him and said there was a job going with a very wealthy man called Sir Michael Fay. He and another rich financier, David Richwhite, own a private 2500-hectare island about 10 kilometres off the Coromandel Peninsula called Great Mercury Island. It was half covered in pine trees and had supported a sizable Maori community in pre-European days.

Fay was the driving force behind New Zealand's successful bid to win yachting racing's holy grail, the America's Cup.

Barclay had to concede that he had never heard of Fay, but on his very last day after 28 years in the army, dressed in his fatigues, he went and met the man who offered him a job immediately.

'We shook hands and he said, "Well, we don't know what you're going to do", and everyone agreed that as long as it wasn't too illegal or immoral I'd have a go at it,' he recalls.

They were just starting to develop the island as a private sanctuary and what eventually became an exclusive $20,000-a-night resort when Barclay took the job.

'I didn't have a job title, because in their company you couldn't ring up to talk to the MD, you had to ring up and say [you] want to talk to a person,' he says. 'I really picked up the logistics and everything had to be barged out to the island. I'd be out there three or four nights a week. I looked after the travel; you had to get people on and off the place, and set up a cookhouse, and employed people to cook for the guys working there. The bloody weather would get shithouse, which it can do there and the next landmass to the east is Argentina.'

Despite the challenges and the pitfalls, Barclay says he really enjoyed the job.

'They had a vision for the whole thing, so we put in roads, and articulated the water for about 20 kilometres, an underground power station. We did all the infrastructure,' he says.

They built large houses for the owners, guesthouses for the paying clients and an airstrip.

Barclay has trouble describing his actual job.

'I never had a contract, I never had a job description, we sort of shook hands, he gave me a car and a fuel card and he told me if I bought a car while I was working for him I was screwed in the head.'

While he wasn't paid a fortune, Barclay said it was like being in the SAS in that it provided a great deal of independence.

'Once I didn't see them for 18 months, they were busy doing their thing. In 15 years I probably got about four briefings,' he says.

When he was turning 65, Fay told him he would have to finish up in about six months' time.

'Well, that went for about 18 months. Eventually, I said to him, "Well, hey, you've got to tell me what's going on and where we're at." So I wandered off.'

Barclay says his SAS training was invaluable during his 15 years on Great Mercury. A key aspect of that was an ability to communicate and to take the initiative.

'You learn very quickly with super-rich people that a lot of people run around talking about them, but not too many have the guts to go and stand up face to face and say, "Hey, I don't like what's going on". They handed me a lot of work back then, and while I might have used that to my advantage, I used it to my employers' advantage too. So I was the filter; all of the shit stopped with me.

'Michael Fay kept telling me, "I'm the boss, I'm the boss." But he was in bloody Switzerland and the guy that's paid to kick sheep has got to talk to somebody.'

Barclay has now retired with Rae and they live in the pretty seaside town of Whangamata on the picturesque Coromandel Peninsula. Fishing and grandchildren are their main preoccupations these days.

Sonny Taniora had mixed fortunes after he left the army. His marriage had failed and he worked for the Department of Labour and then took a job in Germany with a tourist company before setting up training courses for an Auckland-based Maori trust. He is now retired and living with his sister and her family at Tauranga while pursuing his love of horseracing.

The two old mates still hook up about once a month for a cup of tea or something stronger when Barclay drives down to Tauranga for medical treatment.

chapter twenty-two

THE MAORI SPIRIT

Sitting cross-legged on the floor of the *whare*, or Maori meetinghouse, it is difficult to imagine that the gentle man of god, explaining the significance of the symbols around the wall, was once an SAS soldier in the Maori warrior tradition.

Anglican minister, the Reverend Kevin Herewini, is one of those positive human beings with a happy disposition that would make him good company in any situation.

As he spoke about the intricacies of Maori culture and the significance of the army *marae* or meeting place and the *pou pou*, or traditionally carved totem poles around the walls of the whare, it was clear that Maori culture has a fundamental presence within the New Zealand army or Ngati Tumatauenga, 'tribe of the god of war', as it is known in the Maori language.

At one end of the house the sacred wall is covered with photographs of deceased members of the community upon whose marae the meetinghouse stands. The latest picture to join the gallery of the departed is Maori SAS Sergeant Graham Campbell, who was killed in action in Vietnam 38 years earlier in January 1970.

Speaking in hushed tones, Herewini tells the story of the elaborate Maori ceremony that had taken place earlier that day on 12 January 2008, to mark the dedication of Campbell into the whare.

As a chill breeze blew off the snow-covered slopes of the nearby volcano, Mount Ruapehu, guests had been welcomed to the army marae at the Waiouru national army camp in the desert country south of Lake

Taupo, by Maori elders and religious leaders with a traditional *powhiri* or welcome.

'There's a set sequence, they usually start off by acknowledging the Creator, then they acknowledge the deceased,' Herewini says. 'This is one of the dimensions of Maoridom that people have difficulty trying to fathom. For example, the photos on the wall, and all our speechmaking, it always goes back to the departed ones.'

For the Maori it is crucial to acknowledge other things as well, such as the sky father, Rangi, and the building, the ancestral home.

Herewini describes the army whare at Waiouru as 'absolutely magnificent', because it embraces all cultures and all people. He says each army unit has its place in the whare and it is no surprise that he is seated beneath the SAS pou pou. Pointing around the room, he says each pou pou represents an ancestor or part of the community such as a tribe or *hapu*.

'That one there is the sacred pillar — the one on the left is the Christian one,' he says, pointing out the various carvings.

Kevin Herewini served for 26 years in the New Zealand Army and 21 of those were spent in the SAS, where he rose to the rank of warrant officer class one and regimental sergeant major. He eventually became a commissioned officer and retired with the rank of captain in the parachute squad.

Born in 1946 in a town called Kaeo north of the Bay of Islands, he joined up as a 16-year-old boy in the regular force cadets. His father had served with the Maori battalion in World War II and had been a POW under the Germans.

Herewini graduated from the cadets in 1964 and joined the corps of engineers for two years before undertaking SAS selection in 1966. In 1968 he was sent to Vietnam as a patrol signaller with 4 Troop of the first SAS Ranger Squadron under Lieutenant Terry Culley, to operate alongside the Australian SAS in Phuoc Tuy province.

Despite the folklore and one or two minor flare-ups, Herewini has nothing but positive memories of his time working alongside the

Australians, reinforcing the Anzac bond forged at Gallipoli 55 years earlier.

'Contrary to what you hear about the relationship between the Australian and New Zealand soldiers, it wasn't until you sleep together, eat together or go to war together that you appreciated how many myths were spoken about the relationship between the Anzac soldiers,' he said. 'We've got a group of people who, perhaps, think out of the square. I guess our role allows us to do that and we rely on one another. All our first patrols were led by Australians, and so they introduced us and, for want of a better word, indoctrinated us — they taught us the skills and the variations to operations. In actual fact there was very little difference. And then, over the year, you get to know people and your friendship and your relationships grow much stronger.'

Although some of the terminology took a bit of getting used to: he recalls his first patrol commander, a digger known as Zorba the Greek, telling him, 'If anyone comes around that track you brass 'em up.'

'I said, "Does that mean that I engage?"'

Terry Culley has a slightly more sombre view of the relationship between the Australian SAS and its Kiwi cousins. Culley remembers the early days under SAS 3 Squadron commander Major Reg Beesley as being quite a challenge.

'On the first day he [Beesley] said, "Right-oh, Kiwis, you're now under my command, so bring up all that stuff here — brand new Land Rover and all — and start coming under our orders."'

Culley had to point out that the Kiwis were under their own national 'command' and only under the operational 'direction' of the Australians.

'He had this impression we were under his command,' he says. 'We were under operational control, which is a different tactical commission. We kept national command and he didn't understand that so in the end I had to ring Saigon and get someone from Saigon to come down and explain what it was all about.'

The pair had a strained relationship from that point onwards.

'Don't get me wrong, we worked well and the group did work very well, and we celebrated success, we socialised well.'

Culley didn't appreciate it when Beesley referred in a later book to the command and control of the Kiwi troop as being 'bloody shocking'.

He thinks the comment relates to an incident the night before 4 Troop was due to fly back home. According to Culley there was one hell of a piss-up and one of the young Australian officers had been needling one of the old, hard Kiwi soldiers. Later that night they met somewhere in the dark and the Kiwi gave the Aussie a 'bit of a shellacking'. There were no witnesses and the younger man ended up in hospital 'pretty crook'.

'No one could find out how it happened or why, there were no witness, but the young fellow ended up in hospital nearly dead,' Culley says.

Naturally Beesley wanted someone's head on a platter with a full-blown court martial.

Such a course would have kept the Kiwis in Vietnam for weeks past their departure date. Eventually the charge of assault was downgraded because the victim was unable to identify his attacker and the Kiwi was saying nothing.

'Because the evidence was there that someone had done something wrong, the guy was charged with one of those nebulous military offences — performing contrary to the good name or whatever, which was worth a loss of pay,' he says.

Culley thought the incident was symptomatic of the 12-month deployments that were introduced for Vietnam at the behest of the Americans. Prior to that, operational deployments had been based on the British model of six months. Ever since Vietnam the Anzacs have reverted to the six-month model.

'At six months I noticed that things were starting to go wrong,' he says. 'I was getting woken up at three or four in the morning when the guys were coming down from the boozer, to tell me stories about their wives playing up, their kids being sick, the car being smashed up at home. These stories were really symptoms of some other problem.

'It wasn't home that was the problem, even though I'd tried to get something done about that. It was actually them saying that were getting a bit tired and needed something. It wasn't that people were being bad on operations but when they were in the base, they were getting into trouble — breaking things, punching people.'

To relieve the tension and boost morale, Culley organised an exchange with American special forces.

There was strict rule that no one was to go on operations. 'You come in, you go down on the range, shoot, join in the drills, do all that stuff. You go down the club and enjoy life. You don't go out and create a possible international incident by getting yourself shot and not being at your home base,' he says.

It wasn't until 38 years later in January 2008 that he found out that his men did in fact go out on operational patrol with the Yanks. 'I said, "You bastards." And they said, "We thought you'd say that, so we didn't tell you."'

Culley says those exchanges lifted morale and kept spirits up for the final few months of the tour. 'It was getting over that hump — more like a hole — in the road. It did bring it home to me, though, that at six months they were at their peak. There was that little glitch that happened just after that.'

After he transferred across to the officer ranks, Kevin Herewini was sent to Waiouru to the officer cadet school to help train young officers. That meant he could maintain his links with Australia as well because the Australians sent several officer cadets to Waiouru each year to train with their Anzac comrades. During this time he met a young officer cadet called James McMahon who would rise to command the Australian SAS.

'He was fabulous. I used to say to him, "Hey, Sir, when you become the General, you call for me, I'll be your batman." And he said, "Oh no, we can do better than that."'

'Guys like that, you just never forget — never forget.'

McMahon showed a keen interest in the Maori culture, so Herewini took him to the marae and taught him to do a simple Maori greeting. 'He told me he loved the way the Kiwis included their cultural heritage.'

Kevin Herewini left the army in 1987 and took a job in a flooring factory. He worked his way up to assistant manager, but there was something missing from his life and he was still searching. He had always had a strong Christian faith and was working as a volunteer with a group called Youth on the Streets when he received a higher calling.

'I was brought up on the marae,' he says. 'I was the "fair one" in the village, and every time I'd go home they would ask me to lead prayers and do spiritual things.'

So he decided to study for the Anglican ministry and he scored his perfect job, working in schools and mentoring young people through the schools and the church as well.

He was ordained a minister in 2002 and began working in school chaplaincy ministering to families and students right through until they went to university.

'This was a Maori project, called a school community liaison project,' he says. 'Like everything else in the government, if something works they pull the plug on funding!'

His next calling was to become a prison chaplain in 2005 and that is his current job. In 2006 he was also appointed to another 'dream job' as territorial force chaplain for the 3rd Battalion.

Herewini is one of three SAS men to answer the call of faith and another, Paul McAndrew who is a Mormon minister, was also on hand for the ceremony at Waiouru.

The links between the Maori and the Kiwi army and SAS have always been very strong. Many fine Maori soldiers have served with distinction and the marae at Waiouru is about honouring that service.

It was at another marae at Te Kaha in the Bay of Plenty south-east of Auckland in August 2007 that the Maori and the SAS had one of their finest hours. A young Maori, SAS Corporal Bill Henry 'Willie' Apiata, was awarded the Victoria Cross for Gallantry in Afghanistan in 2004.

The 32-year-old then Lance Corporal Apiata had carried a badly wounded mate off the battlefield to safety under extreme fire, before reloading and returning to the fray to help rout a Taliban attack.

He is the twenty-second Kiwi to be awarded the VC and only the second Maori.

The Kiwi SAS has served in conflicts with the Australian SAS from Vietnam to Afghanistan and they operated successfully as joint Anzac forces in both Vietnam and East Timor.

'The unit itself has a wonderful tradition,' Herewini says. 'I'm so grateful to have been part of that family.'

WHEELCHAIR BOUND

chapter twenty-three

THE FIGHTING MAN

Ken Webb has no memory of how he came to be lying face up on a cobbled London street with a smashed spine.

One minute he was standing on the balcony of his first-floor flat, in an old hops warehouse in Southwark not far from London Bridge, and the next he was unconscious in the street.

It was a quiet Sunday morning in late November 2002 and the former SAS major, on the eve of his fortieth birthday, had been in London working on a 'security' project. He was preparing to return home to Perth for Christmas when the accident changed his life forever.

Born in Perth in 1963, Webb was a natural sportsman. After finishing school he started playing professional soccer to pay his way through university when a reality check occurred. A friend who was also playing professionally damaged his knee and had to give up the game. So instead of pursuing soccer Webb joined the army reserve officer training scheme and found that he enjoyed it.

He was soon drawn to the special forces side of the house and after completing his reserve training his next step was to apply for selection to the Commandos. He undertook the selection course in August 1990 and joined the Commandos' signals squadron in 1991.

'It's different from the SAS selection course because the role of commandos is different from the SAS,' he says. 'The commandos are more strike and they operate in company strength [100 troops] where the SAS is more long-range reconnaissance, behind enemy lines on patrol, small teams and specialist recovery.'

Under the Special Operations Command (SOCOM) structure, the Commandos and the SAS Regiment do a lot of work together. In Afghanistan they are working side by side in the Special Operations Task Group based at Tarin Kowt.

Despite the close working relationship there are tensions between the two units, and commandos have been known to start brawls with their better-qualified and better-paid comrades in the SASR, especially after a late night on the town.

'On commando operations there'll be SAS guys with them and also SAS guys on the ground before them, doing the reconnaissance, and if there are SAS guys in trouble it will quite often be the commandos who come to rescue them. So they quite often work in tandem,' Webb says. 'I would say commandos would be considered elite conventional while the SAS would be considered elite unconventional.'

During his training he found himself at the Swan Island unconventional warfare school. The top-secret facility is located in Port Phillip Bay, close to the Victorian city of Geelong.

'That's where I got my introduction to special operations and I found I enjoyed it.' Webb says the best part of the course was meeting some of the outstanding guest lecturers who visited the shadowy facility such as the World War II heroine Nancy Wake.

'You get trained in what they call unconventional warfare so you have people like Nancy Wake come and lecture you and I remember sitting there trying to drink her under the table at the Krait Bar,' Webb says.

The bar is named after the *Krait*, a small former Japanese fishing boat. The boat was used as the mother ship for Operation Jaywick when 11 Australian and British army and navy personnel from 'Z' special unit raided Singapore Harbour in September 1943 in kayaks to destroy Japanese shipping.

'You're being taught . . . very much the delineation between black and white, the grey side,' Webb says.

Wake didn't mince her words in her tales about killing Germans and her time with the French Resistance. He remembers how much she emphasised the importance of learning the culture of the people you're working with, how to earn their respect, how to be open-minded, not to do it very much doctrinally and more importantly how it all came down to leadership and management.

'Leadership is all about respect — you've got to earn the respect of the people that are wanting you to lead them, but you've also got to show your respect to them and work as a team, very much a team-based approach.'

He found it so satisfying that he said to himself then and there, 'I'm never ever going back into the mainstream army. I want to stay like this.'

As for drinking Nancy Wake under the table — forget it. 'I thought that after a bottle of red wine she would have had enough. We're sitting there throwing rocks across the bay watching the stones skim over the waves and we just kept drinking and I kept thinking, "She's just going to have to collapse soon", and here we were at three o'clock in the morning and I felt as if I was the one who was pissed and she was the sober one. She was a very inspiring person.'

Life in the Commandos included counterterrorism exercises such as one four-yearly exercise where Webb was role-playing 'the enemy'.

'We were sent over to Indonesia; for example, I was organising the enemy for this four-yearly exercise and I had to try and work out how we could come into here against the conventional forces. So you go and hire fishing trawlers, and that's how you assert yourself, you go to Bullo River Homestead where Sarah Henderson's place is and you fly in there in a light aeroplane and you sit there and you have the army intelligence corps trying to find you, so you just grow a beard and get a hire car and drive around, it really is a good time.'

Then one day in December 1992 he was in Melbourne having a drink in a bar at about three o'clock in the afternoon when he ran into a couple of SAS mates he had met at Swan Island. One was the operational commander of the training squadron and the other was still at the island, but later became regimental sergeant major.

'What are you doing here, guys?'

'Oh, we're doing the SAS selection boys for Melbourne today and we're obviously using this place to do it. What are you up to, Webby?'

'Oh well, I'm a Perth boy and I want to get back to Perth and spend some time with the family so I've applied for a posting to an army reserve unit over there next year.'

'Why are you going to army reserve, why don't you come across to the regiment?'

So Webb underwent an interview the same day and was slotted in to a selection course on 10 February in Perth.

'I came back here to Perth for Christmas and spent my whole time running around with a 40-kilo pack on my back and a steel pipe to carry as a weapon and ran up and down West Coast highway 20, 40 ks [kilometres] and then went on the course in February and got through.'

Like everyone else who has ever been through the SAS selection course, Webb has his own stark memories of the extreme physical and mental endurance test.

'The first three days were basically becoming accustomed to it and it's not what you envisaged,' he recalls. 'It was quite clear to me that you weren't on the course to be tested for your physical ability because number one you wouldn't have got on there in the first place. It became quite clear to me that what they were after was your mental ability and that was what they were judging.

'And my memories of things? Walking around naked out in the bush, sitting there at three o'clock in the morning watching a black-and-white typing movie from 1950; they'd had me sit an exam on that typing movie at the end of it, after you hadn't had any sleep. The officers are expected to do it at a higher standard than the soldiers. So at three o'clock in the morning the officers are in a tent out in the middle of nowhere watching a black-and-white typing movie for an hour and then they've got to sit an exam and answer questions related to that movie they've just watched.

'Then you go to bed and about two hours later after you've got a couple of hours of sleep, whiz bang, grenades go off outside the tents and wake you up in a big flash and you've got to get out there within about 30 seconds, otherwise you start doing push-ups for penalties, those type of things.

'That just gets you selected for the regiment, and then you've got to do all the other things before you earn your sandy beret. And that includes things like a patrol course where you learn all your contact drills with live ammo, firing rounds, those types of things. I was already paratrooper qualified so I didn't have to go off and do that. Language training . . . so it's basically a six- to nine-month process before you're eligible to be a member of the regiment. I felt quite privileged too that I got to do the training with the commandos and . . . with the SAS. 'Cause you learn both.

'And the main thing I found was the mateship and the unity — that everyone realises you're all up against it and you help each other out. And there are times when you find out who are your mates and who aren't, regardless of rank, and I've found that now with my experiences that have happened to me since, you find out who your mates are.'

The aspects of SAS work that he found most interesting during his four years in the regiment were unconventional warfare and change management.

'I finished up as adjutant and then I was promoted to major and made special projects officer.'

Then came the day that a lot of SAS officers dread.

'Ken, you've been too long in special forces. We're posting you over to Canberra to strategic ops division and you'll man a desk for a couple of years.'

He said, 'No, I joined the army to lead and manage men, not to do stuff like that.'

'So that's when I left and did my MBA,' he says now.

But tragedy had already struck the Webb family, who had two daughters and a son. Their son, Matthew, died in 1996 of brain cancer, aged six.

Webb's wife did not want to leave Perth and her parents were about to retire and so, on leaving the SAS, Webb bought into the family air conditioning business.

For him, there were two difficult aspects of the transition to civilian life. The first was personal pressure.

'Your wife and kids are so used to you not being around and when they are with you it's quality time, so that's what you focus on,' he says. 'Then you leave the army and you're with them every day and from their point of view they love it but they're not getting the quality time. So they have to make the transition of having their dad around them all the time in a totally different mantle and then from your own personal point of view you find it difficult because you get bored, you don't get challenged.

'You lie in bed at night with your wife talking about things and it's totally foreign to you because the last 15 years when you were married you didn't do that type of thing. You didn't have to — you were used to how each other worked, you could second-guess each other. It was different and I suppose that all comes down to that change-management thing, it's how people manage that change.'

On the business front, what he found most difficult was what he calls 'the trust factor'.

'To me, [the] civilian world here in Australia is very corporatised — capitalised, I suppose — and so there is a huge culture of greed,' he says. 'When you're in the army, particularly where I was, you've got the mateship culture, you trust everyone. You know each other; your life depends on the other person around you. It's not like that in the civilian world. It's very much everyone's out to feather their own nest.'

Webb found himself falling back on his unconventional warfare training when dealing with this new-found culture of 'greed is good'.

'I made a successful transition but I found it quite boring that I'd just gone from managing some pretty complex stuff, 120 people and risky stuff to managing an air conditioning service business in Perth. I found it quite boring.'

So he started doing other things, using the British passport he had received courtesy of his English-born father.

When the marriage failed he left the business and went to London to explore opportunities in Europe. That was what he was doing when the accident happened.

'I had no alcohol in my blood or anything and I woke up four to five weeks later after being in a coma in intensive care.'

The only thing he remembers is opening up the French doors to his balcony and leaning up against it.

'It was the first floor and I fell. If you can imagine, it's not your normal bitumen road or anything; it's basically just a bunch of old cobblestones and that's what caused my spinal injury. I landed right where the bricks were jutting up and that's what smashed my spine. I'm so glad it happened [in London] because the emergency procedures there are great — they have a paramedic system where they've got paramedics who ride around on motorbikes and they can be anywhere within about two or three minutes. And they took me to the best neurological hospital in London. You couldn't go to a better hospital for a spinal injury.'

X-rays showed that two vertebrae at the base of his rib cage were smashed beyond repair and that his spine was dislocated.

'They came close to turning the [life support] machines off three times,' Webb says.

The consultant neurosurgeon refused to operate immediately because the operation could have killed him, and as he later told Webb, he knew he had a fighter on his hands. So when he was strong enough, the vital life-saving surgery was performed. To this day whenever he is in London his surgeon takes him out for a bottle of French champagne.

'We have a drink and he says, "I wish everyone was like you in terms of your attitude to what happened to you." You find out who are your mates and who aren't in situations like that. And I was looked after. I was flown back from England after I had my treatment there and I had an intensive care nurse next to me the whole way,' he says.

When he arrived in Australia he was whisked through the airport.

As his life spiralled, Webb's old army mates quickly recognised that despite his catastrophic injuries confining him to a wheelchair, his mental capacity had not dimmed. One day one of them, 'Groover Gordon' (Major General Ian Gordon, AO), the former deputy chief of the Australian Army, phoned him and suggested he undertake a PhD in national security and terrorism.

'So you're lying in hospital thinking, "Okay, why don't I go and do my PhD in a university as essentially part of my vocational rehab?" And that's what I've done and I've finished that now and it's so satisfying,' Webb says. 'You end up getting back into the world you were in before where you were comfortable and you find it quite challenging. Sure, for family reasons, it was a lot more pressure on them, but you are better in yourself as a result.'

His timely PhD thesis, entitled, 'Managing Asymmetric Threats to Australia's Security using the Information Operations of Terrorist Groups as a Foundation', has enabled Webb to travel the world plugging into the rapidly expanding network of counterterrorism thinkers and practitioners.

'Basically what I've done is come up with a model for Australia to manage asymmetric threats — principally terrorism and information warfare or a combination of the two — a hybrid,' he says. 'I've also come up with a management approach to handle that and to handle national security generally, called "Explorential Operations".'

The global network of counterterrorism academics has mushroomed to such an extent post 9/11 that Webb might find himself at a conference in Karachi one day, speaking to generals and senior officials from the new front-line states, and at another in London the following week talking to senior coalition officers and security officials.

'You've got to earn their respect and once you've earned their respect they want you, and that's what it's all about — offering value,' he says. 'You offer your value; you don't go and advertise yourself. I don't have a business card. They come to you and if they come to you, they come to you on negotiable terms rather than you going to them and taking whatever they give you. So you end up in the position where you start to control your own destiny. But this relates very much to the SAS mentality. It's the way that you did things before and you do them subconsciously.'

Webb reckons there are essentially two types of ex-SAS men operating in the world these days.

'There's the type that takes on that borderless thing where they look at the modus operandi, the methodology, the way of thinking, you can apply that to any situation, and they work anywhere around the world wherever they want,' he says. 'Then there's the guy who is still focused on purely the infantry mentality of a weapon and the gear and you go and do a task. Sure, it might be in a different part of the world but you do exactly the same as you were doing 12 years ago.'

However, he believes many SAS soldiers get out and find the big, wide world is not what they expected. He says the regiment is part of a wider army community that to a large extent shelters its members from many of the realities of the world.

'You get out expecting it to be the same and it's not and you get quite bored,' Webb says. 'You can't get back into the system because you've been out for too long, so you are going to start seeking out other things. And that's why guys are over in Africa, all round the world doing these challenging and mentally stimulating things. It's all about pursuing the next level and the last thing you want to do is go backwards. That's part of the mentality of passing the selection course, you don't want to go backwards so you're constantly out there seeking. It's like me at the moment — I've just finished my PhD and I'm going, "Oh my God, what am I going to do: I'm bored, I know something will come along but I need a challenge." And so what are you going to do? You talk to a few people and they try and do something for you and that's the mentality.'

Even with their amazing skill sets, former SAS soldiers have to work hard to be accepted into the non-uniformed world.

Webb's personal life has improved dramatically. He is happily remarried to Jeanne whom he met after the accident and they live in

Perth with her son Zac in a house they specially designed and built. His two daughters visit frequently.

Having completed his PhD, Webb turned his sights on disability rights. He joined forces with WA Liberal Senator Alan Eggleston to try and change some of the outdated and discriminatory disability laws and practices in Australia.

Rather than scream and shout, Webb has learnt to adopt a measured approach.

'I've found that in every aspect of life, your training teaches you that you never take a system head on, you find the holes and you go through them. The last thing you want to do is take on the bureaucrats.'

He has had plenty of first-hand experiences to draw on, such as an occasion when he was flying interstate. After the plane arrived at the gate, Webb the paraplegic was left until last to be offloaded as usual, but this time they forgot about him altogether.

After about 15 minutes a cleaner came along.

'Who are you?'

'I'm just a passenger and they've forgotten all about me,' said Webb.

'So they then go into a mad panic,' he says. 'Your wheelchair has been down, going around this turntable where you pick up your baggage for half an hour by the time they get you out. You're just treated like a second-class or even a third-class citizen.'

Things are no better on international flights. On another occasion Webb landed in Singapore and the same thing happened. They simply forgot about him in his customary last row seat. When he finally left the aircraft he spoke to a flight attendant.

'I said, "This is ridiculous. Why don't you put me in an exit row, because if there is an emergency you can just open up the side door and push me down the slide. How else are you going to physically get me from the back of the aircraft and drag me to the exit?" "Oh, don't worry," she said. "If we ever have an emergency you'll be the last one off the aircraft."

'That's when I realised how discriminatory it is. I'm finding cases like this two or three times a day and that's why you find in Australia that people in wheelchairs tend to stay at home indoors because they just don't want to go outside. You look at governments, they call them disability services ministers, they treat you as if you are a vegetable — as if you can't contribute to society.'

When it came time for Webb to leave hospital after his accident and to adapt to life in a wheelchair he encountered obstacles at every turn.

'I was lying in bed thinking, "Okay. I can't get public transport", because we've gone and tested that with the occupational therapist. "I can't get on the trains and buses, so I'm going to have to get a car to drive around."

'So I thought, "Okay, I'll get a PT cruiser, I've [tested] the shape of it, I can pull a wheelchair across my lap, all that stuff."'

He remembers talking to a nurse one day, when she came in as he was looking at a brochure.

'Look, this is my new car. I've ordered one from America,' he said.

'But you can't drive,' the nurse said.

'Yes, I can, it's got hand controls!'

'But you don't have a licence,' she snapped.

So he pulled out his wallet and showed her his driver's licence. 'I've had it for 20 or 30 years.'

'Oh no, but that licence has been taken off you now,' she said. 'You'll need to go and sit your learner's permit again, do your driving instruction again and be issued a whole new driving licence.'

Webb said, 'Stuff you guys. I've got an international driver's licence from England, I'll just keep driving around on it.'

Eventually he found an instructor in a car fitted with hand controls and after proving his worth behind the wheel, he went for his licence test. The examiner looked up the computer file.

'I'm sorry, I can't take you for a test. You don't have a learner's permit.'

'But I've done a learner's permit.'

'When?'

'Oh, about 25 years ago!'

By now the exasperated examiner was digging deep for his sense of humour.

'No, no, you're supposed to have done a new one now. Well, I can't even take you for a driving test.'

Webb talked him round and convinced him to go for a drive and when they returned the office quietly issued him with a new disabled driver's licence.

His series of run-ins with an unsympathetic system culminated in an incident at a federal government office in Perth.

'I couldn't get into a government building and when I eventually did get in a fire alarm went off,' he says. 'They all evacuated the building and left me stranded. This was a federal government agency that's supposed to be setting an example.'

Webb took them to court, but the case was dismissed.

He says, 'If there is a message for Australian society it is this, "Look, I didn't expect myself to end up in a wheelchair, I'm really sorry for someone out there who will end up in a wheelchair tomorrow and they wouldn't expect it. I didn't expect it but when you get there you will realise how much change is needed in this country to make you equal."'

The discrimination is everywhere, from disabled car parks being hogged by non-authorised vehicles, to the office of his local state MP that has only stairs.

'It is shocking and I am ashamed of this country for the way it treats disabled people,' Webb says.

He had had some experience of the inequality of the system during his SAS days, when he was involved with the formation of the SAS Resources Trust following the 1996 Black Hawk tragedy.

Ironically, Webb had worked tirelessly for the welfare of the families of the dead and the wounded, including trooper Gerry Bampton, who was left confined to a wheelchair.

Now Webb is in a chair himself and he well and truly understands what it is all about.

'It's just Australian society and I don't think it will change until someone like the prime minister ends up with a spinal injury.'

But he is determined to fight on. 'I suppose this comes from my military background — you're used to fighting for your life and you've had people die by your side fighting for your country and you fight for your country. You can't accept this, you've got to cause a change and this is why you fight.'

chapter twenty-four

STRENGTH AND GUILE

Down at Port Hamworthy Royal Marines barracks in the pretty port town of Poole on the south coast of England, a former SAS soldier pulls up in his Land Rover outside the shack that houses the Special Boat Service (SBS) Association.

Chris (he does not want his surname divulged) reaches into the back seat and grabs his super-light, titanium wheelchair and attaches the frame to its wheels that are strategically placed, within easy reach, on the front passenger floor. One thing that a disability such as paraplegia teaches you is patience.

After he assembles the chair and places it on the ground next to the driver's door, Chris uses his toned upper body and strong, athlete's arms to ease himself down into the chair. Token offers of assistance from awkward bystanders are met with a courteous, 'She's right thanks, mate,' and off he zooms for another day's part-time work with the association.

Today's challenge is organising a major charity ball and a steady stream of very fit young marines, who make up Britain's elite SBS, call on Chris to pay their money and book their tables. Their motto is 'By Strength and Guile' and judging by the group of very impressive-looking men, it is taken very seriously indeed.

Chris, who was born at Mascot in Sydney in 1951, was serving with the SBS when he fell from a helicopter and broke his back during a training exercise in Central America.

He came to soldiering at an early age and joined the cadet unit at J.J. (Joe) Cahill Memorial High School in Sydney at the tender age of

12 years, immediately falling in love with military life, thanks to the school cadet corps. Firing an old World War II Lee Enfield .303 rifle and Bren machine gun at the Maroubra rifle range was a great thrill for the young lad. Like thousands of other boys in the post-war years, he quickly memorised drills such as 'piston, barrel, butt, body, bipod' to strip down the Bren.

'I still remember as a young kid that .303 over your shoulder and, being left-handed, I fired left-handed. I tell you what; it just about blew me off the mound! It was good,' he says.

Chris had the army in his blood. His grandfather was a digger in World War I and his father, Harry, a Riverina boy, served in Borneo and New Guinea in World War II, so when it came time to leave school at 16 he knew where he wanted to go — the infantry.

His dad, who was a postal worker, had different ideas and would not allow his under-age son to join up, so Chris began his working life as a file clerk at the Department of Motor Transport. Harry suggested a stint with the civilian militia, the CMF, would be good for the youngster, but that merely fuelled his passion for army life.

As soon as he turned 18 he joined 1 Commando Company based at Georges Heights in Mosman as a reservist. During his commando training he had a parachute instructor from the SAS who was about to embark on his second tour to Vietnam, and the seeds were sown.

'I thought I'd like to join up with SAS, and go to Vietnam. That was my aim, so I told my dad. He said, "Okay, you are 18 now, you've seen what the military is like, it's up to you now if you want to join up", so that's what I did,' he says.

After a brief stint at the recruit training centre at Kapooka in southern New South Wales, Chris and two mates were transferred to Ingleburn camp near Sydney. It was from there in early 1971, with less than a year in the regular army and not a single day with a battalion, that he flew to Perth to undertake the SAS selection course. He passed and embarked on a long and successful special forces career.

After missing out on Vietnam, a brief mental flirtation with the Rhodesian SAS, postings to Papua New Guinea, Indonesia and a short exchange with US Navy's SEAL team 1 in San Diego, Chris was posted on exchange to the SBS at Poole in October 1980. He stayed for more than two years and the idea was born of a permanent move to the Royal Marines.

'I was over here when the Falklands were on but the two troops that went from SBS were conventional troops,' he says. 'I was with the counterterrorist group, the maritime counterterrorist group. At that time maritime CT group would remain in the UK and another CT group in Scotland would remain in Scotland so those troops on line and the British squadron had to stay as well. So the Falklands were on and I never got to go.'

It wasn't for a lack of trying or lack of will on the part of his commanding officer.

'He turned around to me before they left — we spent the whole weekend gearing up the boats — and he said to me, "Right, if your troop gets called out to go to the Falklands, you are the team leader, you'll go and I'll sort the situation out with Australia House later on."'

Chris had been told in no uncertain terms by the diplomats at the Australian High Commission in London that he was absolutely forbidden from fighting in the Falklands. 'You are there to learn how to train, and that is it.'

In February 1983 he went back to Perth to work in the counterterrorist training wing with an early SAS CT expert, Red Webb.

This was the quiet time for the Australian SAS. Vietnam was a memory, Bob Hawke was in power, defence spending was under pressure from the so-called 'peace dividend' and the SAS was desperately trying to define a role for itself. Counterterrorism was the panacea, but the lack of an enemy generated some very lean times.

Chris figured that the uncertainty meant that he was unlikely ever to see operational service so he decided to quit the SAS and seek a job back in the UK with the SBS.

He discharged from the Australian Army in July 1985 and, with his wife Cathy and young son Matthew, moved to England to join the Royal Marines.

His first task was a commando course before he marched into the SBS in January 1986. Soon after that he was made a patrol commander with 2 Troop, honing his jungle warfare skills. By the end of the year he had been to the jungle training area in the former British colony of Belize, bordering Mexico and Guatemala in Central America, and had been promoted to troop sergeant major.

After two years in that job Chris was appointed chief instructor with the training wing and the die was cast.

'One of my major tasks was to organise a training package in Belize for the SBS guys and to teach them special forces jungle warfare,' he says. 'Some had been in the jungle before, some hadn't. I had three months to organise it from dot.'

It was a five-week dry-season training package using helicopters. In March 1989, on the very last day of the initial training exercise, the instructors and three others, one of them not abseil qualified, were due to abseil from a chopper, simulating a rescue team.

'I woke up about a month later in Miami in the spinal unit,' Chris says.

Unfortunately the helicopter that he had ordered for the exercise was incorrectly sent by the headquarters elsewhere that day, so he was left with a Search and Rescue machine that was fitted with a completely different abseiling set-up.

The chopper was hovering about 20 metres above the ground when the men began their descent. When Chris's turn came he jumped out but his rifle, which was slung over his back, caught on the helicopter's skid. The crewman and an instructor leant out to see if the abseilers had hit the ground and they saw Chris hanging unconscious in space, with his weapon sling around his neck choking him.

'The crewman tried to drag me in but he couldn't — he couldn't get to me. I think he thought I was dead.'

The crewman's own communication line had become disconnected as he tried to rescue the stricken patrol commander, so he was unable to talk to the pilot.

Standard RAF operating procedures clearly stated that any obstructions on a helicopter during abseiling had to be removed. Unfortunately for Chris, the crewman took this literally.

'He must have thought I was dead so he cut the sling. I dropped 60 feet.'

His life was saved thanks to an Australian abseiling innovation that he had introduced. The British style of abseiling is to connect the man only at the waist, so that his pack hangs around his backside. Fortunately, he had introduced the Australian method that connects the rope at both the waist and the shoulder, through a shoulder harness. This allows the soldier to remain upright and abseil with a heavy pack below his feet.

'So when I did drop, thank God I dropped feet first. If I had dropped any other way, the best thing that would have happened is that I would have been a quadriplegic; I would have broken my neck. If I had dropped 60 feet on the side of my head I would have been killed.'

He harbours no ill will towards the crewman. 'He knew me well, he was a good bloke and if I saw him tomorrow, I'd still have a beer with him. I've got no regrets — he did what he thought was the right thing,' Chris says.

He suffered a compression fracture to his numbers two, nine and ten thoracic vertebrae.

'I slammed in, the first thing they reckon to hit the deck was my weapon, the next thing was me — "thump, thump".'

His mates performed a tracheotomy after his heart stopped for the third time.

'The reason I'm alive today is because of what those blokes did and those guys saved my life, I have a ton of respect for them. They are still serving, so I can't mention their names, but they are top hands and all the blokes, I had a lot of time for them . . .'

When he woke up a month later in a Miami hospital, he thought he must have been on a bender. He had a rotten headache and double vision although he could see his wife and young son through the blur. He was eventually shipped back to the UK, but unfortunately he had picked up a resistant *Staphylococcus* bug known as MRSA so his hospital recovery time was extended by more than five weeks. He was in hospital until the end of 1989 and then he moved back to the SBS to undertake some work with the training squadron before he was medically discharged in August 1991, destined to spend the rest of his life in a wheelchair.

Post-retirement he undertook some training courses before becoming involved with disabled sports. He learnt how to operate a racing wheelchair, met some British paralympians and began racing, before moving on to a hand cycle and eventually into competitive triathlon.

'Two guys lift you out of your chair, get you to the water, you do the swim phase, they pick you up put you back in the race chair then it's up to you to do all the transfers yourself. They will help you out of a wetsuit but that is it,' Chris says.

At the end of 2003 he heard that an old mate of his, Willy, had taken over as Secretary of the SBS Association. He applied to do some voluntary work with Willy one day a week, but he found out that he could do up to 15 hours a week and the Ministry of Defence would fund it without affecting his pensions.

Had he not been disabled, the family had planned to return to Perth in 1992.

Sixteen years later, they decided to make the move in 2008 to live in a home they purchased at Scarborough on the coast. Chris will continue to compete in chair racing and triathlon and will work with the SAS Historical Foundation for about 15 hours a week.

He says the training he received in both the SAS and SBS has stood him in good stead to cope with his disability. 'The things I reckon that assist blokes in doing well once they are out of the military, and in our case special forces, is one, they can organise themselves, they can organise groups, therefore start a business, they can be involved in security work, organising equipment, selling, running a business.'

He says that if he said he never got depressed, it would be the biggest lie in the world. 'Mentally you have to say, "Get your finger out of your arse and make the most of it; don't be so much of a pain in the bloody arse."

'The people that are really affected are the family. They are the ones that have to put up with the whingeing, the moaning, the crying, a lot of crying, they've got to put up with that. The good thing Cathy said to me is, "Come on, Chris, get your bloody act together, stop being a bloody whinger."

'I'd been swearing and cursing and carrying on; my son was only five, and I was swearing, f'ing this and f'ing that and carrying on like a bloody idiot because I couldn't get up out of the couch,' he says. 'Okay, you have a disability but you still have a brain, it is still ticking over. If you don't use it you are a pain in the arse. You've got to get your act together, otherwise you are a shit bag.'

THE BROKEN ONES

chapter twenty-five

DAMAGED GOODS

Their medical files are up to 20 centimetres thick.

These are broken men and they were broken by the army in the name of defending Australia from the scourge of terrorism.

Sitting around a kitchen table in a house in suburban Perth in September 2007, it is difficult to imagine what these five overweight, limping, depressed or just plain sad men were once capable of. Whether storming a room, shooting static targets with sub-machine guns while their mates cowered in between, hoping not to be hit by the live rounds, or getting so close to deadly explosive charges that their ears bled, they did their duty without fear or favour. It never occurred to them, as they stood among targets on the sniper range during demonstration shoots for politicians, while high-powered rounds slammed into the watermelons placed on the top of the human-shaped targets just centimetres away, or as they were being gassed in a room until they dropped, that they would be abandoned by the country they had volunteered to protect.

But that is exactly what has happened to the men who pioneered SAS counterterrorism tactics, techniques and procedures (TTPs). Australia is a safer place today because of these brave blokes, but many of them find themselves isolated and suffering from terrible physical and psychological injuries. Put simply, they were ordered to break most rules in the army's safety handbook, and a swag of civilian laws to boot, so that their fellow Australians could rest easy at night.

On the eve of celebrations to mark the fiftieth anniversary of the SAS in 2007 they had gathered to discuss the one issue that drives and torments them — the desire for recognition.

These men — Dave Howe, Glenn Shaw, Roger Croucher, John Bromham and Mick Connelly — are the lucky ones. They can at least function in polite society and put their case in a compelling and reasoned way. There are other SAS veterans who live in the bush, too afraid to venture into town for fear of what they might do. Some have been placed on police watch after threatening elected officials, but there have been others who ended their torment at the end of a rope or the barrel of a gun.

The story of the first SAS counterterrorism teams is a Boy's Own adventure story of courage, service above and beyond the call of duty and of official neglect. And it is a story that until now has been largely untold.

These men operated in a secret world, a world they couldn't even discuss with loved ones, but they lived it and they were scarred by it. They were told that at a moment's notice they might have to commit murder in the name of their government and they were trained to do just that.

Glenn 'Rube' Shaw, 52, remembers the early days of the CT teams, as the troops experimented with human tolerances to explosives. There was no handbook but he recalls the drill as if it were yesterday.

'Explosive charges on wood normally require a 300-metre safety distance. Well, in this case it was reduced to 2 metres, or closer depending on the structure of the building you were dealing with,' he says. 'So it brought in a whole range of things that we had to work out: "Well, can you stand that close to a charge?" It was all suck it and see.'

According to the army safety manual, when linear metal cutting charges were fired the user had to be at least 900 metres away, lying down with a steel helmet on.

Linear charges are used widely by special forces troops to breach heavy metal doors. They come in continuous lengths shaped in the form of an inverted V and when detonated the V-shaped metal liner with an explosive core produces a uniform cutting action. The early CT operators detonated them when, in some instances, they were less than 1 metre away.

Roger Croucher remembers how, when he was a young lance corporal, he was left unsupervised on the range with another trooper and a big bag of explosives.

'Under the safety manuals, for a lance corporal or a trooper to use explosives in any sort of situation you'd have to have a minimum of a sergeant supervising you,' he says. 'The two of us undertook an experiment on how to breach double-thick walls. The rest of the team were miles away and here we were with a big bag of explosives just doing whatever we wanted, to work out a good way of blowing double-thickness walls and being as close to them as possible without endangering any people around.'

Explosives generate a pressure wave that travels through the human body. The danger this might have posed to them at the time was never an issue. Tests were supposed to be conducted to assess the impact on the men's bodies, but that never happened.

'The closest analogy to this is a boxer,' Croucher says. 'When a boxer is punched in the head a shock wave is transmitted through the cerebral fluid in the brain. The fact it has been delivered by a hand or a glove is no different to the fact that you have high-pressure shock waves surging through that are doing the same thing. So what happens is each time the brain is rocked a little bit — well, we all see what's happened to Muhammad Ali and the heavyweights who have taken the big hits and the big punches. We were all aware of this because we could feel the effects on our lungs, let alone what was happening where we couldn't feel it.'

Gassing was another regular occupational hazard.

A derelict bus would be filled with volunteer hostages, usually reservists or members of the army band, and the CT team would assault the vehicle using CS gas. On one occasion they used a gas canister called an area ride that was not supposed to be used indoors under any circumstances. It was designed for outdoor crowd control.

It actually landed on the chest of one of the 'hostages' and exploded. There was so much gas inside the bus that troops with gas masks on could not even see their hands in front of their face. One of the passengers smashed the rear window of the bus and had to be revived after he stopped breathing. Another was left behind and was almost unconscious. Many of the men involved in extreme gas training have suffered years of lung and bronchial problems.

Paul Kench's name sits with 46 others on 'The Rock', the granite memorial to SAS dead outside the headquarters at Campbell Barracks. Such is the extreme nature of SAS service that all but a few have been killed while practising their deadly craft and by far the most have died undertaking counterterrorist training.

The lack of recognition really hits home for the men when they talk about CT team members who have been killed, men such as Kench, who died in a diving accident in Bass Strait in December 1992. His son Kyle would place a wreath on the rock each year on the anniversary of his dad's death. Sadly, he was never able to march with the unit on Anzac Day because he had no medals to wear.

All of these old soldiers have wives and children who are proud of what they did, but they cannot reconcile their service because the government says it was not operational and that they were not on active duty.

'We just need some recognition of the fact that our service was real, "Welcome home" or "Yes, your service was real and meaningful and exists", particularly for next of kin of the dead, for the wives and family of the injured,' John Bromham says.

As they recount some of their experiences, there is no sense of regret about the decision to do the jobs they did, but just profound disappointment that after a quarter of a century no government has properly said 'thanks' for a job well done and recognised their extreme military service.

They do not want compensation or cash rewards, they just want recognition in the form of a medal and better access to what is rightly theirs under veterans' entitlements schemes.

Under existing military rules, to qualify for 'operational' recognition or an Active Service Medal, the soldier must have served on an 'operational' deployment. Given that the military does not operate inside the borders of Australia unless under extreme circumstances, that means overseas. Then the degree of recognition is graded on the basis of 'warlike' or 'non-warlike' service, which invariably opens another can of worms. For example, troops who served in East Timor in 1999 were on 'warlike' service while those who went to the Solomons in 2003 were on 'non-warlike' service.

When the first CT teams, 'Gauntlet' (on land) and 'Nullah' (on water) were established at Campbell Barracks in 1980, their service was considered the same as any other military service. Compensation was the same and recognition was the same despite the hazardous nature of the work. So these men, who went to work every day and risked their lives, were lumped in with the postal clerk and their extreme training accorded no greater status than driver training.

Official correspondence from the time says, 'The aim of the course is to train a TAG [tactical assault group] and OAG [offshore assault group] to full operational status . . .'

The troops were formally advised that they were on operational service for a prescribed tour of duty in response to a 'Headquarters Australian Defence Force operational requirement'. As far as these men are concerned, 'operational' means just that.

The SAS commanding officer at the time of the first counterterrorism squadron, retired Lieutenant Colonel Dan McDaniel, told a review panel in 1982 that he was left in no doubt by then Prime Minister Malcolm Fraser and the Chief of Defence Force as to the 'operational' nature of the CT team's mission and the relaxation of normal peacetime safety and occupational health considerations.

'Many training situations would not have been acceptable within any other unit of the ADF at that time or any time since,' Colonel McDaniel wrote. 'Too many of these fine men are suffering various ailments for it to be coincidental. Remember we are discussing the best of the best and in my experience these are not men who want to bludge on the system if there is a viable alternative. In fact for many it's a matter of some shame to admit their problems.'

The five former diggers gathered around the kitchen table sipping tea and nibbling chocolate biscuits are beyond shame. They are simply as mad as hell.

Dave Howe can't even walk through the gates at Campbell Barracks without being physically ill. He loves to catch up with his old army mates, but he cannot do it at the camp.

Roger Croucher can make it through the gates, but he can never stay for very long.

John Bromham says the simple fact is that these young, fit people were ordered to do a job and they were told it was under 'operational' service conditions.

'Therefore safety didn't apply. Now as far as I'm concerned, that's fine and I was quite happy to do it and I'd do it again, but when you leave and the government turns around and says, "Remember that operational service, well that doesn't exist anymore", well that's bullshit,' he says.

During Roger Croucher's time as an SAS counterterrorism operator in the early 1980s he suffered enough injuries to cripple lesser men. The English-born soldier spent 10 years in the SAS and for about half of that time he was on CT duty.

'At one stage I fell out of a helicopter while it was still flying and damaged my back. I eventually left the regiment because of that,' he says.

After 10 years as an instructor with the army school of transport his back became so bad he was medically discharged in 2000. He now works as a private transport consultant to the oil and gas industry.

Croucher, 53, has been married several times and has three children.

'I've been married more times than I can remember. Some people collect postage stamps, I collect wives,' he says.

The ex-soldier is on a 70 per cent totally and permanently incapacitated (TPI) pension.

'They won't give me a 100 per cent pension, even though I've got rods holding my back together and rods holding my feet together,' he says.

Croucher has numerous other physical injuries to his chest, lower leg, ear nose and throat, right foot, left foot, leg, ankle, and eyes, as well as cuts and abrasions.

His medical file reads like a man who worked as a prize fighter and rodeo rider during the week and played rugby league and went motorcycle stunt riding on the weekend.

'I was told by a surgeon that an SAS soldier, by the time he reaches 40, has the same type of skeletal frame of a person that is 60 because of the stress.'

While physical injuries are easily identified and rectified, it is the mental scars that have been most difficult to isolate and treat. He says he can barely remember anything about his SAS service because he has made himself forget.

'The easiest way of dealing with it, is not to think about it, that's what the psych told me,' he says. 'I have had professional counselling. I am mad, I am literally screwed up. They've said the only thing that keeps me sane is I can't remember a lot of stuff.'

He also suffers from recurring dreams about one accident that occurred during training. Another soldier walking behind him was about to throw a grenade when it exploded in his hand.

'He lost all his fingers and I remember saying to the doctor, "Where are his fingers?" and he said, "Most probably down the back of your flak jacket and your neck." They were peeling the bits off me: fingernails, bones.'

One of the major issues for the men was actually admitting that they had any psychological problems.

Mick Connelly couldn't bring himself to own up to any mental weakness when he approached the bosses to discuss his future. His case concerned serious back and leg injuries that he had sustained during a roping exercise from a Wessex helicopter.

Another soldier panicked and ended up on top of him as they proceeded down a 30-metre rope with their 40-kilogram packs. Connelly couldn't brake and so his lower legs and spine were smashed when he hit the ground with his mate on top of him.

'When I was fronting the commanding officer to bring my issues out in the open, I couldn't bring myself to say, "I think I'm having problems psychologically" I couldn't do it,' he says. 'In the end they said to me, "You can go to training squadron if you want to, you can go to Q store", and I said "Well, I didn't join to do that, I joined to be a soldier."'

Rather than confront the system and some of his demons, he left the SAS and joined the Australian Federal Police.

'Even with my discharge I was hesitant to tick all the boxes and say what my injuries are because I didn't want it to backfire on me with getting into the police and the last thing I wanted to do was tick myself as being some insane nutter,' he says.

A mate in the police force eventually told him that he thought he was suffering from a major depressive disorder, so he finally made an appointment with the psychiatrist, whose message was simple.

'Mick, you've got to make a choice. You keep going to work, kiss goodbye to your family, or finish work and say hello to your family.'

'So I chose the family.'

He is now on anti-depressant medication and sees his psychiatrist every few months. He wishes he had been more open about his condition when he was in the regiment, but concedes that it is difficult to be open in an elite environment like that.

Dave Howe comes from Binnaway in the far west of New South Wales. He joined the army at 17 and was posted to 5/7 Battalion where he served under a young company commander called Major Peter Cosgrove. He played rugby with the future defence chief and moved across to SAS in 1977.

After completing the usual round of reinforcement training and serving in a squadron, he was assigned to CT training in one of the first courses in 1979. These were the transition days and resources were thin on the ground, so leftover Vietnam War flak jackets and shotguns borrowed from the police were the order of the day. Soon afterwards the money began to flow into the CT Squadron and they were training up a storm with a seemingly unlimited supply of ammunition and explosives.

The newly married soldier with a baby daughter was on short-notice call-out 24 hours a day, seven days a week and like all on-line CT operators he was forbidden to travel more than 30 kilometres from Swanbourne.

By the time he came off the CT team he was a mental and physical wreck.

'They discovered I had two vertebrae fused together, my neck had almost totally fused together,' he says.

Following stints in the Q store and briefly back on-line he was medically discharged in 1986 as a result of his physical damage, but his mental scars took years to identify.

'You were always [under] extreme pressure, like working in a pressure cooker. In fact if I go back and see the guys — and I love to see the guys, but it makes me feel physically ill to go near that place — all that stress comes up again, and that is why a lot of the guys don't go there, unlike the Vietnam veterans. They love going out, they can't leave the place, they had happy times there. We had mates seriously injured and killed in that base. They [Vietnam vets] went overseas so all their problems are overseas. Ours are here . . . you go in there and you see all the guys, even these old cripples, they go through the gate and then they puff themselves up. I won't go down there.'

Anxiety attacks are commonplace among the former CT operators.

Roger Croucher says he usually lasts about 30 minutes at the SAS Association House inside the barracks before a cold sweat sets in.

'I've felt pretty good going through the door, and within half an hour I feel as though the whole world has fallen in, I can't stay there,' he says. 'I'll go and meet a mate for a beer and then make excuses to leave, all good intentions to go and meet somebody, but I just can't do it. What I find is recounting the stories, the emotion, that's what screws me up. So I'm like John. I just think of the future, I don't even think of last week.'

Just before he became a TPI pensioner Mick Connelly went down to the House to support Glenn Shaw who had become president of the Association.

'It used to gnaw into me, I used to shake. Even though I was down there working behind the bar and helping guys, serving drinks, that type of thing, I used to dread going there, and in the end I had to pull the pin after six months and I haven't been back there in two years, except for the fiftieth birthday celebrations,' Connelly says.

Another big problem for the blokes was the stigma attached to being a TPI veteran at 50 and no longer being in the workforce.

For Glenn Shaw it was the shame of not working that was the most difficult bridge to cross. He says the former CT operators had confronted that issue and mostly moved on, but in the early days it was a struggle.

'You wouldn't seek out people, you were almost ashamed to confront your mates and say, "Oh no, I don't work, mate", "mumble, mumble", and hopefully get past without too much scrutiny,' he says.

According to him, the worst thing about the men's treatment is the feeling of betrayal. He says they gave 100 per cent and did all that was asked of them and more, but when it came time for some help in the other direction there was a stony silence.

'The expectation is that people will turn around and say, "Yeah, we do recognise your service as being valuable, at least comparable with service of other people around the place", so when it comes to medical treatments and reasonable compensation you are not left in a place you can't afford.'

He says a classic case in point was dental treatment for his two young daughters.

'All kids have straight teeth these days 'cause everyone goes in and puts them into the dentist and spends thousands per kid to get them done that way. We found ourselves in a position where we couldn't afford to do that, and straight away you think, "This is a hardship as a result of my service." You feel put out.'

Nobody, as he says, ever becomes a TPI veteran for the money.

chapter twenty-six

RECOGNITION

John Bromham's wife Lesley has sat patiently through a 90-minute interview, listening intently but not uttering a word.

She is one of the many wives who, along with children and extended families, continue to suffer by proxy the damage their menfolk have endured.

She gives the impression that she has never heard these men speak so openly before about the issues they have raised. She says proper recognition would not change what has happened to the men, but it would allow those who have been unable to move on to get on with their lives in peace.

'It has to affect the families, leaving something that has been so much a part of their lives — and a special part that a lot of people never experience — and they are not prepared for civilian life,' Lesley says. 'The fact they weren't supported, they were just left to go and make their own way . . . affects the families, the wives, the kids, it can't not affect them when you've got someone in the house dealing with all this.'

Mick Connelly believes that formal recognition for the CT teams would allow many damaged men who are in the shadows to emerge and seek some help. It would allow them not only to be able to stand shoulder-to-shoulder with an active service veteran, but to get help because it is owed to them.

The men bear no ill will towards others who have been recognised.

'We are not denigrating anybody here, but when they brought out the National Service Medal, fine, there were some blokes that did *x* amount of years, they got the National Service Medal. Fine, they got recognised for what they did, most of them got it for their peacetime activities; they didn't go to Korea, they didn't go to Vietnam,' Connelly says. 'Then they introduced the Australia Defence Medal and they gave that to everybody, to people who were in the army reserve, they said four years in the army reserve relates roughly to a year in the regular service. They are saying it is the same for a regular soldier to do four years and get the same medal, okay, fine.

'But we did a job that no one else in the Australian Defence Force could do and we got no recognition for it whatsoever. If anything, they put us away in a corner and said, "No, no, no, what we told you was wrong, you were just doing training."'

Martin Hamilton-Smith gets very angry when he talks about the lack of recognition for his men on those early CT teams.

As the first officer in command of the Gauntlet team, the current Liberal opposition leader in South Australia was intimately involved in breaking the rules and damaging men, himself included, in the name of achieving an elite capability.

'We broke a lot of rules, a lot of soldiers were injured, some very seriously, both in this team and the teams that followed,' he says.

One of the men, Lance Corporal Peter Williamson, was shot dead during a live ammunition training exercise in October 1980.

'A lot of people were busted and blown up,' Hamilton-Smith says. 'The system broke every rule in the book and a lot of soldiers paid the price, psychologically, and I'm very concerned, very concerned that their suffering hasn't been recognised appropriately because they weren't overseas in a Vietnam situation or Iraq situation, they were on operations here and it was regarded as training. It wasn't training,' he says.

Hamilton-Smith says the men on the teams were on operational duty for a year at a time and that is reflected in both the pay records and the operational records.

'Now during that period there was no operational deployment, there was no counterterrorist event that required us to deploy and fight, but there were quite a lot of periods of high readiness and quite a lot of intelligence warnings indicating there could be an issue,' he says.

The former head of Special Operations Command and ex-SAS boss Duncan Lewis pauses thoughtfully in his office at the Department of Prime Minister and Cabinet in the leafy Canberra suburb of Barton. As deputy secretary of that department with responsibility for national security and international policy, he is fundamentally the prime minister's national security adviser.

For years Lewis has grappled with the issue of recognition for the CT operators and each time he reaches the same conclusion. Their service was not operational and they do not qualify for the Active Service Medal.

Put simply, says Lewis, the work these guys did does not satisfy the definitions of active service. 'That's not to diminish the work they did at all, because it was extraordinary and it should be recognised,' he says. 'I don't have any problem with recognition. But this issue about operational service, whether it was operational service or not is something that we just, in my view, can't clear the bar height on.'

Lewis says the CT operators are not the only ones in this situation.

'There are a whole bunch of people out there in different categories of military service who have done pretty remarkable things but have not been able to get recognition for operational service,' he says. 'If you're a bomb disposal expert for example and you go down to a bomb disposal in Sydney city and you blow your arm off, now I regard that as an extraordinary sacrifice and that is about as operational, if you like, as it gets, but it doesn't clear the bar height for "operational service" in the military context. It's service and it's dangerous service and it's extraordinarily valuable service, but it's not operational service and that's how I see those blokes — and I was one of them, you know, I was involved in this myself for many, many years.'

Lewis believes they should keep plugging away at some form of recognition, but as a member of the Council for the Order of Australia, he understands better than most just how complex honours and awards can be.

'There is no clear-cut answer,' Lewis says.

He says he is acutely aware of the circumstances of the men because they were his cohort.

'Had I not just served those extra few years that took me past 9/11, I would have been exactly in the cohort of this group that served for 20 years with no operational deployments of consequence during that time,' Lewis says. 'You serve a lifetime, you spend many, many years conducting counterterrorism training here in Australia and being on standby ready for operations. There's issues around [questions like] are you on operations because you go to the Commonwealth Games? . . . Was that an operation? They're very awkward questions and they're hard to manage. I'm in that group, that's where I spent my time doing that stuff, but it didn't qualify as operational service, to do with being [on] active service.'

The issue affects him personally because he served in Lebanon during the war in 1982, but he served with the United Nations force.

'We got a service medal, an Australian Service Medal but it wasn't an Active Service Medal because we were with the UN. Now being in Lebanon in 1982 was pretty exciting and pretty dangerous too, you know, when you're under artillery fire or rocket fire, but it didn't clear the bar height and that's where we're at, I think, with this CT training. But it's not to diminish it and I think it should be recognised.

'And where they are scarred they should receive recompense of some sort and they should be properly recompensed.'

Mike Silverstone takes a hard line on the question of damage and compensation.

The SAS commanding officer from 1994 to 1997, he was in the chair when the regiment suffered its worst counterterrorism disaster — the 1996 Black Hawk crash near Townsville.

Silverstone is sympathetic to the plight of men suffering from depression or post-traumatic stress disorder (PTSD). He went through a bout of depression himself following the Black Hawk tragedy.

'Our wives and girlfriends at the time were quite happy to put up with our distractedness, our mental and physical involvement in the joy of the job, [but many of the men] find themselves in circumstances 30, 40 years later depressed and looking back and perhaps regretting some things they did at that time,' he says. 'Frequently there is a butcher's bill to be paid. My view is they need to remember what fun it was; yes, it was challenging, but we were doing a job. We relished it and did the job really well and so in terms of what is the cost, well there is a bit of a cost — we all get arthritis and tingly ears and everything else but it is like footballers with bad knees — it is part of the business.'

Silverstone believes the compensation system needs to provide better support to those in need, but there is a degree of personal responsibility as well.

'There are people who work in the ambulance service and police service and bus drivers who have seen terrible things on highways,' he says.

'People look back on these things, see sorrow and get depressed, many people look back and say, "Right, that was an experience, what can I take from that, let's get on with our lives."'

'There are real challenges to the way we view these things in society, the way we deal with PTSD, what sort of behaviours are acceptable and not acceptable. I think the diagnosis and treatment of people needs to address those issues as well; it is my personal view that PTSD has been given too much freedom in terms of excusing behaviour.'

Silverstone says he parts company with the psychology if or when it says, 'You are damaged and therefore you are excused from behaving that way.'

'But do we have to excuse your anger all the time? Do we have to excuse you being drunk, do we have to excuse you wallowing in self-pity? Sometimes the answer is no.'

He argues that the most important debriefing process is the one that happens as a team, as a result of things that have occurred.

'That is the at the core of the way the SAS do their business . . . but for everybody who flourishes after the military, there are other people who fail to flourish and you've got to ask the question: why?'

Former army psychologist Dr Nick Reynolds has seen countless damaged soldiers as both a military and a private psychologist. He says the easiest solution for the CT operators would be special recognition. He agrees with Duncan Lewis that their service will never qualify as 'operational' under the current official definition.

Reynolds argues that being trained up and on-call to do a job, no matter how extreme and lifelike the training was, is not the same as deploying and actually doing it.

He too would like to see a new category of service to formally recognise what they had done.

'Whether you call it exceptional service and recognise that there is some form of exceptional service, then you don't get that bureaucratic hurdle that they are not on operation. They were doing extreme service for their country; therefore, recognise it in a special way so we don't have to recognise it as operational,' he says.

He thought the casting of a new Extreme Service Medal might be the most palatable option for the powers-that-be.

'That definitely would be possible.'

Major Grant also strongly supports the push for recognition. The SAS executive officer said the men paved the way under demanding circumstances with no occupational health and safety frameworks to protect them as they trained to an operational pitch.

'You look on that rock [SAS memorial], there are very few blokes that died on active service,' he says. 'The names on that rock are only a few that suffered, many more would have been injured.'

Grant says a lot of the problems suffered by the men stem directly from the lack of proper recognition.

'I've always supported the awarding of some sort of medals for these fellows and recognition of their services. For crying out loud, we are giving the ASM to people; I've got an ASM for my Butterworth experience you know, that was not a dangerous activity. I was serving my country but it was nothing like these guys had done, so I support them.'

He agrees that the men do not meet the criteria for 'operational' service, but he wants to see that changed.

'A lot of these blokes are not chasing financial remuneration, they are chasing recognition. They are no different to anyone who has worked their guts out for the collective purpose, some form of recognition.'

He says gongs such as the Defence Medal do not cut it when you examine the sacrifice the early CT operators made and the extreme risks they took.

Chris Roberts is another former CO of the SAS Regiment. A tough, no-nonsense leader, his relationship with some of his former soldiers in the early CT teams is best described as 'tense'. Roberts was the commanding officer from late 1982 to mid-1985 and became the army's first Commander Special Forces in 1990.

He has already had one go at trying to help the CT operators, but it ended in tears some years ago, largely due to differing views about tactics and timing of the push to get recognition.

He regrets this unfinished business, because he has no doubts about the merits of their case.

'They should be recognised', he says bluntly. 'We've lost more dead in counterterrorism training than we've lost on active service. That speaks for itself.

'I can truly say this, having been on active service with the SAS and having seen what the guys did in those early days of counterterrorism, there is absolutely no doubt in my mind that they performed an incredible service to this country. Those young men who went into those killing houses, went into those extreme training environments, I mean you have never seen anything as extreme as [what] those young men went through. There is absolutely no doubt in my mind that these men need to be recognised. They need to be looked after . . . in exactly the same way as the war veteran is looked after. Because they performed a service to this country that went above and beyond the call of duty in Australia, in the training environment that nobody else participated in, whether they were navy fellows who were attached to us at the time or whether they were SAS guys in the regiment.'

He says their training was far more extreme than any he went through and in terms of stress was akin to the duties that he and his SASR comrades performed on active duty in Vietnam.

Now that he has retired, Roberts is keen to take up their case again. He has recently joined forces with a retired brigadier in Canberra to work on a new approach to the problem. He agrees with Duncan Lewis that the current regulations and the way they are written do not allow the men's contribution to be categorised as active service, but he says the argument needs to move beyond that.

'So what I'm trying to do is say, "Let's take a completely different tack", rather than just say, "The current legislation doesn't . . ." Let's get them recognised as a special right. A lot of people when they see a regulation or a new idea come up look as to why it can't be done. [Let's] look at how it can be done. Let's look in favour of the soldier. Let's forget about what is on the legislative books now. Let's put a case up that says this is another form of dangerous service, another form of hazard service, that because it hasn't occurred on active service, because it hasn't occurred overseas doesn't mean to say that it shouldn't be recognised.'

Roberts says the CT operators did all they were asked to do and more in situations that would have been too extreme for lesser men.

'They worked to provide a capability that would save people in a hostage situation at such a high standard so that the government wouldn't wear egg on its face. And now we've just swept them under the carpet. That's not right, that's un-Australian.'

chapter twenty-seven

THE KIND OF MEN

The stereotyped image of the macho, gunslinging SAS soldier is very far from the reality. Anyone who looked around a room full of serving and former members of the SAS regiment would see men of all shapes and sizes, drawn from all over Australia and all levels of society.

They range from the 'class clown' who always has his group in stitches to the nerdy genius manipulating some esoteric piece of software in the corner. One thing they do have in common, particularly the serving soldiers, is that they are fit and have noticeably clear, alert and thoughtful eyes.

But there is more to it than that.

Psychologist Dr Nick Reynolds spent years in personnel support, including screening recruits and those seeking career transitions, including to the SAS. He says that there is a predominant personality type in the SAS regiment — the 'stable introvert' who has a high resilience to stress.

Reynolds, who hails from Adelaide and is a Flinders University graduate, says men selected for the SAS usually have very few negative traits. In a sense, the selection process filters out negative traits and leaves a pool of intelligent and highly trainable individuals.

He says that in the military there are five grades of soldiers, ranging from the untrainable, rated as fives, to the brilliant, graded as number ones.

'The selection groups one and two were the higher-level people who would verge into where the officer intelligence levels were and that is where you select in the Special Air Service people,' Reynolds says.

He says the major factor separating the fives from the ones and twos was speed of processing or intelligence.

'If you are talking about the situations SAS people are in, the ability to think in a very agile way and react under pressure is most important,' he says. 'Basically, it was looking at the overall ability of the people fairly quickly, a quick screen, but choosing fairly bright people.'

But psychological screening is not just based on intellect. It also examines personality types. The process focuses on two key psychological constraints called neuroticism and psychoticism.

Psychoticism obviously relates to psychotic or abnormal behaviour, which is often revealed in late teenage or early adult years. According to Reynolds the military selects out the psychotics very early in its screening processes. Screening for neuroticism is in a sense a more difficult.

He is currently conducting some work into the selection of people who may be less prone than others to post-traumatic stress disorder (PTSD) and says neuroticism comes into play here, along with what he calls 'internal control', which is the ability to take responsibility for one's actions and what is going on.

'There is a dark side of that which is related to neuroticism, where they start blaming themselves for things they couldn't have had anything to do with, or they will take responsibility for [such] things,' he says. 'So you select out those sorts of people because they are not going to cope with stresses of military service.'

This characteristic may be part of a trigger for PTSD, which in itself he calls a 'dose response' to significant traumatic events over time.

'They used to call it the "old sergeant's syndrome",' he says. 'One of the major generals I used to work for was a company commander in Vietnam and he said to me, "Nick, I didn't really believe the PTSD stuff until one of my brave sergeants started showing symptoms of it." And that is related to a lot of continual exposure to dangerous situations. The same thing happens to ambulance drivers. They will go to 600 road accidents, deaths etc. etc. but there is one that will resonate with them that will actually cause the PTSD. It may be the exposure to a child that is the same age as their own child that may be the trigger. So it really is [that] people have coping mechanisms.'

He says that what they used to emphasise in relation to PTSD was that those likely to suffer from it were not normal people in normal situations; rather, they were normal people in abnormal situations that were also far more intense and threatened their lives and those of the people around them.

But he has come to the view that SAS soldiers may be less prone than other soldiers to develop PTSD. 'So if you are talking as a group of Special Air Service people being exposed to a lot more of those situations pro rata compared to any other group in the military . . . the fact that not many of them go on to form PTSD — now, I don't have any stats on that but it is my experience — is because you are actually choosing very resilient people, very emotionally tough people. So what we are choosing for is a lack of neuroticism; that is stability, very stable people.'

The ability to cope with stress is vital, and this is tested during the SAS selection course itself.

'For the SAS the stresses increase, so you are putting a fine-tooth comb over them, if you like, and selecting the ones who are stable. The other part of it, interestingly enough, and it was not one we used for selection, more the other end, was the introverts. The SAS people tend to be stable introverts,' he says.

'If you have a look at one of their prime roles, deep penetration behind enemy lines, you are putting ones and twos behind enemy lines, they had to live off the land, they had to be very self-sufficient. You can't choose party animals that have to have stimulation, they had to be people who could look after themselves with their own devices.'

That's not to say that the regiment has no party animals. Comedy is a very important commodity during a long, lonely SAS patrol and for defusing fraught situations. Yet Reynolds thinks that most of the comedians in the regiment are still by their nature introverts who are happier entertaining a small, intimate group rather than appearing cold in front of a large audience.

It is a trait they share with many successful comedians who have traditionally been introverts, such as the late TV star Graham Kennedy.

'I am sure he had tension every time he did it, fed off that adrenaline, because it was going against time, but [in his private life] he would stay at home, very self-contained away from that TV setting,' he says. The late British TV comic Benny Hill was another well-known introvert who lived alone.

Reynolds recalls a colleague saying to him that it was always the 'boring' soldiers who made it through SAS selection.

'What she was relating to was the fact that they were introverted. She didn't see them overtly out there in the bar doing all those things,' he says. 'They were all very self-contained, stable, able to cope with situations and pressure. Those sorts of characteristics are the ones, not cracking under pressure, making logical decisions, going forward, reasoning things out, they are all things that will make people very successful.'

In addition, the type of men who make the best SAS soldiers also get on well with people and are very good friends to have.

He says another important trait that is not picked up during the initial screening process is tenacity. 'That is the ability to push through adverse situations, to do the job no matter what it takes, and do it efficiently with a minimum of fuss.'

Tenacity appears during the SAS selection course when the applicant is pushed to breaking point and then pushed some more.

'You get them to do a challenge, then they have to do another challenge and then they think they are getting out and then they have to do another challenge,' he says. 'It is that constant thing of having to push through and come out the other end. That really is the selection and it's not something you can train into people. It's a trait within the individual that they use and develop further.'

So when it comes time for an SAS soldier, or indeed a commando, to move on from the military these traits that have made them 'special' in the military context are very marketable.

'Given what they can do, their ability to learn and adapt, they will adapt to it very quickly, so once they are put into a job they will succeed quite admirably, I'm sure.'

Jerry Hilder, a former SAS senior soldier who is now a nurse, is very aware of the value of psychological support, but says it has to be appropriate support.

'I talked to one of the guys who had come back from Afghanistan who had a wife and a couple of kids,' he says. 'He said he had a young girl counselling him about what he had just done in Afghanistan. She's got no idea of what he's just done, doesn't have any kids, doesn't have a husband and she's trying to help him into life back in Perth.'

The result was that the soldier just told her what she wanted to hear so he could get the hell out of there.

'They really need to be talking to people that have the knowledge and the understanding,' Hilder says. 'You don't have to have been through what they've been through, but you do need an understanding.'

He says many men who leave the SAS are suffering from heavy stress and they haven't quite discovered what's important. 'By the time they do it's too late because they are on the drugs for depression. Some of them have lovely wives and families, but because of the mental illness they destroy it. I can't help them, I'm not a psychiatrist, and most of them probably wouldn't listen anyway.'

George knows what PTSD is and he has seen the terrible impact it can have on soldiers, including some of his mates. Many of the troops from the Rwanda mission were diagnosed with PTSD, but despite a very active military career, including missions to East Timor and Afghanistan and a close encounter at the 1996 Black Hawk tragedy, George appears unaffected.

'I appreciate the Australian Army for this; they do debrief us about everything. After the Kibeho massacre we had psychologists all over us like a rash and I've noticed it particularly since then,' he says.

George doesn't believe he is a heartless bastard, but says he has no problem reconciling anything he has seen or done. 'I've seen some horrific things but I found it very easy to remove myself from feeling any responsibility or anything,' he says.

A very dark sense of humour helps him to break the hold of the unimaginable horrors that he has witnessed. 'Every time I tell a psych that I was in Rwanda the alarm bells go off as though I am going to start crying and pissing on the floor.'

Still, he is grateful for their efforts. 'Everywhere I've been — Timor, Afghanistan, we always get held up and have to go through a process before we come home.'

But he shares Hilder's view that the psychologists don't always seem up to the task. 'After the Black Hawk accident, that very night, we had psychologists there,' he says. 'We were toying with them, virtually, because we'd lived and [we] saw what the fuck was going on, so we felt better talking to each other than them so we were fucking around with them,' he says.

Sometimes it was impossible to resist taking the mickey. On George's way home from his final mission in Afghanistan the psych debrief was conducted by an old hand known to the soldiers as 'Mike the Psych' and a fresh-faced lieutenant by the name of Potter.

'I called him Harry throughout the thing,' says George mischievously. 'He'd be sitting there asking me questions and the whole time he looked uncomfortable, but he never raised it. He'd be asking, "Oh, what did you see?" or "How do you feel about this?" And I'd say, "Well, Harry, I'm glad you asked", and you could see it was irking him no end.'

Whether or not George has an inbuilt resistance to PTSD, he seems to have escaped with little or no lasting psychological damage. That is not, however, the case with all SAS soldiers and PTSD is not the only extreme behaviour exhibited by some.

Of the 2700 or more men who have qualified and served in the regiment during its 50-year history, a small number have actually gone right off the rails in terms of criminality.

One of the most notorious was David Everett.

He first came to the notice of authorities when he was working as a mercenary for the Karen National Union in eastern Burma in the early

1980s. The Karen has been fighting an insurgency along the Burma–Thai border against the rogue military government in Rangoon since 1962.

Everett made the mistake of appearing in a documentary film about the insurgency.

A former executive officer of the regiment remembers it well.

'He was a dead-set mercenary so he went straight on the shit list,' the officer recalls.

When Everett returned to Australia in the early 1990s he went bad and began a life of crime that led to him becoming Australia's most wanted man. At one stage he was wanted in Perth for armed robbery, kidnapping, faking his own disappearance and blowing up a munitions store.

He linked up with a couple of other former soldiers and the gang committed a number of brazen armed robberies netting $116,000. In January 1991 they kidnapped the manager of a Perth cinema and his pregnant wife and drove them to a derelict house. She was blindfolded and handcuffed and the husband was driven to his cinema where he was forced to open the safe and hand over thousands of dollars. The same tactic was employed with a bank manager at suburban Midland.

At one stage during his fugitive days, Everett and his gang were holed up in a safe house right next door to a police station, putting an entirely new spin on the SAS motto 'Who Dares Wins'.

After serving a lengthy prison sentence, Everett was back in the news in April 2007 accused of stealing and burning two tractors in outback Western Australia near the Northern Territory border.

In the most recent case his lawyer successfully argued that his client was not a risk because he was a disability pensioner and was under medical care for depression.

Everett had been on the run across Australia and was almost captured on Magnetic Island in North Queensland, but narrowly escaped before returning to Perth where he was finally apprehended and convicted.

Despite his colourful career since the SAS, he was back at Swanbourne in September 2007 to join the fiftieth anniversary celebrations. He recently published a book about his eventful post-SAS life.

One of Everett's accomplices in the early 1990s was later caught trying to import a yacht full of cannabis into Australia.

While he waited for trial his lawyer told him that if he was convicted the government would confiscate everything he owned including his home. So he took an early guilty plea.

'He pulled a plastic bag over his head and tanked himself so the missus would have everything. He was a tough dude,' the former executive officer says.

Another couple of ex–SAS men introduced rappelling into Australian criminal history. Roping down the side of a building or from a helicopter is a core skill of the SAS soldier. The soldiers-turned-crims would enter buildings through the roof and rope down inside, grab the booty and scramble back up the rope.

'The cops couldn't work out what was going on, "Who are these guys, supermen? No sign of forced entry or anything",' the officer says.

The most recent SAS soldier to run foul of the law was convicted in February 2007 for conspiracy to conduct an assault against a woman who had become pregnant to him. His name was suppressed, but the Iraq and Solomon Islands veteran was sentenced to more than three years in jail for the plot to make the woman miscarry the baby.

In August 2004 a senior and well-regarded SAS soldier, Corporal Grant Rushby, was jailed for 20 months for his role in the ill-fated plan to bash the woman.

Rushby was also fined $4000 over firearms offences. Both men were discharged from the army as a result of their criminal offences, and the crimes brought great shame to the SAS Regiment.

Some armchair critics seize on these cases as evidence that the SAS turns soldiers into psychopaths and then unleashes them on an unsuspecting community. Many senior military officers take the view that these people should have been filtered out during the rigorous selection process, because by definition they were prone to be 'bad eggs' and not the right people for the regiment.

Yet those who have turned to a life of crime are remarkably few, given the numbers who have gone through the regiment and some of the traumatic experiences they have faced during their extreme service.

Dr Nick Reynolds is not surprised that the number of SAS soldiers to have gone bad is so low. He is also not surprised that some of those who have turned their skills to evil instead of good have been somewhat successful.

'It is a function of a person in the environment,' he says. 'Now if they are in an environment that is not being good to them or some trauma happens, it could push them in that direction. Some people go back and analyse their story later and say, "Oh yes, that's what it was". It may not be something in their makeup, it may be an experience they've had which has essentially pushed them in a different direction.

'To my knowledge there hasn't been that many that have gone off the rails at all, considering.'

THE SPICE OF LIFE

chapter twenty-eight

KEN ACKERS

Ken Studley has one of those faces that just makes you want to laugh.

The Tasmanian is regarded as one of the funniest men to have served in the SAS and during many difficult missions he kept morale up with his jokes and his antics.

During one long patrol in the frozen mountains of Afghanistan in early 2002, Studley transported his fellow patrol members, who were dining on lukewarm tea and a dry cracker biscuit, back home to their favourite restaurants. By the time he was finished his mealtime commentary the shivering, hungry diggers were eating fillet steak or lobster overlooking the Swan River.

Humour is a bankable commodity on any SAS patrol and those lucky enough to have served with Studley had it in spades. Like a true professional, he is very aware of the need to not go over the top.

'Not necessarily a big cheesy grin, but right when people are about to fall asleep you come up with some little cracker that makes everyone laugh,' he says.

His comedic abilities first shone through at school in Tasmania in the early 1970s where his reports regularly referred to the 'class clown'.

Born and raised in the pretty town of Huonville about 45 minutes south of Hobart, he had an idyllic childhood with regular camping, fishing and shooting trips with his older brother. He was at home in the bush and the army was a natural fit for the boy whose father had died in a forestry accident 20 days before he was born.

His journey into a uniform was not immediate, however, and after he completed Year 10 he joined the Wrest Point Casino as an apprentice electrician, a job organised by his stepfather. At 17 he joined the army reserve.

'There would be about 20 blokes there. You'd turn up in your greens, play with SLRs and M60 machine guns and muck around marching up and down in the hall,' he says. 'That would go for two hours and then you'd go back to the boozer and get on the piss until five in the morning. I thought, "If this is what they do part time, I want to do it full time."'

Much to his mother's dismay, he left the apprenticeship in May 1985, just shy of his eighteenth birthday, to join the army. He took to the military life like a duck to water. His ability was recognised early and he was soon sent on a sniper course at Singleton army base in the New South Wales Hunter Valley. A crack shot from his roo shooting days, he blitzed the course.

'Succeeding in the military is wanting to do what they are teaching you and I really enjoyed it and loved it,' he says.

Back at the battalion he was posted to the reconnaissance platoon. His marksmanship was recognised with selection to the army sniper team, They travelled to Hong Kong in 1989 to shoot against nine other countries. The diggers won and Studley returned to the rifle company in time to organise his section for the battalion military skills competition. They went on to represent 8/9 Battalion at the Duke of Gloucester Cup, the army's infantry skills competition and suddenly he was the section commander of the winning team. After a seven-year Gloucester Cup drought for the battalion, they were welcomed back like conquering heroes.

'They had limos and a band waiting at the airport; we were on parade when we got back,' he recalls.

Soon afterwards, his second in command in the section, a soldier called Eddie, decided to have a go at SAS selection, but Studley was reluctant to join him.

'I was always too scared to do it, because all I'd seen were half a dozen guys doing the selection course every year and half a dozen coming back,' he says. 'No one ever got in, and that was very frightening for a lot of guys within the battalion who wanted to try and give it a shot and I was one of them. [I thought] "What do I need that for? I'm flying along here, doing really well."'

At about this time word came through that he had been selected to become a batman for a general in Land Command. This hit him like a bolt from the blue and he told his superiors he would rather leave the army than be someone's batman.

'All I wanted to do was proper pack-on-your-back, gun-in-your-hand soldiering,' he says.

He had been watching his mate's progress towards the SAS selection course and decided he would give it a go after all. He rang SAS and spoke to the regimental sergeant major who virtually said he was too late and to come back again next year.

However, word filtered through the channels that this top young soldier and Gloucester Cup-winning section commander was keen to attempt selection. Next thing he knew, he was summoned to his company commander's office to take a phone call from the officer in command at the SAS Training Squadron, Major Tim McOwan (now Major General McOwan and head of Special Operations Command).

He told McOwan straight that he knew he was late, but he had made up his mind and would not be one of those blokes who pulled out. He begged for a shot and promised he would be ready to go.

After passing the fitness and psych tests and following an interview with an ex-SAS regimental sergeant major, he was in Perth and on the selection course two weeks later. The officer in charge of that particular class was an SAS veteran of two tours to Vietnam, Terry O'Farrell. He and his team gave no quarter, but Studley survived and passed, even though his mate Eddie did not.

He joined SAS in 1990 after completing the water operator's course, which he believes was more difficult than selection.

'For six of the 13 weeks it was just 18-plus hours a day, non-stop absolutely physically and mentally exhausting,' he says. 'Luckily I was always a mad keen swimmer so I've always been comfortable in the water, but there were a few guys that weren't and they didn't make it. Not that it mattered because they always said in the regiment, "If you can't make it in water ops, there is always vehicle mount or free-fall."'

The SAS vehicle and free-fall courses are much shorter and less physically demanding than the water operator's course. But Studley stayed in the water, won the 'top fin' merit award, and just lapped up the detailed theory and practical work that was thrown at him.

'When it came to learning anything military I just had a brain for it,' Studley says. 'They'd tell me something and it would go in and stay in, in exact detail, all the quotes from theory I could quote off the top of my head right now. It got quite technical with descriptions and being able to just rattle them off. Tabulated data for weapons, I knew it inside out and upside down. When you have people under you and you question them, you've got to know more than they do, otherwise you've got no credibility.'

His year of reinforcement training, or his 'reo year', was one of the best of his life.

'You are doing courses with your mates who you got through selection with and they become your best mates,' he says. 'The friendships that were bonded that year are forever, they are phenomenal. You are working so hard that the only way to get through it is through laughter a lot of times. That year of work, you just couldn't top that with anything. It was fantastic.'

He had maintained his passion for comedy throughout this period and had come to realise that genuine stand-up was much more difficult than being stupid and making your mates laugh at you.

'I had an idea I would love to do stand-up comedy one day and during my trips away I'd write things down in little army notebooks, but I never got the guts to have a crack at it,' he says.

So as he was going on leave in 2000, he said to his mates, 'When we come back I will be doing stand-up at the Last Laugh or the Comedy Club [in Perth].'

He drew on material that had been largely written during lengthy bush patrols when he was sitting in the 'muck and heat' for days and weeks on end.

'The reason I told the boys was because I wanted to use my time on leave, knowing they were expecting it, to practise my routine.'

When the big first night came his mates and their wives and girlfriends turned out in droves. His routine went down really well and at the end one of the organisers approached him and suggested he enter the amateur section of the Melbourne Comedy Festival. He did so, won the Perth heats and was getting ready for the final in Melbourne when he got called out on a job. His stand-up career was cut off before it even got going.

The year 2000 was a busy one for Ken Studley and the SAS. He was posted to the Solomon Islands where he had to secure and distribute Australian cash being handed out to rebel leaders. He and his men guarded the cash on board the navy ship as it moved from Australia to the troubled nation and then handed it out.

'When it got distributed out to the different factions we made sure that it was all going to the right spots,' he says. They also escorted rebel leaders to Townsville and back for peace talks.

The next job was one of the worst in his entire SAS career.

In April 2001 the Argentinian-owned and Togo-flagged fish-poaching vessel, the *South Tomi*, had been caught red-handed stealing prized Patagonian toothfish from Australian waters near Heard Island in the middle of the Southern Ocean, south-west of Perth. The vessel refused to stop and was being tracked west across the ocean towards Africa by the civilian patrol vessel *Southern Supporter* under charter to Australian Fisheries.

The Perth-based SAS tactical assault group (TAG) was ordered to fly to South Africa on a Qantas flight, proceed out to the ship with the help of South African navy and special forces, capture her and return her to Perth under the command of two navy officers who would join them on board.

They conducted an armed boarding about 500 kilometres south of Cape Town using South African special forces boats.

'That was the worst three weeks of my life, sailing back on that boat,' he says. 'It shattered any thoughts I might have had about buying a yacht and sailing the seven seas. Cape of Good Hope to Perth in a smelly fishing boat, absolutely reeked, it was shocking. It was small and unseaworthy and the seas were huge.'

The trip, especially some of the bathroom scenes, would provide plenty of material for his next stand-up routine, but the voyage back to Fremantle was an ordeal that he wishes never to repeat.

Music was working its way into his comedy routine and he spent more of his down time practising guitar and working on funny songs. A good mate is married to the daughter of the Australian bawdy comedian Kevin Bloody Wilson. After hearing about his songs, Wilson invited him to his Perth home for a few beers and a jam session. So one Friday night he went around to the Wilson home as nervous as a kitten.

Wilson is popular among diggers and is a big supporter of the army and the SAS in particular. Studley did his song entitled 'My Brown Door', and the audience, which included Wilson's mate, Vietnam veteran and Australian singing legend Normie Rowe, fell about laughing.

Wilson invited him back, they worked on songs together and eventually Studley backed him at a gig in a Perth hotel. And so 'Ken Ackers' was born. They originally wanted the stage name 'Ken Oath', but sadly that was taken.

His transformation to the part-time 'Ken Ackers' was complete, but his stage career was again cut short by his day job. In September 2002 the navy's amphibious transport ship, HMAS *Manoora*, was steaming towards the tiny Pacific island of Nauru with almost 1000 foreign boat people on board. Mainly Afghani and Iraqi asylum-seekers, they were more commonly known as illegal entries under the Howard government's so-called 'Pacific Solution'.

Studley's troop boarded the *Manoora* off Darwin to relieve the 3 Squadron troops who had been on board since the SAS intercepted the ship off Christmas Island.

'We were spewing! This was a babysitting job,' he says. 'What do they need SAS troops to sit there and guard refugees for? I guess they trusted us to not escalate anything and to look after everything.'

More than 200 Iraqis were housed in the troop deck and 440 Afghanis were living in the tank deck underneath. It was hot on the ship so they were allowed out once a day into the open air.

The Aussies had established reasonable relations with the Afghanis on board, but the behaviour of the Iraqis left a lot to be desired. Studley and his mates had been forced to hand-deliver food to the women and children because the Iraqi men had deemed that any hunger striking would not be done by the males. Then, during one of the fresh air sessions, things turned ugly when a group of Iraqis stood up and began chanting and wailing. A group of sailors from the *Manoora* was watching from a platform above and it was clear that the Iraqis were putting on a show. Studley told the sailors to move away and suddenly two women had grabbed two small children and began banging their heads together.

'They were threatening to throw them [the kids] overboard, they were banging them, holding them towards the side of the ship,' he says. 'We had blokes all geared up with fins and life jackets and rings ready to jump in after them. As soon as we turned our backs, we kept a sly eye on them and got rid of any other onlookers, but when they had no audience they realised they were hurting the kids for no reason and they stopped. They threatened all sorts of situations and they hurt their own for their own selfish benefits. I was really annoyed.'

Just under two years later, he was in Afghanistan fighting on the same side as some of the people he had been guarding on the *Manoora*.

When he returned to Perth, Kevin Wilson invited him to join him on a national tour as his support act. He manoeuvred himself into a job that would allow for a month off and hit the road.

'I didn't tell [SASR] what I was doing. Only very few people in the unit knew and I made it very clear to Kev that there could be none of this SAS stuff while I'm out there [on stage],' he says.

The tour was just like a road movie, with a new pub every night and loads of laughs.

They toured South Australia, Victoria and Tasmania and then back to Victoria, with Ken Ackers doing a half-hour spot in the middle of the show to give Wilson a break.

'He'd introduce me and my other signature song, "Australia, You Fuckin' Beauty", which is just a whole lot of things about Australia. Kev loved that song, he keeps ringing me up saying, "Can I do it, can I do it?" I'd do that one and there is a little line in it about Kevin Bloody Wilson and Kev would come out and we'd sing the last two choruses together. It worked brilliantly, the show would finish and I'd be signing chicks' hooters, it was great.'

People would ask him how his wife felt about that part and he would say, 'Fine, it's not as if I touch them, it's just a pen.'

Studley has been married to Kylie, a Perth girl, for 15 years and they have three children. Theirs is a strong marriage and he is deeply admiring of the hardships she has suffered during his lengthy absences, including having three kids under 18 months, two of them twins being toilet trained, and all with chicken pox.

He even managed to pick up some fans along the way and after the tour was over played at some bucks' nights and other gigs. For a while he became the poor man's Kevin Bloody Wilson and was being regularly booked at $1000 for a 30-minute show.

On one memorable occasion Ken Ackers was booked by a Perth motor car club. He explained to the organisers that his act was quite rude, in fact it was 'really fuckin' rude', but they didn't seem to mind. When he turned up, however, the average age was 65 and all the wives were dressed in ball gowns.

'My opener was called "Fuck Me Drunk" and I tried toning things down where I could,' he says. 'I tell you, being in the military has some hairy situations at different times, but standing in front of an unappreciative crowd is bloody tough.'

His spot was cut to five minutes and an embarrassed Ken Ackers took his $1000 and headed for the door. This was followed by a gig that Wilson had organised in a pub owned by someone connected with the outlaw motorcycle gang, the Coffin Cheaters. He had no idea of the connection, so turned up as the interval entertainment for a totally naked Moulin Rouge-style cabaret show every Friday night.

'It was a perfect crowd, young blokes, perfect. I could do different stuff, the same stuff, it didn't matter because it was mostly a different crowd, and I did that job for six months. Every bloody Friday night I'm backstage and I didn't know where to look, I'm tuning my guitar and there are all these lovely girls and they haven't got a stitch on, I'm like, "My God, what do I do?" I was tuning my guitar a bit, I had to keep my eyes down.'

He then found out who the boss was and although he had never tried anything untoward with Ken Ackers, the army had been scandalised by links with bikies in Darwin and had issued a strong warning about any bikie gang affiliations.

'I had to terminate the association. I would never have risked my job or reputation or the regiment's reputation.'

So that was basically the end of Ken Ackers's professional career.

'Comedy was great and I did look seriously at it but I reckon I'd need to be 15 years younger without a family,' he says. 'There is just too much risk. If you are not achieving like the top few comedians out there then you are not making enough money to bring up a family.'

These days he does some footy club shows and private parties for friends and that is about it.

Studley spent the next two years with the reinforcement troop, training new SAS soldiers and running the selection course, before he had his final posting into his dream job — troop sergeant with E Troop, the water operations troop. The next step for him would have been warrant officer and his days of pulling on a pack and working at the coalface would have been over.

But his oldest daughter was already nine and he had missed a quarter of his children's lives.

'I was thinking, "Another nine years she'll be eighteen. How can I tell her what to do or have any input into her upbringing?" That struck me pretty hard to have that realisation, never ever driven by my wife. She was happy — obviously not happy I was going away, but it was a well-paid job, secure, and everything was fine.'

Once the realisation struck, he gave his six months' notice and was out by Christmas 2004. He worked until the day he left, 24 December.

His mother owned a very successful rural real estate business back in Tasmania and at Christmas in 2003 she had sown the seed in his mind about returning home to join the family firm. Money, job security, his personal security, a sound future for the family and a great lifestyle eventually won the day and the family moved to Tasmania in January 2005.

Sitting in his den perched high above a pristine valley in the shadow of Mount Misery, it is not difficult to understand the strong pull of his home country.

As the family's sheep and horses, including his own mount, Ian, graze happily in the warm afternoon sun on 12 hectares just 30 minutes by car from Hobart and five minutes from his office, he reflects on 20 great years in the army and his life beyond the SAS.

Still, his daredevil days are not quite behind him. His daughter now has a horse and he rides with her and also with a group of mates.

'We go on these mountainous tracks, Man from Snowy River style, riding down hills, real hairy stuff, brilliant fun.'

It is a long way from swimming off a nuclear submarine somewhere under the Pacific Ocean, but there are plenty of photos on the wall and the memories are sharp.

A couple of old SAS mates have bought blocks just down the road, so the yarns and the jokes will go on for decades to come.

chapter twenty-nine

THE DOOR KEEPER

When it comes to unusual post-special forces jobs, few come close to former Royal Marine and Special Boat Service operator, Willy.

After retiring from the marines following a distinguished career that included a Mentioned in Dispatches (MID) during the Falklands War, Willy took a job as doorkeeper in the House of Lords at Westminster.

Only retired warrant officers could apply for the job when he was appointed in 1995.

His special forces training during 12 years in the SBS, which included working in the national maritime counterterrorism role, proved invaluable as he dealt with some odd characters and tricky situations involving hereditary peers and those members appointed to 'The Lords'.

So at age 45 and after an extensive interview process, Willy left the marines to begin life commuting from his home at Poole in Dorset, where the SBS is based, to London and life in the Palace of Westminster.

There are two sets of doorkeepers inside the English Houses of Parliament, one for the Lower House or the Commons and one for the Upper House or The Lords.

Both houses operate independently so the doorkeepers never work together except for state openings of parliament or other very special occasions.

No one, other than members of the Lords, the doorkeepers and now police during sittings, is allowed into the House of Lords chamber and it is the doorkeepers' job to see that the sanctity of the chamber is not breached by a commoner or a stranger.

'We assisted in taking messages to lords, looking after the clerk or parliament, and also looking after the government ministers who were being advised by their advisers,' Willy says.

They were also responsible for controlling visitors to the Strangers' Gallery.

'Some people might think it is a security job, but it is a lot more than that,' he says. 'We had to understand the legislative procedures, all the stages of legislation, how it actually worked. We didn't necessarily understand what they were talking about all the time, but we had to understand what stage they were in.

'Quite often a lord would come in and say, "What's happening today?" And you'd have to tell them, or they might say, "We've got to vote" and quite often they'd say, "Who should I vote for?"'

Another important job was keeping some of the more seasoned lords awake during proceedings.

'You also had members of parliament who were not allowed to sit in there, but would stand and they would often enquire, "Who is that?" or "Who's this?"

'When I started there they had 1500 lords and I knew every one of them by name, but it took about two years to learn all those names, what they did and what party they belonged to,' he says. 'You had the Liberals, the Conservatives, the Labour, the cross benches, so there was a lot to learn. The good thing about that particular job was the quality of life. I only worked four days a week. Thursday night, that was it until Monday morning, but I met a lot of really interesting people. It was a good job.'

The job gave him a ringside seat to some of the most significant events in modern British history, including the address to both houses in Westminster Hall by South African president Nelson Mandela and the lying in state of the Queen Mother in 2002.

Westminster Hall dates from 1097 and features the largest clear span medieval roof in England at 73 metres by 21 metres. It was the venue for the trial of Charles I. A speech in Westminster Hall is the highest honour that Britain affords a visiting dignitary.

'When you hear of somebody coming in and addressing parliament and they do it in the Great Hall, you know that is the highest privilege. If they do it elsewhere you know they are not that important,' Willy says.

Members of the House of Lords are not paid a salary but, like politicians the world over, they greatly value their allowances.

To qualify for the daily sitting allowance a lord must spend time in the chamber or be seen in the chamber. It falls to the doorkeepers to keep a roll off all lords and to check them off on the board as they enter. They must be checked off on two of the three boards to be able to claim the allowance.

'So what you get is a lord you probably haven't seen for a while who will come in and say, "Morning, doorkeeper. Have you ticked me off?" or, "Has Lord So and So come in?" He'll look down your list to make sure he's been ticked off and that then qualifies him for the allowance, so it's quite humorous.'

Unlike in the Commons, members of the Lords are not directed to vote by party whips. They are 'requested' to come into the chamber for a vote. But once they are in, the whip takes up guard duties at the door and will not let them escape until the voting is done.

Willy was on duty late one evening and a well-known baroness aged in her eighties was keen to go home. She was in the Prince's chamber just off the main chamber and when he asked how she was, she replied, 'Not very well. That woman over there [the whip] won't let me go home.'

Summoning all his military guile, Willy directed her to a chair within earshot of the whip and a few minutes later he reappeared with a message.

'"M'lady you have a guest at the entrance." And I made sure the baroness [whip] heard and the other baroness was able to walk out. Halfway down she turned and smiled.'

Willy enjoyed his time at the House of Lords and was particularly fond of conducting guided tours for members of the public.

'I used to do two generally every day and you never knew who you would be talking to,' he says. 'You might go down and find 16 little prats you had to take around so you had to gear your tour to children's talk, and the next day you might have 16 High Court judges, or top public servants or a women's institute so you went down and geared your talk.'

He found the job of educating people about the role of the Lords and its function as the house of review, very satisfying.

'Often the interpretation is that because they were not elected they shouldn't be making laws,' he says. 'In fact it is instrumental, because the House of Lords is full of experts on any subject you wanted to speak about: top lawyers, top doctors, top scientists, top charitable people, right across the board. You've got former defence secretaries, you've got about seven or eight former chiefs of defence staff. So if you wanted to speak about defence you've got those people, and former secretary of state for defence on either government benches, so the level of debate in there was far more intellectual than it was in the Commons.

'Now you say that to the Commoners, the MPs, and they get quite upset, but that is actual fact and the fact is the House of Commons don't have time to discuss in detail on any new legislation, they almost all brush it, whereas in the House of Lords they will go through it, line by line, word by word and make sure everything is in place.'

After eight years in the job Willy decided it was time to head back home to Poole. He had been working voluntarily for the SBS Association, which is the welfare organisation supporting the unit, and when the job of full-time secretary came up he took it.

It was a hard decision because the hours were longer and the workload greater, but the pay was higher and there would be no more travelling up to London.

'I knew I was going to take on more work and more responsibility, plus I had to have two roles, a military role and a charitable role and of course the Ministry of Defence would not pay for someone to run a charity,' he says.

Since he joined the association in 2004 it has grown substantially in terms of both membership and funds.

'We are now providing more information, the magazine is far better and also the relationship between the association and serving members has greatly improved,' he says.

The magazine is run by former Australian SAS soldier, Chris, who became a paraplegic when he was injured while working on exchange with the boat service.

He was due to return home to Perth during 2008 and according to Willy he would be sorely missed.

'I think it's been good all round, good for Chris from a therapeutic side of things, keeps him active, keeps him interested in what's going on, but also it's a morale thing for the unit to see we are looking after him, one of our own that had become injured, and so really it's been good all round for the unit to see that, to see people are supported and assisted and it's good for Chris, so he will be missed when he goes.'

As association secretary, Willy is also part of the SBS command structure at Port Hamworthy Barracks at Poole and as such his key responsibility is to support the families when a marine is killed or badly injured. As the visiting officer it is his job to organise the funeral, repatriate the body, sort out the military headstone, cemetery, any probate, his estate and any sort of issues on the support and assistance.

'When they are negotiating pensions, probate, I get heavily involved in that, so I'm heavily involved in the first two weeks, but the work drops off after about a month.'

Unlike the SAS Resources Trust in Perth, which raises funds to support the families of dead and injured SAS soldiers, the SBS Association is more focused on entitlements and ensuring those entitlements are met.

'Just recently I've been heavily involved in a court case where one of our ladies, her husband died four years ago from an illness related to his service life, is fighting the Veterans Agency,' he says. 'We went to the tribunal and managed to sway the tribunal to actually pay her a widow's pension relating to her husband's death . . . [and] back-dated four years. We then provide her with advice and support.'

Willy is keen to examine how the SAS Resources Trust operates and to implement a system of family support at Poole.

'We have looked at that for the future and we have a fund-raising campaign going at the moment for the next 18 months and I hope to raise five million pounds,' he says.

At present the coffers hold about £600,000 and when it reaches two million it will generate income to run the association and to offer the support it wants to give to families.

Meanwhile the SBS, like all other special forces units around the globe, is competing with the private sector to keep its operators.

In Willy's day it was the oil rigs, but today it is the global security companies that offer the big money.

He says the training and the operational experience equips the marines in the SBS very well for life outside the military.

'For example, a corporal who is speaking at all levels within an embassy, or different government agencies at the highest level. You wouldn't see a corporal in a regular battalion even talking to a commanding officer,' he says. 'We've got our guys — and I'm sure it's the same in Australia — we've got these guys actually briefing generals and ministers about what is actually happening and they've got the confidence to do that.'

chapter thirty

THE BRIEF MAN

Noel Duigan loved brief missions.

The former SAS trooper was happiest when he could go on a job and be back home either the same day or a few days later. He would trade the long tours and lengthy patrols in East Timor and Afghanistan for short, sharp tasks any day.

Just after completing the Olympic Games counterterrorism operation in September 2000, he was taking a shower and getting ready to hit the town when he was summoned urgently by the boss. He ran to his office with a towel on, still dripping wet, and within two hours was on a plane heading to Christmas Island in the Indian Ocean.

The mission was to intercept an Indonesian people-smuggling vessel that intelligence had suggested would be carrying the 'Mr Bigs' of the people-trafficking syndicates.

The troop of SAS men were armed with linear-shaped metal charges to blow their way onto the vessel if necessary. In the event, they waited for four days but the boat never came, so they went home.

Another quick job occurred a few years later when, in March 2003, the North Korean drug-smuggling ship, *Pong Su*, was steaming off Sydney and refusing all requests to heave to. The SAS tactical assault group (TAG) was activated and Duigan and his colleagues flew in from Perth. Once again, shaped linear explosive charges were in their kit in case things turned ugly. He was part of the raiding party that rappelled onto the deck from a navy helicopter at the same time as another boarding party scaled over the rails from fast boats.

Not only was it one of his favoured 'quickie' missions, it was the day that he learned that not all of his SAS comrades were as willing as he had assumed they were, and nowhere near as gutsy as they made themselves out to be.

He was the first soldier inside the ship, dressed in black and with his carbine locked and loaded. He had no idea what they might find inside the doorway.

'So I went into the room and cleared my area and turned around looking back to the guy who was meant to be backing me up and he sort of poked his head in and had a look! I said, "You fucking little prick." You see people in a different light when it comes to the real situation.'

Firmly established in the busiest unit in the Australian army, Duigan had also deployed to both East Timor and Afghanistan and it was during the latter that he had learned the true value of special forces leadership.

One day his patrol was sitting in a disguised lying up position (LUP) when the cover was blown by a young Afghan goat herder.

'He was a very small kid and when our patrol commander, who was a SB [British Special Boat Service] guy on exchange, reported into headquarters they said, "Get out of there as soon as possible."'

'So we packed up and got going, and headed up the creek line and we could hear some gunshots which we assumed was going back into our LUP and then we just laid up in the creek. About 100 metres away a four-man enemy patrol walked past. We could have just taken them out then and there, and we didn't.

'Again about five minutes later, another four-man patrol, so that is eight of them in single file came past and I thought [not killing them] was pretty professional . . . I thought it was harder to do that, to not shoot them. It would have been easier to shoot them.'

Their job was to gain intelligence and remain undetected, not to engage the enemy unless they had no choice.

'I respected his [the Patrol commander's] decision, although he sort of made it harder because they took off up the hill and we had to follow them to get to the landing site to the helicopter.'

Duigan admits that part of him would have liked bragging rights to a gunfight, but he respected the commander's decision to remain undetected and not to engage the enemy.

'It could have been good, a little bit of gunfire, to test yourself and see how it was but I think more professionally, he did what he was asked to do. I know for a fact that other people engaged just to say, "I've been in a gunfight."'

Born in Hobart, the son of a teacher and a nurse, he has four sisters and a brother and he developed an interest in the military when he was about fourteen.

'My dad and I would sit and watch war movies and I thought that looked pretty interesting,' he says.

As well as teaching maths and religion at St Virgil's College, his father also ran the cadet corps at his school and was not surprised when young Noel announced after one particularly heroic American movie, 'I want to be a marine.'

His dad simply said, 'If you want to do something special, why don't you try and join the SAS?'

So at the age of 14 in sleepy Hobart that became his ambition.

'I didn't really enjoy school that much, I knew I never wanted to go to uni, that was a definite given,' he says. 'I'd sit there and my teacher would say, "Where's your homework?" And I'd say, "I haven't done it", and he'd say, "Right, I want to see your father up here tomorrow morning. What sort of sons are you raising?" It was pretty good.'

After serving with the army reserve while he was still at school, Duigan signed up for the infantry in 1993 and undertook recruit training at Kapooka near Wagga in southern New South Wales. He joined 1 Battalion in Townsville and undertook SAS selection in late 1996.

After his reinforcement training he was posted to B troop in 1 Squadron in mid-1997 just in time for the start of the regiment's busiest period since Vietnam.

His first overseas deployment was to Kuwait in 1998 and after a tour to East Timor in 1999 he moved across to 2 Squadron for the Olympic Games job and the Solomons soon afterwards.

With East Timor likely to remain a problem for Australia for some time, the SAS was sending as many of its soldiers as possible on Portuguese language courses, so he completed that before he joined the first deployment to Bagram air base in Afghanistan.

But then, after six action-packed years, he began contemplating his future. He had fallen in love and had always vowed that if he were ever to marry, he would not stay in the army.

'When I was in battalion and I'd see these guys down at the boozer, on Thursday nights and this big fat chick would turn up in a mini van with 14 children beeping on the horn,' he says. 'Her husband would come scurrying out, jump in the van and get berated by her and off they'd go. So I thought if I ever get married I'm never going to stay in the army, I just don't want to do it.'

The couple became engaged while he was in Afghanistan and he decided during that tour to stay true to his vow and leave the army. So when he returned he took six months' leave and began the discharge process before getting married.

He was dabbling in real estate and didn't really have a plan when he was offered a job in Abu Dhabi as a trainer with the United Arab Emirates Special Operations Command.

Unfortunately the marriage ended after 10 months and Duigan, who was 30 at the time, puts it down to immaturity on his part and the fact that his wife was just 23 years old with no friends her own age in a foreign city. The expatriate life can be difficult for partners, particularly if they have no children or contact with others their age. In the UAE it was either married couples with children or single blokes on the tear, so the outcome was inevitable.

'She was 23 years old with no friends, she had to hang out with all my mates' wives who were a lot older than her with different interests,' he says. 'She is a fantastic girl and if I could be with her now in the stage of life I'm in now, I'd be pretty happy, but the way I was back then, I just wasn't ready to settle down and commit. I just wanted to go out and at that time of my life, she was probably the right girl, but not the right time.'

He stayed on after she left, spending three years working for the SOC as an amphibious operations trainer. He observed and endured all the frustrations that come with working in a foreign culture.

He says many of the Australian trainers tried to import their personalities and their training concepts straight from Swanbourne to Abu Dhabi.

'It's like we are taking their army and trying to turn it into our army, but that's not what we should be doing, we should be taking their army and making their army how they want it,' he says. 'Everyone comes over with preconceived notions of how things were in Australia and that is how they are going to do it.'

It was this conflict of ideas and a disagreement about personal travel arrangements that led Duigan to leave the command.

He was cashed up and was planning a major housing project back in Australia on a 43-block subdivision he had bought in Tasmania. So he was in no rush to decide his future when Cupid intervened. He met a Lebanese lady in Dubai and his course was set.

He had long been interested in furniture design so he began pursuing the idea of manufacturing high-class furniture for the up-market hotel trade.

'I talked to her about it, she's got some friends who are decorators and interior designers and showed them my designs and they thought they were pretty good,' he says.

So off he went to China to talk to manufacturers and he linked up with three other designers, in Perth, Dubai and Beirut, to get the business under way.

'They are doing fabric designs for me and I'm at the stage now where I'm at the production stage so hopefully I'm going to launch this furniture in 2008.'

He plans to base the business in the Dubai free trade zone and export from there. 'I will tailor and market it to interior designers and all I need is one hotel and I'd be laughing,' he says.

In the meantime and to keep the till ticking over he took a job as a security consultant with London-based Control Risks Group (CRG).

Motoring down the freeway in his high-performance Audi, Duigan explains that his job has been to assess hotels in the region and to write security audits for the hotel management. This has also provided him with the opportunity to check out the interior design of 18 top Middle Eastern hotels, from Istanbul to the Sinai Desert.

He has taught himself about crisis plans, evacuation plans and business continuity plans. His work is evaluated further up the tree and during the next year he will complete a consultant's course and move into sub-contracting where the real money is and his time will be his own.

'At the moment trying to get things organised, on the weekends I fly to China to try to sort stuff out and it's a little bit hard to manage.'

His job does offer some interesting diversions. While he was in Karachi, Pakistan, evaluating a hotel, he was called on to assist the evacuation of two clients when trouble blew up. They were two Britons who worked for a large power company. Duigan took command of an armed escort, travelled to where they were operating, escorted them safely back to Karachi and on to a flight out to Dubai.

Having come from the financially sheltered world of the military, he admits to being a little shocked by the money-oriented ways of commercial security and the cost–revenue realities of the business world.

'In the military you are not trying to make money off these people,' he says.

There are 14 expatriates working in CRG's Dubai office and until recently he was the only Aussie, the lone digger among a gang of ex-British officers. 'It's a good company, it has footprints around the world so there is opportunity to move around.'

His other major observation of the commercial security sector, when compared to his own experience in the military, is the lack of training.

His first commercial security job was as an unarmed escort of the global president and vice-president of a large American energy company who were on a business tour through Algeria. Duigan had never been there before.

'After that this hotel job came up. They said, "We've got 18 hotels that need to be reviewed." I'd never reviewed a hotel in my life! The first one, I had to sit down with one of the regional managers and audit it . . . Talk about put the spotlight on you!'

After conducting the audit and realising that most hotels did not even have a crisis management plan, he felt much better about his knowledge base and soon picked up the essentials for that kind of job. Yet he also finds this aspect of the work quite boring and does not see himself doing it for long.

Unfortunately the relationship with the Lebanese girl ended in disappointment and he found himself single again. So for now, the 34-year-old is content to work as a consultant, pursue his furniture business and keep a weather eye out for the next Mrs Noel Duigan.

'I think it is starting to get to that point in my life when I'd like a few children.'

He managed to sell the land in Tasmania at the top of the market and for now he is financially secure.

He has not absolutely ruled out a return to the SAS, but as time goes on that is looking increasingly unlikely.

If he were to return home it would probably be to Melbourne, but right now he has no desire to live in Australia. 'I'd be quite happy to meet someone from a different country and travel. I've been in Australia for 34 years, I know what it's like. I might meet a nice little Italian girl and settle in Italy for a while. Brazilian would be my first choice.'

chapter thirty-one

THE KITE SURFER

Ian Young is happiest when he is riding a wave off one of Perth's beaches or is in his studio sculpting a piece of art.

The former SAS officer was a pioneer of the sport of kite surfing in Australia and the windswept Perth beaches are ideal for a sport that combines the power of the wind and the swell of the ocean.

A classic blond, blue-eyed and bronzed surfer, Young lives with his family in a well-to-do beachside suburb not far from SAS headquarters at Swanbourne.

He began his military career as a trainee technician in the Signals Corps and was a foundation member of Norforce in Darwin. It was there that he first encountered soldiers from the SAS and they had a profound impact on him. He underwent selection in 1983 and was posted to 2 Signals Squadron. In 1986 he moved across to the officer stream and transferred to the Royal Military College, Duntroon where he graduated as top cadet and winner of the Queen's Medal. A brief stint with 1 Signals Regiment followed before the newly married officer moved back to Perth and the regiment as a freshly minted lieutenant.

He had told the then commanding officer, Lieutenant Colonel Jim Wallace, that he was happy to undertake officer selection, but Wallace saw no need for that. He wanted Young to get to work immediately as a bereted signaller.

After a posting with 3 Brigade to Somalia in 1993 he returned to headquarters special operations command in Canberra before moving back to Perth as officer in command of the signals squadron. While in

Canberra, he made a brief visit to Rwanda to conduct some contingency planning for the evacuation of the Australian medical team working with the United Nations.

During his five months in Somalia he started to seriously contemplate life beyond the military. 'I was at a senior enough level to be getting insights into political processes, not just within the military, and there were some pretty political processes there, but also in terms of deployments and caps on numbers of people being deployed and all those other limitations that governments put on the military to do a job. Even the rationale of why we were there in the first place, so I started to question a lot of that sort of stuff.'

It was clear to him that the reason he and his colleagues were in Somalia had more to do with the so-called 'CNN effect' than any deeper policy considerations.

'You see the images of starving kids and the western world feels it has to do something about it,' he says. 'There were obviously a lot of non-government organisations trying to get food to those people who needed it and of course there was a civil war and that is why military intervention was required, but the first thing I found difficult to understand initially was why a lot of Somali people didn't really want us there. Not just the warlords; these were people on the streets, in Baidoa where the first battalion group went.'

As he went deeper into the countryside with US special forces and the more he examined the situation, the more concerned he became.

'We were there to break up the warring factions, to feed people who are starving, but then I learnt that a lot of Somali women have a whole lot of children,' he says. 'This has been a famine belt, a place that gets regular droughts for thousands of years, nothing has changed there. The culture was such that they had lots of kids and maybe only two of them survived to what they consider to be an old age, which is middle age to us. So you start questioning different cultures' value of life and why they make those decisions. I felt we are going to save one generation of kids, but what happens to the next generation? The land is not capable of feeding the next generation, especially if they have as many kids as the previous one.'

He very quickly reached the point where he asked himself, 'What right does western civilisation have to come and impose its values on people like the Somalis?'

'It is always the little people who get crushed in these conflicts and you feel for them,' he says, 'but I am of the philosophy, even with my own children, that you can't help people who aren't prepared to help themselves. You can give them opportunities, but you can't force them down a particular path and that is where I felt the western world was trying to force the Somali people in a direction they didn't necessarily agree with.'

He says the Australian government (led by then Prime Minister Bob Hawke) wanted to be a good international citizen, but with little forethought about what job actually had to be done.

'The Australian government had already set a ceiling on the number of troops to be deployed, without even knowing what the tasks were,' Young says. 'I thought that was just stupid. I wouldn't say I was disillusioned, but I was getting an insight into the political processes.'

In the background throughout all this soul-searching was the memory of his father who had served as an army officer, retired and died 10 years later.

'I thought, "I'm not going to spend 30 years in the military, I don't want to be a major general and I'm not going to be one", even though I was highly reported at the time and I had a good career path,' he says. 'I wasn't going to be coming back as commanding officer of the SAS [and] my heart was in special forces.'

After a stint at headquarters Special Operations in Canberra, he returned to SAS as officer in command of the signals squadron in 1996. He was in that job, as well as executive officer of the CT force, when the Black Hawk tragedy occurred and claimed three of his signallers.

His most vivid memory is of walking into the operations room and seeing the names of the men who had died.

'I lost three of my guys in the accident as well, from my signal squad, so I had to break the news to those three girlfriends and wives,' he says. 'It's the worst thing and you keep on replaying it in your mind and think, "Shit, I could have done so much better than that." Of course you can't; that's life, unfortunately.'

Like all SAS officers he was forced to watch on as several of his mates were hung out to dry by the top brass during the investigation.

'Bob Hunter is a very close friend of mine, as is Sean Bellis, and I was extremely disappointed with how they were treated,' he says. 'I know all the details that came out in the investigations and a lot of other stuff that wasn't disclosed, and that was extremely disappointing to me. To hear the Chief of Army on *Four Corners* say that lack of resources is never an excuse for unsafe practices, was just totally hypocritical. To use Hunter and Bellis as scapegoats to me is just sort of, "Jesus, they say mateship is an ethos of the service."'

One aspect of the saga that makes his blood boil is that many of the facts concerning the wider management failures of those at the top of the military chain were never disclosed, in the name of security.

'Because the investigation had security caveats on it, the classified documents, directives from the Chief of Defence and the Chief of Army that basically detailed the level of capability and the resources allocated against those capabilities, were never tabled. They pointed the finger straight at the CDF and straight at the army-chief and those two people were never accountable.

'I know, I've seen the classified documents and I know it had been brought to their attention for years, that the level of capability was suffering because resources were not being allocated. To see that it never gets disclosed and they hung guys like Bob and Sean out is to me just unforgivable.'

The Black Hawk saga had a major impact on Young's decision to resign his commission. Although he lasted in the army until 1998, his heart was never really in it after the Black Hawk inquisition.

chapter thirty-two

NOT HAPPY JACK

Jack Robertson graduated top of his class at the air force training academy at Point Cook in Victoria.

At the 1987 graduation parade he carried the same Sword of Honour that was won by his uncle, Donald Dare Robertson, in the first Point Cook graduating class of 1951.

Donald was killed in action while flying a fighter during the Korean War.

Jack Robertson bore his sword for the very last graduating parade at the RAAF academy before the three services amalgamated into the Australian Defence Force Academy (ADFA) in Canberra.

Robertson, whose SAS officer brother fought in Iraq and Afghanistan, is no left-wing pacifist, but at the height of the debate about the Iraq War he took a stand that would see the pro-war lobby virtually label him a coward and an appeaser.

He argued forcefully and logically against the war on journalist Margo Kingston's web diary and subsequently in her book, *Not Happy John*.

He says he knew exactly what would happen to him, but he went ahead anyway. Five years on and with the US and its coalition partners mired in Iraq, his strategic and moral arguments against the war have mostly been proven correct.

After obtaining a science degree in 1986, Robertson moved into fighter jet training, but was 'scrubbed' about halfway through the course. He left the RAAF in 1987 and transferred to the army to fly helicopters, joining 162 Reconnaissance Squadron in Townsville, followed by 161 Squadron in Sydney where he did the bulk of his flying aboard two-man Vietnam-era Bell Kiowa helicopters.

The late 1980s was a very quiet period for the Australian Defence Force and for the young officer it was an endless round of exercises, training and more exercises. This included some flying with the SAS during counterterrorist training on Bass Strait oil rigs and on their annual 'yippee shoot' to Woomera, where they shoot off all the surplus ordnance from the previous year.

'The thing about being with the army in those days is, it was a reasonably non-operational period,' he says. 'I mean, even when we deployed people to Namibia for some mine work, that was quite an exciting thing. And then the Cambodian election, there were some pilots who went to that and that was a big deal.'

In 1993 Captain Robertson was posted to his last job in the military when he was appointed Aide-de-Camp to Governor-General Bill Hayden. The ADC is obviously not a cutting-edge operational role, but is regarded as a big tick in the box for up and coming military leaders.

It was an opportunity to broaden his horizons outside the military. At Government House in Canberra he met a variety of interesting people, ranging from heads of state and politicians to artists and journalists, including the eclectic political reporter Margo Kingston, who would storm back into his life some years later.

'I got a real insight as to what was out there and I found it hard to contemplate towards the end of that year another 15, 20 or 25 years slowly floating towards the top of the military chain,' he says.

Despite the frustration of being an army officer without a conflict to test his skills on the battlefield, Robertson regards this period as a golden age of world sanity. It was to end in spectacular fashion for the Australian military in East Timor during 1999, but it was a time of mixed emotions and great frustration.

'I remember thinking precisely along the lines that [John] Howard used as a lever afterwards,' he says. '"The world's run by lefties, and they don't understand the military, they don't understand the conservative outlook."'

At the end of his stint at Government House, he could not find a valid reason to remain in uniform, so he quit the army. He has observed the ensuing operational frenzy with a tinge of envy. 'I think there's a lot of my cohort — guys in their early forties now, who would have been captains around the late 80s, early 90s, who do occasionally lie awake at night and think: "What if? What if I'd stuck it out?" Because we see our peers doing hard-core serious — you know, Boy's Own — stuff now,' he says.

After a brief stint of reserve service, he was out the gate once and for all by the end of 1995. The following year he moved to Bathurst in rural New South Wales with his then girlfriend to pursue his interest in writing.

'Partly because I'd been exposed a bit to a more cerebral, intellectual stuff through Bill Hayden and meeting journalists, artists, writers, politicians and thinkers, you think, "Fuck me, you know, there's a big life out there",' he says. 'You don't have to fly aeroplanes around to be adventurous. Ideas can be consuming and I guess I wanted to buy into that, but I wasn't sure how.'

Thus began a period of experimentation and de-institutionalising as Robertson tried to figure out how he could get his foot in the writing door. He had always planned to travel overseas, so after 12 months he set off with a pack on his back to see what the world had to offer.

After a stint in Europe he arrived in Java in 1998 and trekked up through the island to the capital, Jakarta. He was travelling alone and immersing himself in the cultures along the way.

'I spent quite a lot of time getting into Indonesia. I learned Indonesian which is pretty simple, and I ended up in Jakarta, and stayed with my old boss who was the defence attaché there.'

This was around the time that the regime of the dictator General Suharto was starting to unwind. At one point Robertson was beaten up by some angry locals and he recalls a lengthy argument with his host about the level of angst in the local community towards Australia and Australians. The army man assured Robertson that everything was fine.

This was also a time of great tension over Indonesian policy between the defence spies in the Defence Intelligence Organisation (DIO) and the Department of Foreign Affairs and Trade (DFAT) and its overseas spy agency, the Australian Secret Intelligence Service (ASIS). The diplomatic spies run a large station in Jakarta and the strain between the two shadowy organisations came to a head in Washington the following year.

DIO agent Mervyn Jenkins hanged himself at his home near Washington after he was disciplined for passing sensitive material about East Timor to the Central Intelligence Agency (CIA). The diplomats had Jenkins in their sights, but he beat them to it.

The top-secret material he passed on highlighted the divergence of opinions between military spooks and their civilian counterparts about what was actually going on in East Timor.

What Robertson experienced was the early rumblings of what was to follow when DFAT was accused of harbouring a pro-Jakarta lobby that attempted to cover up Indonesia's excesses in East Timor. This view held right through the 1999 crisis, when the Howard government tried to blame 'rogue elements' of the Indonesian military for violence that was orchestrated at the top levels of its military. He believed that his old boss was a bit too supportive of the 'steady as she goes' course with Indonesia and in particular the Suharto regime.

He travelled back to Europe to pursue his writing dream, but further travels reinforced his observation of the growing tensions between Muslims and the west. He saw well-educated Muslims working as tour guides for fat, rich westerners and was convinced of the inevitability of a culture clash.

'They might have a double degree in Engineering and European History, but they can make better money showing rich Americans around the souk,' he says. 'I was really aware of this; in fact, it was the central part of this bloody great masterpiece I was trying to write, that there was something brewing. And I felt it in Java, I felt it right throughout Turkey,

Morocco and Europe. It was unformed, I wouldn't have been able to sit down and say, "Look out, something's going to happen", but it didn't surprise me in the least when 9/11 came along.'

On that fateful September day in 2001, Robertson sat in front of his television set and cried and cried. 'I knew that there would be this aggressive outpouring of nationalism. Which isn't a problem in itself until it starts to fuck up operational and strategic decisions like it did in Iraq.'

What he failed to fully understand was the impact the reaction to his anti-war stance would have on him.

He returned home in 2002 and started writing on Kingston's web diary. Regardless of his more conservative political leanings he was labelled as one of the 'Not Happy John' brand of lefties. Despite, or perhaps because of, his military pedigree and the weight of logical argument in his anti-war position, he was exposed to the full fury of the pro-war right. Conservative columnists let fly with both barrels and his reasoned arguments about the strategic folly that was about to take place were overwhelmed with charges of cowardice and appeasement from the neo-cons' cheer squad.

History has proven him correct, but there is no way that any of the pro-war brigade would ever concede the point, so he remains a bitter man.

'I knew that Muslims would be radicalised and polarised in Australia,' he says. 'I knew we would make everything worse, because I'd seen enough of the way that good intentions badly applied can exacerbate this divide between the haves and have-nots in the world.'

The one-sided fight between a web diarist and the pro-war elements of the mainstream media turned nasty.

'Things just got to the point where it became like an undergraduate game. It seemed like a pantomime.'

Jack Robertson realised how serious his problem was over a beer with one war supporter who told him, 'Look, I know Margo's not that bad. She a bit rough round the edges, she's a bit of a nutter, but it's all good fun.'

'It might be good fun for him, but when these pantomime characters start driving policy, which is what happened over Iraq, it is no joke,' Robertson says. 'If you step back as a former military professional, and try to view what we've done in Iraq with "uncoloured" eyes, it is incomprehensibly a blunder. Is it recoverable? I don't know.'

He concedes that the coalition cannot simply walk away from Iraq but all the strategic options, particularly for the United States, are extremely unpalatable.

'We may well recover, and the future may be better in many ways but it certainly will go down as a terrible mistake, and I'm glad to have opposed it.'

When Kingston raised the idea of *Not Happy John*, he jumped at the chance. His contribution began as a single chapter, but ended as a major part of the structure of the piece.

'I hate the whole left/right division, the pantomime divisions and I was trying to say: "Look, it's not as simple as this." If you go back and look at what we were arguing, and read Margo's book, a lot of the propositions we were arguing are now forming the mainstream,' he says.

His brother, the former SAS officer, says that while he himself was fighting in Iraq he was not really aware of the vilification Jack was enduring back home in Australia.

He puts it very bluntly: 'My brother is an ex-Sword of Honour winner, an ex-serviceman, he served with distinction and worked with Bill Hayden as ADC. He was one of the reasons I joined the military; he was an example to me at the time and we have a close relationship. He is not an idiot and he knows what he is talking about. Now a [commentator] who has never put on a uniform implying that my brother, after 15 years' military service, is a coward, just makes me sick.'

THE HUMANITARIANS

chapter thirty-three

FROM LITTLE THINGS

'Why are people racist, Dad?'

The question from his 11-year-old son took SAS Major Grant by surprise.

How do you explain to a middle-class white boy from Perth, who has just spent six weeks with his best mate and his dad living as guests in a remote Aboriginal community, why people discriminate on the grounds of skin colour?

'It was a fantastic question from an 11-year-old,' Grant says with pride.

He had been staying in the coastal community out from Broome to conduct research for a PhD in coastal land management, after completing a postgraduate diploma in coastal management from the University of Western Australia.

While he undertook his field studies, the boys joined the young men of the community to hunt and gather and to provide food.

'They were spearing salmon and stingrays, collecting the food which was going to feed us each day. So the day was broken up with workshopping, hunting and gathering and then communal eating,' Grant says.

The boys worked hard and were invited back whenever they want.

It wasn't that his son was looking through rose-coloured glasses; he has seen troubled indigenous communities as well. But as they drove home to Perth, where racism runs close to the surface, he wanted an explanation.

Racism is not new to Grant and working in indigenous community development has exposed him to plenty of extreme views.

The most common refrain from white Australians is, 'This is just another taxpayer-funded project that is bound to fall over.'

'My answer to that is, "Hang on!" We've got true capacity to develop capabilities, succession planning, identify the up and coming blokes, how to get them involved and develop their leadership and management skills,' he says. 'Mentoring is a big part of it. I'm really confident, if we chip away at it for the next four years, we'll get it going.'

In a crowded room nobody would pick Grant as an SAS soldier. The slightly built, fair-haired and blue-eyed 46-year-old looks more like a teacher or an accountant, but he is the quintessential SAS officer.

The son of a glass designer/book binder and a piano teacher, he was born and bred in Adelaide where he completed his schooling at a state agricultural high school at suburban Unley. He went off to the Royal Military College, Duntroon in 1980 and after graduating in 1983 was sent to 1 Battalion in Townsville. After three years he became training officer with the Far North Queensland Regiment based in the Torres Strait.

That was his first real exposure to indigenous Australia and the beginning of an interest that would endure beyond his military career.

He completed officer selection for SAS in 1988 and in November that year joined the regiment as a water operations troop commander. That role included leading his troop on tough training missions in Bass Strait. They dived off Oberon Class submarines carrying heavy loads on long underwater swims to 'assault' offshore oil platforms.

'If you stopped swimming you'd sink, you would be carrying simulated chargers, sledgehammers and of course the climbing apparatus. If you went deeper than 12 metres you ran the risk of oxygen toxicity so you kept diving at 8 metres, but frequently you'd find yourself at 20 metres, just the weight of the stuff,' he says.

'That was very demanding work and of course we'd come back from the platforms and have a good time, as a troop. It was very bonding, [the] troop environment, we'd go on the piss together and have a good time.'

An SAS soldier during a training patrol in Western Australia.

JOHN FEDER NEWS LIMITED

Former commando and SAS major Ken Webb and his team undergoing some extreme cold weather training in the Australian Alps. Webb would become a paraplegic in an accident in London.

Ken Webb married Jeanne on 17 November, 2002 with her son Zac and his daughters Bronwen and Hilary in attendance.

This rare photograph from the early 1980s shows just how close the early SAS counterterrorist teams came to explosive charges as they developed new CT techniques.

SNIPER DEMONSTRATION

Trooper less than 2 meters away. Note MX 360 on belt and KT26 runners

Targets head is shot off

Snipers fire on command from 100m away

SAS counterterrorism operator Mick Sim stands among targets being blasted by sniper fire from 100 metres during a demonstration for visiting politicians. Realism was a vital but extremely hazardous part of the early CT training.

RAAF cadet of the year Jack Robertson carrying the Sword of Honour in 1987 that had previously been won by his uncle Donald Robertson at the Point Cook pilot academy in Victoria.

Ken Studley as Ken Ackers (right) on stage as the support act with Kevin "Bloody" Wilson.

SAS trooper Ken Studley oversees the transfer of *Tampa* refuges from the *HMAS Manoora* onto Nauru during the infamous 'Pacific Solution' in 2001.

Former SAS officer Ian Young following his passion for kite surfing off a Perth beach.

Noel Duigan, during a patrol in the mountains of Afghanistan. He has since swapped his SAS M4 carbine, beard and jungle greens for a new career as a security consultant and budding furniture designer.

Six years on and Australian SAS troops are still patrolling the rugged and dangerous mountains and valleys of Afghanistan.

South Australian Opposition leader Martin Hamilton-Smith in his SAS days.

ALP candidate and ex-SAS major and operations officer, Pete Tinley, with his almost boss, Prime Minister Kevin Rudd, during the 2007 election campaign. Tinley failed to wrest the seat of Stirling in Perth from the Liberal Party.

Former Navy clearance diver and SAS operator Paul Papalia (far right) with a navy colleague and British engineers inspect a cache of sea mines near Khwar Az Zubayr in Iraq after the 2003 invasion.

Ex-Navy clearance diver and SAS operator Paul Papalia (second from right) and colleagues in the UN chemical disposal group in front a pyre of deadly chemicals in Iraq in 1992. Papalia, who is now a state Labor MP in Western Australia, was confident that no weapons of mass destruction would be found during the 2003 invasion because he had helped to destroy a large amount during his tour with the United Nations.

Grant eventually became the commander of 1 Squadron, then the counterterrorist squadron. But after three years on active duty, it was time for the now married major to move into a desk job and try to tick some promotion boxes. He had married Bridget in 1990 and she had an early taste of SAS life when he was separated from her for several months soon after the wedding. They have two children.

The then Brigadier Jim Wallace, whom Grant regards as a political master, was running special forces command in Canberra and he needed some eyes and ears closer to Land Command in Sydney, where the reigning general apparently wasn't too keen on the SAS.

'My job really was to look for opportunities for special operations, whether operationally or training, to be an adviser to the various environmental commanders and make sure J.J. Wallace was across what the issues were of those operations,' he recalls. 'That was a great job because I got very good exposure to that joint operational environment and from there I went to Staff College, and that was a good year and my son was born as well.'

The next phase of his career would be very tough for Grant.

'I was told that I wasn't competitive for a promotion and I saw the peers around me getting promoted. I didn't take it too well, deep down, [though] I didn't show it, because up until then I believed I was on track,' he says.

Once he recovered from the setback, he realised there was a lot that could be achieved by officers at his level and it also meant he could get off the promotion treadmill and back to what he loved — the SAS.

A crusty old lieutenant colonel who had mentored him had once told him how much influence an officer could have from the middle ranks. Grant discovered he had been absolutely right. 'I really had influence. Now my mates are going on to major general, so you have that indirect influence, and if you've got the credibility with these people then they listen to you, so it was best, particularly because SAS was becoming operational again.'

The regiment was entering the busiest phase in its 40-year history and Grant would be right on the cusp of it.

The operational tempo began to heat up in 1998. He was initially appointed staff officer to the commander of Australia's 200-strong military commitment to the then latest US operation against Saddam Hussein. But the staff officer job fell through and Grant was at home at Williamtown near Newcastle in New South Wales pulling the clutch out of his car one evening when he got a call telling him to be in Sydney at 8 a.m. the next day.

'I got up at 4 a.m. next morning, shot down, didn't know where I was going . . . and found myself on a plane over to Kuwait and came back four months later,' he recalls.

He found himself posted as the military support officer with the Australian embassy in Saudi Arabia that was establishing a branch office in Kuwait City. There he met a colleague from DFAT and set about liaising with all the stakeholders, including the allied special operations group, the government of Kuwait and various foreign embassies under Operation Pollard.

That involved a Boeing 707 air tanker and an SAS contingent that was intended to act in a search and rescue capacity. But after several months, UN Secretary-General Kofi Annan defused the situation in Iraq and early in 1999, Grant returned to Perth as the SAS training officer under then commanding officer Lieutenant Colonel Tim McOwan.

Life, however, would be anything but humdrum. The situation in East Timor was deteriorating by the week and the training demands on the regiment grew rapidly, although the resources didn't. When the SAS deployed to East Timor later that year, the workload for officers left in Perth increased dramatically.

'If you didn't deploy you were doing two, three, four jobs just trying to keep it together,' he says. 'While you have a commitment overseas, you still have to maintain the capabilities and the ongoing reviews and what-not that the SAS still has to comply with.'

He eventually deployed to Timor as the officer in charge of the rapid response force, which became the reconnaissance force along the border with Indonesian West Timor. Its job was to patrol the border and to prevent incursions from Indonesian-backed militias still operating inside West Timor.

Returning to Perth, Grant became acting operations officer and regimental executive officer as SAS deployed forces to the 2000 Olympic Games and the Solomon Islands.

On 9 September 2001 he went to see his then boss, Lieutenant Colonel Gus Gilmore, who by then was SAS CO.

'I was just burnt out. I needed time out so I told him then that I was going to resign and the reasons why and he supported that,' he says. Two days later September 11 happened and he went back to Gilmore and said, 'I can't jump ship now, forget what I said, I'll hang on.'

He remained on duty until early 2003 when he took long service leave and enrolled in the postgraduate diploma in coastal management. That led him back to his beloved northern Australian coastline in Arnhem Land and eventually to his PhD.

When he was serving previously in the Far North Queensland Regiment, Grant had developed a strong affinity with the indigenous people and had become fascinated by their approach to managing the fragile landscape.

'I've always been concerned about environmental issues and social justice issues. Initially I wanted to get out and do more a marine science based study but then I soon realised if I was to go down that path, chances for a job afterwards are pretty poor,' he says. 'As a pure scientist you don't have the opportunity to influence policy and project management as you do from a management perspective.'

He completed his diploma and travelled to Maningrida in Arnhem Land to examine a project run by the Bawinanga Aboriginal Corporation that employs indigenous rangers in land management projects.

'One of the projects they do has a commercial base as well, where they collect crocodile eggs and incubate them, collect the hatchlings and sell them to the crocodile farms at two weeks old so they haven't got all the overheads,' he says. 'They collect the eggs using traditional methods and they make an income out of it, so I went up there, read up on all the risks associated with indigenous management and looked at NT government policy which is very good in regard to sustainable industries.'

He stayed with the rangers at Maningrida for a week and developed a management model that formed the basis of his PhD scholarship submission.

Many of the management issues he had dealt with during his time with the Far North Queensland Regiment had commonality with his research.

'If you compare my thesis that I put together for the research project there is a lot of application of what I learnt as a platoon commander in FNQR and as an officer in SAS,' he says.

Having won the scholarship he sat down with his supervisor to find a suitable project.

Grant was keen to get into the Kimberley region to try and create a management model and build a sustainable industry. He travelled to Broome in northern Western Australia to examine a number of coastal communities. By good fortune his wife was working as a teacher at Trinity College in Perth where the Aboriginal liaison officer approached her. The school operates a scholarship program for about 30 indigenous boys from the Kimberley and a traditional owner runs the program from the Bardi people on the Dampier Peninsula, a renowned pearling area.

'He was very interested to hear what I was doing because he eventually wants to go back to his country and establish an opportunity for his people, his family group. This family has custodial claim over about 15 kilometres of coastline just south of One Arm Point.'

The property is about six hours' drive north from Broome on the isolated and beautiful Cape Leveque.

'I didn't know where to start and we decided to give it a go,' says Grant. 'So first opportunity he took me up to his country and introduced me to people in his community, then we went out to his country and there is nothing there. It first established itself as a family outstation back in the early 1990s and like all government policies with regard to Aboriginal people, they are set up for failure, they really are. They create these opportunities through funding and say, "Okay, we want you to go live on your family country with money to do it."

'So these people went out, won some funding to build pretty rudimentary accommodation to live there — nothing else, just to live there. There was no program to actually develop any enterprise, any community building, any conservation program, nothing, just go live on your land and be happy. They stuck it out for five, six years but no servicing levy, no education for kids. These people have numeracy and literacy and they are concerned about getting an education for their kids, so the outstation collapsed.'

He found some of the classic problems confronting many remote indigenous communities that white governments try, with good intentions, to rebuild.

'You've got distant family groups coming together with all their baggage trying to establish an enterprise or a program for a finite period of time. So the government funding is there for three years. If nothing happens after that it falls over, if key personalities leave after three years it falls over,' he says.

Grant realised that to succeed, projects had to be more in tune with the cultural custodial link that a family has with its land.

Kakadu plum or wild green plum is known as *gubinge* in the Kimberley region and it has the world's highest fruit concentration of vitamin C; 500 times more than an orange. They calculated that a small, irrigated plantation of about 200 gubinge trees could generate an income in excess of $150,000 a year.

'On top of that there is opportunity for niche, low-overhead, low-effort enterprises, such as niche tourism, not mass-market tourism, but tourism targeting schools for youth development organisations, bringing these people to the country to live for a week with Aboriginal people who are caring for their country and participating in the work they do,' he says.

There would be opportunities for businesses, particularly the resources sector that has generated wealth from the region, to do some mentorship and take up development opportunities with Aboriginal people.

'There is also an opportunity for native seed collection . . . low overhead, simple operation, collect the seed and give it to distributors that are already established.'

On a more complex scale there is aquaculture and a host of other niche endeavours.

'The important thing is [that] this gives the opportunity for family members to participate in the corporation. Some will choose to become heavily involved, some will choose to become involved in community management and others might choose to get involved in land and sea care management.'

Grant's PhD thesis is based on the model for this traditional indigenous community enterprise, which he hopes will lead to better educational opportunities for young members of the community.

'One of the key things that's come out of it is the methodology. How do you sit down with an Aboriginal family group and develop their plan so there is thorough ownership of it? How do you facilitate what they want from the heart and head, how do you articulate that vision and then how do you put it into a plan that wins government and industry support for funding?'

In his view it is all about ownership and breaking down the barriers that prompted his young son to ask, 'Why are people racist?'

His experience in SAS is a source of great ideas and inspiration.

'Nothing gets achieved in SAS without ownership by the regiment. By ownership I mean not just the executive level; capability development is a mixture of input from the troops, the squadrons, the executive management of the organisation. Nothing happens in SAS that sustains capability without input from all facets of the organisation,' he says.

'To me it's a bit of a no-brainer. If you can identify leadership in a community, if you can work with that leadership and, let's face it, some of the communities don't have that leadership, but if you can work with that leadership to articulate a vision, and drive a project at a localised level that leaves people with their country, then it's got to have more chances of success than a government coming in and imposing a paternal solution onto a community without their input.'

His thesis was submitted in early 2008 and he plans to push tertiary institutions for monitoring projects and industry for funding. 'I would really love to get into an environment where I've got the charter and the funding to manage a series of projects based on developing capacity around natural resourcing.'

Money has never been a major personal driver for him, but the plight of indigenous Australians has.

'It's always stuck in my throat in this country, particularly at the moment with incredible surpluses at state and federal level and incredible opportunities, that we still have a section of our community that are living Third World,' he says. 'Look at the pastoral industry in northern Australia, it is an incredible demand on Australia. Part of my thesis talks about what the Kimberley pastoral industry takes from government in terms of subsidy and what it actually contributes to our economy — and it is actually a loss. We are funding a lifestyle. Now that is a bit harsh; the northern Australian pastoral industry does contribute in some way to our Australian character and to a degree our GDP, but it is a net loss. Incredible amounts of subsidies are going into it and an incredible amount of that subsidy is going into a pastoral industry that is getting bought out by millionaires.'

Grant says that fundamental to the future development of indigenous Australians is providing them with a choice to exercise their custodial claim to family land and care for resources on their country.

He says it is no longer valid for governments to simply influence how these communities live with the stroke of a pen over numbers pulled from nowhere.

'One government policy says priority will go to communities that are 200 people and larger. Now where the hell do they get the figure of

200 people? Why can't it be 25 people, why can't it be five people, as long as they are achieving some choice of living and contributing to the management of our natural resources? [It] may be as simple as managing the population of turtles that transition their land.'

Once again he put his studies on the back burner and returned to the regiment, Grant agreed to return to the SAS for one more year in 2008 as executive officer, as the unit struggled with a high operational tempo and lack of numbers.

He hopes to have his doctorate by the end of 2008 and plans to get into indigenous community development work when he leaves the SAS for good in 2009.

chapter thirty-four

THE NURSE

Jerry Hilder hit the skids when he was confined to a dark hospital room for weeks on end waiting for a kidney transplant.

The former SAS sergeant had endured a lot of discomfort during his army and special forces careers, but nothing like the agony of uncertainty and isolation of a long hospital stay in a dark and lonely room, fighting for a second chance at life.

As he waited for someone to die so that he could live, he had plenty of time for reflection.

A Sydney boy, he was born in December 1955 to middle-class parents and lived at Willoughby on the north shore. The eldest of three, he was educated at Crows Nest Boys High where the intricacies of schoolwork tended to pass him by. He dreamed of being a soldier. His dad had served as an anti-aircraft gunner in the Middle East and then as an infantryman in New Guinea during World War II. 'I read a lot about the war and listened to my dad and his mates talking,' he says.

Leaving school at 18, he joined a hardware store as a shop assistant and at weekends he served in the transport wing of the army reserve. Finally in April 1975, at the age of 19, he joined the army and undertook recruit training at Kapooka camp near Wagga. After infantry training at Singleton he was posted to the 2nd 4th Battalion in Townsville as a rifleman in A Company.

'I didn't enjoy it that much; I didn't like the spit and polish,' he says. 'To me it was almost like walking 20 kilometres and digging a hole, then sitting in the hole for a couple of weeks, then filling in the hole and walking back again. It was repetitious, it was very regimented and I found that difficult. I found the structure difficult between diggers and officers and sergeants. It was very segregated, they didn't seem to work well as a team. So I bit the bullet and applied for the SAS cadre course in April '76.'

The SAS philosophy was like a breath of fresh air for the young digger. He even enjoyed the selection course.

'The instructors were professional. There wasn't a lot of yelling and screaming, they just talked. You don't have to yell and scream to get your message across,' he says. 'They were professional, they knew what they were showing you, it was a good place to be and everyone was committed to the same thing. I think the cadre bonds people together and in the unit it seems a much stronger bond. You meet people that you haven't seen for years and it's like you just stepped out for a coffee and walked back into the room.'

Hilder sometimes wonders if men who join the SAS might not be a bit weird. 'It is just total commitment, I met guys in the battalion that would be really good in the regiment but they didn't want to do it, they just wanted to go home every night, I don't think it makes you better than anybody, it is a different commitment, a different life.'

He served in the early SAS Gauntlet teams, which pioneered the counterterrorism tactics that formed the standard for counterterrorism operations today. He escaped the mental and physical scarring that damaged many others during that extreme training, although he admits to having been a very angry man during this period.

It was his own health that eventually drove him out of the regiment he loved so much.

He was a patrol sergeant, which to many diggers is the best job you can have in SAS, but his kidneys began to let him down and eventually he could not go on. Tests revealed a degenerative, genetic renal disorder and his reaction to the news was even deeper anger.

He says he took his predicament out on his then wife and on his soldiers and he now deeply regrets this period of his life.

'The stress was mounting, I went off [CT] team and went to 2 Squadron and it wasn't as intense and I think the kidneys seemed to be stabilising so the mood improved, although I'd have occasional flare-up,' he remembers.

Like many tough men he didn't discuss his health problems with his first wife. 'My partnership was with the military and if my wife came along that was good, if she didn't, too bad, and when my kidneys were failing I just couldn't deal with it and the easiest thing to shed was my marriage,' he says. 'I treated her abominably and I can't make that up to her. [It is] sad.'

They separated in 1985, the same year he had to tell the unit about his kidney disease. Fortunately they had no children.

'She has moved on and I've not met her since then, but I've heard she is doing really well and that's good. I can't take back what I did to her,' he says. 'In the unit there are a couple of guys who I [also] treated quite badly, just with total frustration and ignorance and I can't take that back. I don't know if they hold it against me or not, but it makes me feel bad. It's easy to use an excuse that my kidneys were failing but I should get over that.'

The regiment offered him a number of jobs, but he felt he had to flee so he left the army.

'I went right away from the unit and went to Sydney and lived there for a couple of years and I just had nothing to do with the military at all. I think that helped me adapt a little bit better.'

He then moved to Auckland in New Zealand. He began work as a crewman on a rescue helicopter, but discovered that he was unable to qualify as a paramedic due to his kidney condition.

During this time he met his second wife, Cathy, who was a paramedic on the same crew. She suggested that he should try his hand at nursing instead. So he did, and he managed to complete his first year at Auckland Institute of Technology while receiving peritoneal dialysis.

'You have a tube in your stomach and you basically run a bag of fluid, like salty water with a bit of sugar into your stomach, and that goes between the peritoneum and the stent so that draws out the toxins and then four hours later you drain that out and put another bag in,' he says. 'So it means you are always walking around with 2 litres of fluid in your stomach, which doesn't help. [It's] almost like walking around with the flu all the time, you never feel 100 per cent. But the school was very good, I used to change the bag at school twice a day then once in the evening.'

His first transplant opportunity came in June of his second year at college, but unfortunately it failed after just three days.

During this setback and the dark period that followed, he found his SAS training kicking in. He was admitted to a small, dark and windowless hospital room.

'I didn't feel like eating or drinking. I was basically waiting to die because they couldn't dialyse me for quite a few reasons. There were curtains that opened up to another room that overlooked Auckland harbour. People would pull the curtains open and I'd get the sunlight, [but] the lady who was in there was quite ill, so they'd pull the curtain and I'd go back in the darkness.

He had some of the blackest days of his life in there and a lot of time to think.

'A lot of the stuff I'd done in the unit helped me cope, not in a macho way, just being in the dark, being alone,' he says. 'My wife would come, she would visit me before she started her shift at seven and come and visit when she knocked off at seven and fall asleep on the bed at night time, she was absolutely totalled. The nurses were fantastic but they had other patients to look after, so during the day I'd get through and at one stage I was so weak I couldn't shave myself and she would come in and shave me, wash me in bed.'

He constantly longed to be able to go to the gym and when he started dialysing again, that was where he headed. He lay down under the bench and put his hands on the bar and thought to himself, 'I'll do a couple of warm-ups.'

He could not even lift it out of the rack. The bar weighed 25 kilograms, which would never previously have been difficult.

He thought to himself, 'Well, what is the point? You can't even lift the bar, you might as well go away somewhere quiet and go to sleep.'

Again his SAS training kicked in. 'I can't lift a bar but I could do a push-up.'

So he started from there and worked his way back up to lifting the bar.

'It gives you — maybe it is stubbornness or determination, maybe it is good for you, maybe bad, but you get that from the [SAS] unit.'

He went back on dialysis and in January 1996 he had a second transplant. 'And that worked and it's still working now, so at the end of the third year I graduated and went to work in coronary care in Auckland. It's the best place I've ever worked [as a nurse], the best nursing manager I've ever had. I learnt more about myself in that unit, apart from when I was in the army, at any time. They are totally committed to their patients, true professionals, a great place to work. I did 18 months there.'

The nursing course, which he completed in 1997, taught him to deal with disappointments, but his illness showed him what it was like on the other side of the ward door.

'You can't always achieve 100 per cent in health, so let's help someone achieve the level of health they can achieve and then push them a little bit further,' he says.

By the time Hilder was in his third year of nursing training, he and Cathy were living together in Auckland and wanted to have a baby. Because his kidney condition was hereditary he had had a vasectomy the year before. So they used donor sperm to conceive their son, David, who was born in January 1997 just a month after Hilder had started work as a registered nurse.

'It is funny, because the doctor was talking to us about [artificial insemination] almost being like a transplant, "You are accepting it as a donation", and we started laughing and he got a bit upset so we explained about the kidney and he was totally on board,' he says. 'Biologically I am not David's father, but in every other way I am. It's funny because people say, "He looks a lot like you."

'Most of the time I don't even think that biologically he's not mine. We talk to him about it, but I don't think he has a true realisation of what it means yet. They advise us to discuss it every now and again and then eventually he will come to realise exactly what it means and he may or may not want to chase up his biological father. He could do that if he wanted to, I'd support that.'

After about 18 months in Auckland working as a nurse, Hilder was missing Perth and his old mates so the family decided to move back to the west where he took a job in the coronary care unit at Perth's Sir Charles Gardiner hospital.

'I've always missed the place, I've tried to explain it to my wife, I can't explain it to myself, it is not just because the unit is here, I don't even go out there a lot,' he says. 'I guess in the back of my mind there is always the thing [that] I never served overseas and these guys have, but they have said if you weren't there we wouldn't be here and that's true. I wish I was where they are. If it hadn't been for the kidneys I'd probably still be in the army. I miss it a lot.'

But Hilder doesn't harbour any deep regrets and he is grateful for his second chance and his family.

'I wouldn't have a career in nursing which I really enjoy,' he says. 'A lot of the guys think it's just changing bed pans and a lot of it is, but my thing is this: the fifth time I clean up a patient with diarrhoea, if you can stop them from being embarrassed about it, if you can make them feel comfortable that this is part of their illness and we will work through it as a team, then who cares, all the shit you are cleaning up has nothing to do with it.'

He finds himself regularly falling back on his SAS training. It is all about the team and knowing when to yield to those who know more than you do.

'I never go in and say I'm your nurse, I say, "My name is Jerry and I'm the nurse that will be working with you today", because I work with them, I don't tell them what to do,' he says. 'I'm not the sort of nurse that says to a doctor, "You need to do this", because I have to respect the doctor and all his training, it is like dealing with an officer. There must be officers out there who would gladly wring my neck because I gave them a hard time, but I learnt that without them there is no team, because officers learn the big picture.'

He is able to use this realisation to understand some of his own limitations as a soldier.

'I was a digger and I never really got the big picture and I have trouble sometimes thinking laterally. My troop sergeants will tell you I was absolute torture because I could see this thing I needed to get done and I wouldn't veer out of the way and they were trying to get me to think outside the box.'

Hilder credits his mum, who suffered a lifetime of kidney trouble and dialysis, for his fighting spirit.

'She never had a transplant, she dialysed, and during one summer the medication and stuff, she got a clot and died, but she was always a fighter,' he says.

He also puts his 'never say die' approach down to the regiment. That willingness to cross the next hurdle or the next mountain goes right back to SAS selection and it has stood him in good stead as he fought his disease.

He now competes regularly at the transplant games, fighting a constant battle between the two sides of his training: the SAS soldiering and the nursing.

'I don't go there to win the races,' he says. 'It's not important to me that I win, its important I finish, and strictly speaking "regiment-wise" I should be trying to win and I do try to win, but if I finish every race, that is the nursing part.'

All the time he reflects that without a lady who died and without her family agreeing to transplant her organs, he would probably be dead by now.

'I think it makes me a better nurse. It certainly would have made me a better soldier. It gives me a better understanding of what the guys are going through,' he says.

In both careers he has learned that you can't always achieve 100 per cent of your goals. In the regiment it was about pushing hard to the next level and in nursing it is about helping people achieve the best they can.

Nursing and his illness have combined to mellow Jerry Hilder. The tough, no-nonsense patrol sergeant has become a much more compassionate and tolerant human being.

'It wasn't until I did nursing and my kidneys failed that I understood that we don't need to walk on people to achieve our goals,' he says. 'Our goals are not everyone else's goals, so let's consider their goals as well.

'You live in that [hospital] room for however long I was in there. Then they moved me to the room that overlooked the harbour. I could see the sun come up in the morning and the sunset in the afternoon and that meant more to me than anything else.'

chapter thirty-five

THE STRATEGIST

For the first time in 24 hours Rob Jamieson allowed himself just the hint of a smile. He could hear the beat of a rescue helicopter and after one of the worst days of his life salvation was at hand.

Then suddenly the desert sand around his Land Rover began to dance. Incoming 7.62mm rounds were blasting his position and as he ducked for cover Jamieson was nicked in the neck by shrapnel, the second time he had been struck that day.

But this was no enemy fire. The British helicopter crew, thinking the men were the enemy, had started strafing them in a classic 'blue on blue' friendly fire incident.

After a quick signal from the ground they stopped firing. But it was an inauspicious end to a bad day.

Jamieson (not his real name), an Australian SAS officer, was working on exchange with the British Royal Marines Special Boat Service (SBS) when hostilities began.

In March, 2003 he was in the Al-Jazeera desert in western Iraq as operations officer in a squadron of about 60 marines.

The ill-fated action began not far from the Iraq–Syria border when a mobile Fedayeen force supported by Syrian elements hit the Land Rover mounted SBS column.

In the Arab context these were hard-core fighters. Australian SAS patrols were confronted by similar forces further south when they invaded Iraq from Jordan but, unlike the Aussies, the SBS squadron had access to limited intelligence.

They were conducting 'hearts and minds' tasks, which meant exposing themselves to the locals and were a long way from their comfort zone, the sea.

'Due to a lack of knowledge about exactly what was going on in the desert we found ourselves operating quite overtly because we needed to interact, but also in a fairly high threat area,' he recalls.

During the ambush the British force lost eight vehicles after they became bogged in the sand and a number of US-made Stinger man-portable surface-to-air missiles also fell into enemy hands. After fierce fighting, in which Jamieson sustained a minor head wound when his car was hit, the British troops blew up their own vehicles to render them inoperable. They were later paraded on Arab TV, a small victory for Saddam in an otherwise one-sided war.

Most of the SBS men were airlifted out after some heroic deeds by coalition helicopter and fixed-wing aircrew operating at the limits of their endurance, but two had become separated and made their way to Syria on a quad bike and on foot.

'I would have to say that getting forced to extract out of an AO [area of operations] is not something I would ever want to do again,' he says. 'That still carries a very bitter taste in my mouth, particularly how things went down and also subsequent events. But I guess you can't actually succeed without failing once in a while.'

Jamieson, who was decorated for his role in the force's successful fighting withdrawal and for earlier service in Afghanistan, had been concerned from the start about the SBS mission under the British invasion plan, Operation Telec.

It coincided with a move in the British special forces hierarchy to provide the boat service with a more general capability, so it could operate across the conflict spectrum from the sea to the desert.

'As a result we had to create capability that was very elaborate on a very short time line. People will always be critical about way we did it and what we were doing,' he says. 'The bottom line is, the nature of special forces means you are generalists and your role is about pushing the boundaries and operating beyond conventional forces. That means sometimes doing things that aren't as well practised as you would like.'

He says it was a true unconventional special forces mission and it was right that it was attempted. 'The guys raised a sound capability within the limitations.'

The squadron was later posted to Basra and the commander removed. Jamieson was appointed officer in command and set about rebuilding the shattered force and getting it back to work. He moved the headquarters to Basra airport and began intelligence-gathering and reactionary tasks in keeping with the SBS motto, 'By Strength and Guile'.

'We were attached to the armoured group down there who were basically conducting the invasion of Basra,' he says.

'We conducted advance force operations for them, multiple tasks with a lot more counterterrorism type work in and around Basra. It was very demanding and as you can imagine we were not at our happiest after the incident in the north, so it was great to regroup and get back into operations.'

The desert debacle shook the boat service to its foundations and left it open to accusations of incompetence and even cowardice from its special forces cousins.

British special forces have long been riven by deep divisions and some members of 22 SAS Regiment, based at Hereford in England, would use the incident to fuel a long-held contempt for the 'shaky boats'.

After its own deep embarrassment over the infamous Bravo Two Zero incident in the Iraqi desert during the 1991 Gulf War, the SAS did not pull any punches.

'They cocked it up, panicked and did a runner,' one unnamed SAS man told London's *Daily Telegraph* newspaper. 'They are like fish out of water on land, if you'll excuse the pun.'

Once they arrived back in the UK, Jamieson and the commanding officer had to defend the squadron against some nasty attacks from Hereford.

However, later briefings with the American Delta operators and the Australian SAS, who were also operating in the desert, were less abusive and far more productive.

During the debriefing process it was revealed that two days after the boat service debacle a Delta patrol, which was due to rendezvous with the SBS squadron, had engaged the same Fedayeen force and had lost a couple of its own operators despite having air support from Apache attack helicopters.

Rob Jamieson came to the SAS regiment via an unusual career path: an air force jet fighter pilot.

After finishing school in country Victoria, he joined the RAAF as an officer cadet at Point Cook near Melbourne before transferring to fast jet training at Pearce in Western Australia. His first posting was to Tindal in the Northern Territory where he flew the infamous Australian-built Nomad aircraft, which had a history of falling out of the sky.

'I narrowly survived that experience with a structural failure on my last Nomad flight as a young officer,' he says.

His next job was at Williamtown RAAF base near Newcastle in New South Wales where he was posted to forward air control, flying Winjeels and PC-9s. The forward air controllers are the flyers who loiter in vulnerable positions over a target to guide in fast jets, ensuring they do not fire on friendly forces. With the advent of better surface-to-air missiles and communications they have been largely replaced by ground-based operators, often attached to special forces patrols, who guide in the air power.

In 1995 he joined a Hornet fighter squadron and flew fast jets until 1998 when he decided to give the SAS selection course a go.

He believes that the jet aircraft world did not come naturally to him and he had to put in a lot of effort to build his flying skills.

'I had to work very hard,' he says. 'A natural is someone whose motivation, basic skills and awareness gives them enough ability to take care of the nuts and bolts of flying and therefore have more brain space to deal with the fighting. I was not one of those.'

A keen rock and mountain climber and martial arts exponent, Jamieson believed that he had some of the attributes required to be an SAS officer. He had been up close with SAS patrols during his time at Tindal and at 28 years old it was a case of now or never. Of the 21 officers on his selection course just three made it through, including him.

'My preparation was rigorous. I was too stupid to know how hard it was going to be,' he says. 'The psychological side to me was not a consideration because I was never going to quit. It was just a matter of pushing on and I was incredibly lucky that I didn't get injured. My feet were numb for months after the course.'

He acknowledges that ego plays a big role in special forces work. 'We like to think we are the humblest blokes around but the fact of the matter is to even strive for that service there is an element of ego within it. It is when the ego gets carried away and we start to believe our own myths that things become damaging. I think there is always a danger of that in any elite unit, whether it is fighter pilots or whether it's SF. Particularly if those myths are heavily cloaked for operational security reasons and hence it is very easy to create a perpetual motion of reputation in lieu of anything else.'

By the same token, many Australian special forces soldiers, either SAS or Commandos, are pretty humble, down-to-earth blokes.

When he was thinking about joining the SAS, an experienced SAS officer had said, 'It's a shit job mate, why do you want to do it?'

'He was exactly right, it is a shit job and you have got to want to do it in your heart and soul, not for any other reason.'

Jamieson could not explain why he wanted to do it and the officer gave him the best advice he ever received, 'You have got to have a fire in your belly.'

'I couldn't tell him why I wanted to do selection and that was the reason he supported me, just because it was a want.'

Having survived selection and the intense reinforcement training, he joined 2 Squadron in the work-up for the 2000 Sydney Olympic Games.

This was followed in 2001 by a transfer to 1 Squadron and the *Tampa* refugee ship operation.

Like many of the men involved in the *Tampa* mission in August 2001, where the SAS counterterrorism squadron boarded the Norwegian container ship MV *Tampa* off Christmas Island to prevent her from landing any of the 438 refugees rescued in international waters, Jamieson regards the use of the SAS as inappropriate.

Once the counterterrorist squadron had secured the vessel unopposed it became a humanitarian mission. The troops did more cooking and social work than soldiering on the *Tampa* and the later voyage to Nauru on the navy ship HMAS *Manoora*.

'I saw it as a gross misuse of the national counterterrorist asset, albeit for political reasons,' he says. 'I thought the guy in charge, the skipper [Captain Arne Rinnan] was subject to some unfortunate actions from the Australian government. For a man who had just saved the lives of 400 people he was caught up in a situation that he really didn't need to be in. It was fairly transparent that the whole activity was an obvious political gesture at the time.'

Several other SAS officers involved in *Tampa* have spoken privately about their disgust at being used as political soldiers.

'The military is a political tool, but it is a national political tool not an individual's political tool,' one ex-officer said. 'When it becomes an individual's political tool, particularly a partisan political tool, then you have got real problems.'

Jamieson relieved the initial force commander on board *Manoora* off the coast of north-west Australia in early September 2001.

By the time he boarded the vessel it had a human cargo of close to 1000 souls after embarking several more groups of refugees from other rickety people-smuggling boats. It was bound for the tiny island of Nauru and the 'Pacific Solution'. The coalition government had paid cash-strapped Nauru and Papua New Guinea, and negotiated with several other struggling Pacific states, to hold the boat people for processing rather than have them land on Australian soil where they would have legal rights. It proceeded to excise all offshore Australian territory to further discourage any refugees from attempting the hazardous voyage from Indonesia to the mainland or nearby reefs or islands.

Mainly Iraqis and Afghanis, the human cargo was kept entirely separate from each other on different decks of the *Manoora*. They were also kept completely in the dark in terms of news, so when the September 11 attacks on the United States occurred, there was a complete news blackout on the ship.

As he discussed politics and history with the Afghanis or tried to placate the increasingly irrational Iraqis, Jamieson could not have imagined that he would soon be in these peoples' home countries — first in Afghanistan, then Iraq — fighting the forces that had driven them to risk everything to seek a new life in Australia.

Yet instead of the free country they had dreamed of, the asylum-seekers were on a navy ship bound for a tiny, poor Pacific island created by bird droppings, being treated as potential threats to Australia.

'The Afghanis were great,' he recalls. 'Great people clearly escaping a very difficult regime under the Taliban at that time and doing well to look after their children and find themselves a way ahead.'

The Iraqis on the other hand were more middle class and manipulative. 'They were much more difficult to deal with and generally the ones that weren't going to leave the *Manoora* because they saw it as a vehicle to get to Australia. They were being very selective about where they went, which doesn't really indicate necessarily solid reasons for being refugees.'

When Jamieson sat down and spoke with the boat people he found the Afghanis usually had a sad tale to tell about a stolen farm or lost brothers who had been press-ganged into service by the Taliban and subsequently killed, or simply murdered in cold blood.

'When you spoke to the Iraqis the best reason they could give was a general, "Saddam is a horrible man." That was also an indicator that perhaps they were more economic refugees at that point. There was just a clear difference to me.'

What the experience also showed him was that he and his fellow Australians had little understanding of refugee issues and tended to generalise far too much about asylum-seekers.

'What the *Tampa* taught me was that refugees are individuals. Every single one has an individual case,' he says. 'They must be treated swiftly, processed swiftly for the sake of their own humane development, and either returned or offered refugee status and that process needs to be fast. We can afford to do it in Australia.'

It also provided him with a salutary lesson about the political manipulation of military forces in a democratic country. 'Most of us [SAS] like to have a pretty good idea of what we are doing for the national interest. When you see clear and obvious, if not deception then certainly manipulation, then you tend to lose faith very quickly.'

John Howard's government had spent hundreds of millions of dollars on new equipment for the SAS, had used them more than any government for decades and the *Tampa* was the payback with interest. In the military, as in politics and business, there is no such thing as a free lunch.

Jamieson was at the cutting edge of the renaissance of the SAS. Between Timor in 1999 and Afghanistan in late 2001, the men of the regiment saw more operational service than many previous SAS soldiers had in entire careers and it was about to get a whole lot busier.

As well as the Sydney Olympics, he had two tours to the Solomon Islands in 2000 so was becoming accustomed to the operational lifestyle. He commanded one of the task forces to the Solomons and there he learned a valuable lesson.

'We body-armoured up and went ashore,' he recalls. 'One of my blokes was a particularly big guy and as he jumped off the RHIB [rigid hull inflatable boat] there was a bunch of expats sitting around having a beer!'

It suddenly seemed that the troops' aggressive posture was way over the top.

'Subsequently I slapped myself around the head,' Jamieson says. Even so, he knew that it was better to look like a goose than to have someone shot because of underestimating the risk.

The military philosophy of overwhelming force and maximum protection was on show again in the Solomons during June 2003 when Australia landed a very large, well-armed force to deal with insurgents armed mostly with home-made guns and spears.

Immediately after *Tampa*, Jamieson went back to 1 Squadron SAS as mobility troop commander preparing men and vehicles for a possible deployment to Afghanistan. By October it was clear that the mission was on and after a frantic few weeks in Perth and at the Middle East staging post in Kuwait, the squadron was deployed.

He was part of the first lift of vehicles by C-130 transport aircraft into Forward Operating Base Rhino about 100 kilometres south-west of the country's second biggest city, Kandahar, in early December 2001.

It was case of literally hitting the ground running for the SAS patrols as they fanned out across the barren terrain to provide their boss, US Marine Corps Commander Brigadier General James Mattis, with some eyes on the ground. Rhino was virtually surrounded by 'tiger' country so the Australians were at the sharp end of the early campaign against Taliban and al-Qaeda forces.

Jamieson and his men undertook the first patrols through the Helmand Valley to Kandahar and they opened up the crossing through Lashkar Ghar. This was very much traditional bread-and-butter SAS work, small self-sufficient patrols offering a long-range surveillance capability to coalition forces. The patrols lasted for between 30 and 50 days and of the 120 days Jamieson spent in country between December and March, 108 were spent out on patrol.

The work varied between hearts and minds operations with local villagers, lengthy undetected surveillance missions and direct engagement with enemy forces including the battle of Anaconda in early March 2002. It covered the weather spectrum too, from snow-capped mountains to baking deserts.

'We achieved all our missions, we didn't lose a man and we didn't have a man evacuated from the field at any time,' he says. 'So by the end the troop was very tight-knit and that's probably what I am most proud of.'

The SAS men covered the country from Bagram in the north to Rhino in the south.

Because they were the first coalition troops to cross the Helmand River, he recalls a great deal of tension among the local population. His troops moved into one village with a bridge and were ordered to observe the bridge.

'We couldn't get close enough to see it without driving over it,' he says. 'We went in with fairly open minds but it was a very tense situation. I have never seen more military hardware in my life. The entire village was at stand-to [armed and alert] even though they were flying a Southern Alliance flag and they looked to block us off.

'We talked and got ourselves through, drove across the bridge, cleared it, opened it and that was the main link from Rhino to Kandahar. We parked out in the open, outside of mortar range and went back in the next day, after a very tense night, and were greeted with open arms.'

The friendly welcome became a little frayed later in the mission when smiles were often replaced with hostile glances or a stone being pelted in their direction.

There is a big risk with operations involving air support. While air power can be easily the most effective form of offensive action, it carries great risks, particularly if bombs or missiles go astray. As a former forward air controller, Jamieson is more aware than most of the need to be 100 per cent certain of who, what and where the target is.

'It doesn't matter how careful you are. Unless there is an active target and you can physically identify it, the only way to tell enemy from friend is by their intention. You can only tell by looking at them. When you start to look at targets that aren't active and calling in strikes on them, you are not really sure who you are knocking off.'

He says that during their 108 days on patrol his men showed

remarkable restraint. Under the rules of engagement they could have fired on many occasions, but they held off and probably saved numerous lives.

'That's the sort of thing I am proud of. We weren't there for a gunfight, we were there to do a mission.'

The irony of his situation was not lost on him as he recalled that just six weeks before landing at Rhino he had been on an Australian navy ship protecting his country from Afghani refugees. Now here he was in Afghanistan putting his life on the line to save the Afghanis from the Taliban.

Jamieson became very fond of Afghanistan during his deployment. He forded its rivers, climbed its mountains and crossed its deserts and was struck by the beauty of the place and the endurance of the people. He gets very annoyed when ignorant commentators, who have never even been there, start describing the country as a 'shit hole'.

'Afghanistan is a beautiful country and I love it,' he says.

He was also 100 per cent committed to the campaign and the objectives of ridding the place of the Taliban Islamic fundamentalists and cutting opium production.

'It was a very tailored and effective response from the United States. It had been a long-term problem area and it was a time when they had significant global sympathy and as a result the coalition was very strong and very involved. It was a multi-dimensional coalition and it was very much seen as getting to the heart of terrorism problems throughout the world. That was very, very good and very effective.'

Jamieson is also full of admiration for men such as the SAS commander at the time, Lieutenant Colonel Gus Gilmore, whose political savvy, salesmanship and close relationship with General Mattis won the regiment many of the complex tasks it was given.

'Gus's strategic manipulation brought a very small country and a very small SAS onto the international public platform,' he says. 'He will always have my admiration for that.'

The Australians filled a role that no other special forces unit could fill as effectively. Others had chased the glamour of short, sharp counterterrorist type roles, but the Australians never lost the ability for long-range vehicle mounted- or foot-patrolling.

'We made our name by doing that . . . which is something I think all of us are exceptionally proud of because we did it well.'

While Jamieson and his men were risking their lives in Afghanistan, the neo-con politicians in Washington were busily cooking up another adventure a little further west.

George W. Bush had been looking for an excuse for years to take on Iraqi dictator Saddam Hussein and after 9/11 he finally had one. Suggesting links between Iraq and al-Qaeda, his hawkish regime built a case based on Saddam's alleged stockpiles of nuclear, biological and chemical weapons. The catchcry of the neo-cons became, 'Imagine what al-Qaeda would do to a western city with a nuclear bomb.'

The fact that Saddam could not have built such a weapon after 12 years of UN sanctions and weapons inspections counted for nothing; nor did the fact that Saddam and al-Qaeda loathed one another.

John Howard and his coalition government in Canberra was one of the US administration's most fervent supporters and went into hyperdrive to sell the message that Australia should go 'all the way with Dubya'.

Like many expert observers and strategic thinkers, many military officers at first saw the build-up against Iraq as clever brinkmanship. Never in their wildest dreams did they believe that Bush would actually push the 'go' button and invade the place.

As the deadline loomed for George W. Bush to carry out his threats against Saddam, Rob Jamieson was confident it was all part of a grand plan.

'In my simple idealism, as we got closer and closer to deployment date I figured it was all working how it should,' he says. 'The military build-up plus UN resolutions and Saddam finally comes out and says, "This is all I have got." I thought there was a wonderful opportunity for a political, diplomatic solution with a very real and immediate threat of force behind it.'

During a brief trip home for Christmas in 2002, he had a chat with his brother, saying 'This is working exactly as it should, mate. We are going to come out of this brilliantly because there is not a reason for invasion, we have won without fighting — Sun Tzu.'

Sun Tzu was an ancient Chinese military general and strategist who wrote the classic military treatise, *The Art of War*.

'I genuinely believed that was the way we were going to go. Subsequently we found there was a momentum established well before, leading to a different conclusion and that was invasion.'

To this day he and many other military officers remain convinced that the invasion was morally and strategically wrong.

'I can't work out what possible advantage there is about the current situation and I couldn't think of it at the time,' he says. 'It was going to be a very difficult campaign that committed resources and global focus into an irrelevant battleground for terrorism and created a battleground. It was actually incredibly ineffective in fighting terrorism as opposed to something like Afghanistan where there was a clear strategy at work.'

By mid-January 2003 it was clear that the invasion might actually proceed.

Jamieson had gone to the UK just a few weeks after he arrived home from Afghanistan. Now he took over as operations officer of the SBS Squadron, moving from being on exchange to being a functional part of the headquarters structure.

The deployment would prove to be the most 'special force type' mission he had ever been on.

'It was very high risk, it involved huge force projection, it involved a lot of unknowns and it was pushing ourselves to the very limit,' he says. 'The combination of all those factors made us vulnerable and we felt vulnerable going out there, but the beauty of SF is that we cracked on and did it. Every special forces unit and capability from the creation of it has had mission failures because we push the limit and it should not be viewed as any different in this context. That is what "Who Dares Wins" is!' Or, in the case of the SBS, 'By Strength and Guile'.

After Jamieson arrived in the UK, he and his mates from C Squadron SBS, the 'green' squadron used for land-based operations, went down to Africa for a training exercise to build up their mobility capability, which was a good fit for the Australian SAS mobility troop commander. In his previous experience with the British SAS it had been clear to him that the British were firmly entrenched in the belief that they were superior.

'One of the great things about working with the SB is that you realise, hey, it is all the same, guys make errors, guys do good things, the blokes are the same, they crack on at their best level,' he says. 'I do think that technically [the Australian SAS] were far more advanced than the English as a general rule. We have a much closer relationship with the Americans on equipment than the British and I think they were left behind a bit at that period.'

When it came to operational experience, however, the British special forces were way ahead after years of battling the IRA and campaigns in places such as the Falkland Islands.

But East Timor had shown the Special Boat Service, which deployed a troop there with the SAS, that the Australian SF capability was very good indeed. Afghanistan proved the point when the American generals' force of choice for sensitive, long-range surveillance missions became the Australian SAS.

In addition to his work building the mobility side of the boat service, Jamieson undertook intensive diving and Arabic language courses. He put the personal moral dilemma about a pre-emptive invasion of Iraq to one side as he prepared for what would be a very tough mission. And during his 16 weeks in country, Jamieson was far too busy to dwell on his own philosophical demons, and besides, like all soldiers, he had signed up to do what his political masters told him to do.

'I don't believe in conscientious objection. You sign an agreement with the government and you do what the government asks in as humane a manner as possible. If you want to register your disagreement you resign when you can without breaking contract and that's what I did. I've got friends who resigned prior and some who conscientiously objected and some who wrote letters under pseudonyms about how the war was unjustified, but none of those are very effective weapons. It is very easy to turn them into irrelevant acts of self-sacrifice.'

He was aware of the debate that was raging in Australia about the invasion and, like many Australian officers, he was privy to high-level briefing material that strongly indicated there were no weapons of mass destruction in Iraq. Saddam simply had been unable to rebuild the stocks following the 1991 Gulf War.

Regardless, the Americans and their allies proceeded to cook up stories about mobile factories and vast quantities of hidden terror weapons that the Iraqi dictator would unleash upon Israel if something wasn't done.

'I was exposed to some pretty high-level briefings from some of the closest political advisers who were stating information that was directly in contrast to what was being released,' he says. 'There wasn't a military man that really believed there would be WMDs.'

From a military point of view and to a soldier about to invade the place, that was of considerable comfort but it still meant that for the first time ever, Australian forces would conduct a premeditated invasion.

'Where did the concept of premeditated invasion for self-defence come from? Since when can a country invade another country in self-defence without any clear show of intent or capability?'

This was one of the points that the Labor Opposition and others opposed to the war had been arguing.

'The country [Iraq] was seriously depleted from 1991 and it was systematically bombed over the '90s, sanctions, surveillance, even from a non-intelligence point of view, rationally you couldn't look at them and think they have somehow squirrelled away a capability to develop something as sensitive as biological or nuclear weapons,' Jamieson says. 'I said that to my boss — this stuff is not there and he said, "I know."'

As his squadron crossed into Iraq, he clearly remembers thinking, 'We are about to waste the high-profile and international support the Americans have enjoyed since 9/11.'

He knew with certainty that he was part of a strategically flawed mission that, from an American perspective, would develop into a slow and declining military failure.

From an Australian soldier's perspective it was the worst of everything.

'We jumped on the gravy train, we weren't as strong as France or Germany to say, "Hey, this is wrong",' he says. 'We committed a minimal force and that force did a fabulous job. But it was a minimal force and we pulled that force out as soon as we possibly could and later on after the invasion there were some limitations on that force.'

It really disgusted him that John Howard was crowing about how good our boys were as a coalition partner, while American and British troops were dying on the streets of Basra.

He says the soldiers did everything to live up the Anzac spirit, but they were let down by their political masters whose motives were not so honourable.

'We got away with minimal commitment, we jumped on the gravy train, we got our free trade agreement, our losses to date have been minimal, thank God, and the public relations was exceptional. There is the contrast between the soldier's perspective and the politician's perspective. And that amongst everything is why I lost the faith.'

What disappointed him more than anything was the fact that his country and his leaders were not interested in doing the right thing.

'They were actually interested in political gamesmanship and that is a hell of a risk with lives. I no longer wanted to have my moral well-being under the control of someone who I no longer morally trusted.'

As he made up his mind to leave the military once the Iraq mission was over, he became increasingly aware of what was happening back home. He says the vilification of good people opposed to the war absolutely disgusted him.

'I have the utmost respect for the anti-war movement,' Jamieson says. 'Those people who have absolutely no moral compromise are the very guys that our politicians should be observing. For the rest of us, the guys like me who can go and take life and still sleep at night, it is very easy to end up on a slippery slope without the guides of those who aren't willing to compromise. We get up to some pretty shitty stuff and you need people to make sure we don't get off the track and end up busting heads in Abu Ghraib.'

He argues that without such guidance from opponents of the war, it simply becomes a propaganda mission. That is risky given that the first casualty of war is truth.

'This is where Mr Howard had totally underrated the impact of the responsibility of what war is. He hasn't learned a lesson because unlike America and the UK, because of our minimal commitment, we don't have Herc-loads of body bags coming home and so he will never learn the seriousness of it.'

Adding insult to injury, when the American Abu Ghraib prison scandal occurred, Australia cowered. While there is no evidence of Australian involvement in prisoner abuse, it was a member of the invading coalition force and therefore shared some responsibility. Despite this, both Howard and then defence minister Robert Hill completely abrogated Australia from its responsibilities as an invading power.

'We couldn't even stand up when times got tough and take responsibility for what we did. Instead we dodged responsibility for what we did. And that's been the worst thing of this whole effort. We tried to ride the coat tails of the coalition but at no point have we truly taken a national responsibility for the acts that the coalition was doing.'

After returning to England and enduring the intense Iraq debriefing sessions, the 34-year-old left England and returned to Australia to sort out his future.

Jamieson went on long service leave from the SAS in July 2004 and finally resigned in February 2005 after 10 years of very high-tempo employment. He had bought a property in England so moved there permanently in 2005 and gave himself until he was 40 to find his next career.

'I went to work in the UN for about six months, putting the Afghanistan election process in place,' he says. 'I was quite dubious about the role of the military in those offshore wars so I sort of sat down with the UN, saw what they were doing, got a bit of experience and left there, mainly for relationship reasons, before the elections.'

His time with the UN provided a glimpse into the complex world of global diplomacy and what many see as the great challenge of our time and the fertile ground for the growth of terrorism — the growing imbalance between the rich and the poor.

The UN bureaucracy was also an eye-opener for the military man. 'It is literally the most dysfunctional organisation I've ever worked with, but that doesn't mean it's wrong. The concept is beautiful, [but] because the concept is beautiful, that's its biggest enemy. It is a fundamentally flawed structure.'

If his stint with the UN taught Jamieson anything it was that all the military action and all the UN and non-government efforts in some of the world's poorest countries count for little or nothing without coordination and the backing of business.

'What the UN has to do is tap into the power of business because business is becoming more socially aware.'

Following his UN stint he established a consultancy working first in the high energy producing areas of Nigeria, the Middle East and Eastern Europe.

'I'm an independent consultant and I pick and choose clients based on first of all the size of their company, their philosophy, whether it meets what I'm trying to do and also their areas of operation,' he says.

At present his major client is a private sector petroleum company operating in Nigeria, Gabon and Kurdistan.

'I effectively manage their global loss mitigation strategy. That includes everything that doesn't involve getting oil out of the ground, such as health and safety, environmental development, community relations and investigations.'

During a two-year period he has convinced the firm to integrate all those processes into a mutually supporting environment. 'Safety, information management and community development to enhance the stability of the operation,' Jamieson says. 'It is a simple structure; it is just about implementing processes that are all supporting each other.'

Having concluded that governments, the UN and NGOs were all failing, he established a formal group to study unconventional solutions to some very big commercial problems. Just like the al-Qaeda terrorist network, it is based on a loose network with its aim being stability rather than instability.

'Energy is the centre of where instability is, where the instability and disproportionate distribution of wealth is, so it is a very good starting point,' Jamieson says.

Community development is the major focus because traditionally that is where energy companies have failed. They grasped the health and safety nettle in the 1980s, but he says community relations is about more than just building a school.

'It's the teachers, the community, the pride . . . the aim [of] community development programs is to actually become interdependent, not dependent.'

He says that in Nigeria, community relations are based on handouts. 'Their pride goes down, their self-care suffers and they end up aged between 17 and 25 when organisations like al-Qaeda prey on them and say, "Come on, strap a bomb on because everything else is lost." It is a romantic illusion for Muslims and unfortunately that's what makes it so powerful.'

To counter this Jamieson goes into the boardrooms of some big companies and talks straight to the directors.

'I talk their talk, take these unpalatable, unstructured concepts which are people and turn it into their language and scare the shit out of them,' he says. 'At the end of the day, corporate social responsibility is a bullshit term, but people [directors] are becoming more and more accountable. So you scare the shit out of them and then if you've got a streamlined reasoned process, instead of having 25 departments, you have one department, one strategy, all interrelated, it saves you money.'

This is a powerful message in a corporate world littered with directors and executives who have happily watched their firms dig large holes, poison communities and then move on to make a pile from the next corrupt Third World basket case.

Jamieson does not take on clients unless he has direct access to the board and the chief operating officer. He is in demand at security conferences throughout Europe and runs workshops in the Middle East. At least some of the corporate world appears to be listening.

THE POLITICIANS

chapter thirty-six

THE NEAR-DEATH POLLIE

Martin Hamilton-Smith has lost count of the number of times he could have been killed. Being an airborne specialist in the SAS, most of them involved aircraft.

He was in a Caribou that ran out of fuel and crashed in a paddock, a C-130 Hercules that hit a bird and almost ploughed into trees, a Chinook helicopter that suffered a hydraulic failure and made an emergency landing and another Caribou that lost an engine and landed on one wheel. But the worst by far involved a UH-1H Iroquois 'Huey' helicopter over the sea near the SAS camp at Swanbourne.

The tough military life of the former counterterrorism team leader and one of the founders of Australia's CT capability provided a solid foundation for his latest, and perhaps most precarious job yet, Leader of the Opposition in South Australia. The Liberal MP for Waite in suburban Adelaide was elected to Parliament in 1997 after a successful military and business career.

His rugged, weatherbeaten features break into a grin and his piercing green eyes glow as he recalls one of his nearest misses.

The chopper had a total engine failure at about 7000 feet and began to fall from the sky. The three SAS men in the back baled out, but unfortunately they were not dressed for a water landing.

The machine crash-landed safely on the beach but the three paratroopers went into the drink. His two comrades, who were water operators and powerful swimmers, managed to scramble ashore with the help of some surfers, but Captain Hamilton-Smith wasn't so lucky.

None of the men was wearing a life vest and Hamilton-Smith was dressed in a flying suit over the top of a tracksuit. After he hit the water, his left arm and leg became entangled in the ropes of the sinking chute. The only thing keeping his head above water was brute strength.

'I was in the water for a long time, maybe 45 minutes to an hour and slowly the parachute sank,' he recalls.

Meanwhile the flying crew somehow managed to get the Huey restarted, and without any thought for their own safety, mounted a rescue operation. There was no boat on standby and no other rescue capacity in the area.

'I don't know how they did it but they did and they came out and attempted to rescue me,' he says. 'The crewman hoisted me once — now this aircraft had a known problem, it had just crashed once and they got it flying again — he then hoisted me a second time and I got pulled back into the parachute on each occasion.'

On the third attempt he made it as far as the skids, but as the crewman was trying to cut the ropes he tumbled back into the sea.

'He came back for a fourth hoist and I just had no strength, I was giving up,' he says. 'Then the movie starts to become a slide show, I was losing consciousness and drowning and I had the parachute sinking, I'm tangled in suspension lines, I've had several attempts, I'm physically exhausted, I'm spitting water and probably vomiting and going under the water, I remember long periods under the water and sucking a lot of water into my lungs. I remember the white light . . . I remember looking down on myself in the water dying, I remember hallucinations and what I thought were out of body experiences, I was drowning and then, it is like a movie shot at this stage, then the helicopter went away. I remember this deathly silence, I remember at a particular point getting ready to die.

'Apparently what happened when I was unconscious and dying, the helicopter returned and a load master jumped into the water with his life vest on, he swam to me and held on to a suspension line which probably saved my life. I was bobbing up for a moment then gone for extended periods, he managed to hang on long enough for a passing fishing boat to come by, they fished me out of the water unconscious, applied CPR and somehow got me back to life.'

He recalls spluttering back to life in the boat, spewing up seawater and finishing up in Royal Perth Hospital on a stomach pump and ventilator. He actually thought he had died and gone to hell — hospitals can be like that.

About three days later he was discharged in great pain. 'I couldn't move, I'd busted every muscle in my body from the adrenaline rush, fighting for my life.'

Back at Swanbourne he walked into the close-quarters combat course he had been on before the incident intervened.

'I remember sheepishly coming through the door, waddling over to my chair and as I came in there was deathly silence because everyone knew what had happened. I'd nearly died, there was silence,' he says. 'The instructor stopped, I sat down, he looked at me and said, "Captain Hamilton-Smith, it is very good to see you, sir", and went on with the lecture. It wasn't like, "Tell us what happened, tell us the story", just, "Very good to see you, sir."'

Martin Hamilton-Smith was born in the southern Adelaide suburb of Mitcham, part of the electorate he now represents.

The first son of a policeman and childcare worker and the second of six children, he won a scholarship to attend the Royal Military College, Duntroon. Two of his classmates, Duncan Lewis and Don Higgins, would go on to command the SAS Regiment and a third, Lou Vincent, became chief of the New Zealand Army.

The young Lieutenant Hamilton-Smith was posted to the 6th Battalion Royal Australian Regiment and in 1978 he undertook SAS selection. He became a free-fall paratrooper and was allocated to the air operations troop.

In February that year the Hilton bombing occurred in Sydney and the Fraser government responded with a plan to develop a counterterrorism capability within the SAS. Hamilton-Smith was chosen to command the army's first ever counterterrorism team, Gauntlet 1.

In those days the regiment ran its own close-quarters battle training, but it had no capacity to train or exercise CT troops. So in mid-1979 he and a senior sergeant were sent to the British 22 SAS at Hereford in England to learn about this new form of warfare. Hamilton-Smith was initially attached to SAS headquarters in Regents Park in London, but British SAS boss Colonel (later General Sir) Peter de la Billiere soon transferred him to Hereford.

'Being the fantastic soldier that he [de la Billiere] was, he realised the best place for a young SAS captain from Australia was at Hereford working with 22, not in headquarters. So he sent me out to Hereford and I spent the whole time there,' he says. 'I was able to get right up close and personal with the British counterterrorist capability, did a lot of training with them — small arms demolitions, CQB [close quarters battle], lot of counterterrorist work; did other things too, did a high-altitude low open [HALO] free-fall course in France, but most of it was counterterrorist related and Northern Ireland-based work.'

The two men returned to Perth in late 1979 and set about establishing the CT team at Campbell Barracks. Hamilton-Smith recalls his time with 22 SAS as a tremendous learning curve. He was part of the team and therefore went on all their exercises and was involved in securing several important meeting places as an armed CT member. Hereford itself was in a state of high alert in case the IRA should try and attack the home of the SAS which was very active in Northern Ireland throughout the 1970s and 1980s.

He raised the first Gauntlet (land operations) team in January 1980 at exactly the time that 22 SAS was resolving the Princes Gate siege in London.

'I remember we were doing our final exercise and watching Princes Gate go in on live television,' he says.

He is extremely proud of the work achieved by Gauntlet 1.

'They were a wonderful group of people and really set the benchmark for what was to follow,' he says. 'If there was a reflection I'd make on all that has been achieved in the SAS in recent times, it would be that this was an incredible transition period. The regiment went from 1978, when it was in the post-Vietnam period and looking for a role, to a highly trained terrorist capability in the space of about 18 months to two years. I was part of that process and it was a very interesting period in the regiment's development.

'All that has been achieved since was built on this transition, all of our involvement in counterterrorism and our involvement in a range of other operations since were largely built on those skills and capabilities developed during this period from 1978 through to about 1981–82. It was an incredible period of transition.'

Some of the SAS men, particularly Vietnam veterans, were not too happy about their new role

'A lot of people were at a stage in their career where they didn't really want to start again; it was this new style of warfare and there were retirements,' he says.

Despite this, many of the Vietnam vets went on the journey. It was also an opportunity for young diggers, who hadn't been to Vietnam, to cut their teeth and prove their worth operationally, and they did.

'We had a new generation of young soldiers emerge who were really good at counterterrorist work. They hadn't been to Vietnam but could establish themselves in their own right. In a sense I was part of that group; I missed Vietnam as well.'

With the then head of Special Action Forces, Colonel Mike Jeffery, pushing hard for the new role in the Canberra bureaucracy, the exercises became tougher and tougher as the men went about redefining a role for SAS in the post-Vietnam world.

The CT team soon expanded into a squadron with a designated land and water role.

After two years with the CT team, Hamilton-Smith moved across to 3 Squadron and back into a war-fighting role. In 1982 he was posted to Land Command in Sydney and spent some time at the guerrilla warfare school at Swan Island near Geelong before moving into Commandos as a company commander in 1984. He stayed there until 1993 when he was appointed commanding officer of the Commando Regiment.

By now a lieutenant colonel, he then left Australia to become Australia contingent commander and number three in the United Nations observer force of 3300 troops in the Sinai along the Egypt–Israel border. He had two terrific years in the Sinai and once his promotion to colonel came through it was decision time. He was still a single man without children and had sampled the delights of business when he had bought into a childcare business with his mum, Barbara.

'For the last two years I was in the army, I was making more money out of the business than I was from the army and I could see that if I got out and built this business up I could make a lot of money.'

He was torn between seeking higher command and making a clean break to give the business a go, so in 1994 he took a year's leave without pay.

'I used that time to build the business and it flew and early in 1995 I took discharge and built the business up,' he says. 'I finished up with six businesses in two states and about 130 staff. It was a multi-million dollar turnover business and I built that up over successive years until around 1997.'

By that time he realised that childcare was not really for him.

'It's not necessarily what every good SAS officer does when they are in special forces, set up a childcare centre, but I wanted to get involved in business and see if I could cut it, the cut and thrust of the private sector,' he says. 'I felt I'd achieved what I needed to achieve: command at each level, CO twice. I now wanted to test myself in the private sector.'

He then turned his mind to how he might continue his public service outside the army. He had joined the Liberal Party when he left the army and in 1997, upon the retirement of the deputy premier and Member for Waite, Steven Baker, he threw his hat into the ring.

'I was actually away skiing at the time on a holiday and I got a phone call saying, "Get your backside back to Adelaide, there is a pre-selection in two weeks' time for the seat",' he recalls. 'I'd only been there for two days. I cancelled my trip, checked in my skis and back I came, won the pre-selection and then won the seat in 1997 and that started what has been a 10-year career.'

After serving as deputy government whip he became Minister for Tourism and Innovation in his fourth year as an MP. That lasted just one year and in March 2002 the voters elected a Labor government for the state.

The opposition went into a period of decline, was thrashed again at the March 2006 poll and eventually Hamilton-Smith won the leadership, knocking off Iain Evans in April 2007.

He regards political leadership as a much tougher job than military or business leadership.

'I do rely a lot on the leadership lessons I've learnt both in the military and in business and apply that to politics,' he says. 'There is a lot that's different. In some respects leadership in politics is the most challenging. You can't pick your own team, you are not directly in control, you don't command, you can't hire and fire, you have to bring people with you if you're elected and you are open to public scrutiny 24 hours a day, seven days a week. It is largely about process, not just about results. These things make politics quite different from business and the military.'

But he sees the principles as being very much the same. For instance, he leads by example. 'I've taken on a large string of portfolios; I work very hard. If I set the example then other shadow ministers will follow that example,' he says. 'You've got to be prepared to do the hard yards.'

He often reflects on the qualities that make an SAS soldier and how those qualities translate into civilian life.

'My theory is if you are going to be involved in something, you've got to aim to be the best. You've got to squeeze the juice of life out of every opportunity that is presented to you. You are only given one life, it is not a rehearsal, so make the most of it,' he says.

'When I was in the army, being in the SAS to me was the goal so I had to make the most of it, when I was in business I wanted to be successful and make some money and I was fortunate to do so, now I'm in politics you've got to make the most of it and if you feel you can do better, rather than criticise or harp from the sidelines, be prepared to roll your sleeves up and have a crack, which is what I've done. So I think that was part of it.'

When it came to his officer selection course for SAS, he pledged that he would either succeed or be carried off on a stretcher.

'I keep reminding the Premier of that. Here, there is an election in March 2010 and I'll either be successful or I'll be carried off on a stretcher and the final point I'd make, thinking back on selection, you have to give it everything you've got, keeping a little bit in reserve for the unexpected. You never completely expend your last gasp.'

Valuing teamwork is the other vital ingredient that the army gave him.

'The army is a lot about teamwork, a lot about getting along with people regardless of background, circumstance, origin and frankly I don't give a stuff whether someone is black, white, yellow, Christian, non-Christian, upper class toff, I really don't care, I'll take everybody as I see them and accept everybody at face value and make my judgements about them.'

A crucial development in his life was his marriage to Stavroula Raptis and the birth of their son, Thomas. He had never found the time to settle down during his military career, but upon returning home to Adelaide he realised at 40-something that it was time.

'I'm married now with a three-year-old, gorgeous little creature, and two stepchildren. One is 23, she is a hostie for Emirates living in Dubai and the other one is an 18-year-old that knows everything, just like I did when I was 18,' he says. 'I'm glad I wasn't the father of this little kid when I was in the SAS because I was doing things, we were all doing things that were life threatening and we were all away a lot. Even though politics is quite demanding in terms of time, I value my time with our kid and it's given me a new insight into how tough it must be for guys in the regiment that have young families.'

chapter thirty-seven

THE WATER POLLIE

Paul Papalia travelled the world during the 1980s and wherever he went he was always proud of Australia.

The Royal Australian Navy officer saw deep social flaws in the United States and in Britain and always assured himself that such things could not happen in Australia.

Then in 1998 the government-backed waterfront dispute took place and dogs were unleashed on Australian workers. In August 2001 the *Tampa* refugee incident triggered a hardening of immigration law and in October of that year, the Howard government used the military to cover up the fact that it had misled the Australian people about children being thrown into the sea by asylum-seekers.

This period had a profound impact on the skipper of a navy patrol boat whose job was to enforce the government's hard-line policy and intercept boatloads of desperate souls and turn them around.

The then Lieutenant Commander Paul Papalia never imagined he would become so politicised by these events that he would become a member of parliament, but he did. Now the member for the safe Perth Labor seat of Peel in the West Australian parliament, he regards that era as a dark period in Australia's political history.

'People weren't allowed to be called refugees. Initially they became asylum-seekers, then illegal entrants — you had to change how they were referred to so they were breaking the law rather than seeking refuge,' he says. 'Our patrol boat was the first one in that era to intercept a vessel on the high seas and turn it around, which then was mirrored in the *Tampa* affair a couple of years later.'

Throughout all of this, Papalia instilled in the crew of HMAS *Bunbury*, ironically the name of his home town in Western Australia, the need to maintain respect for the boat people they had to confront on the high seas.

'My objective was to instil in my people a respect for the people we were dealing with as human beings worthy of appropriate respect,' he says.

That approach was not necessarily consistent with what the government was trying to achieve, which was to intimidate asylum-seekers into not setting sail for Australia in the first place. He believes that excessive force was used, with troops escalating situations that did not need to be escalated.

'That occurred not because of the troops involved but because of the leadership right up to the political level,' Papalia says. 'They [the government] politicised the military, they compromised the integrity of the military and particularly the navy.'

The Howard government's hard-line attitude was also reflected in the way Immigration officers handled refugees. In one case, HMAS *Bunbury* was involved in the transfer of 120 people from Scott Reef to Broome. They had been abandoned by people-smugglers without food and had not been noticed by Australian aircraft for four days. All that the men, women and children had to sustain them was a 44-gallon drum filled with tepid rainwater.

'My troops carried a lot of them over the reef, aged people, to get them to the boats to bring them to our patrol boat,' he says.

They arrived back in Broome and one frail old man was assisted off the boat by two crewmen. 'He could hardly walk, he had a couple of my blokes on either side of him. They handed him over to Immigration and they treated him like a prisoner and made him struggle his way up the gangway and onto the bus. Their complete attitude reflected their political attitude. I thought that leadership was inadequate and not appropriate. They vilified people who were vulnerable and subsequently were proven in 95 per cent of cases to be genuine refugees.'

Papalia has no doubt that the 'get tough' policy was not only morally wrong, it was extremely costly to the Australian community.

'Why did we treat them like that and throw them into detention when in reality it would have been more effective and cheaper in the long run for the nation and more healthy for our psyche and most of them if they were dealt with very quickly and placed into the community while the process was taking place?'

Papalia has never been a trade unionist, but his sense of fair play was deeply confronted during the 1998 waterfront dispute.

'I thought it was wrong, it was a conspiracy against our own people, dogs on the waterfront in Australia in that era, shocking, ridiculous and I had no respect for Peter Reith,' he says.

When Reith became defence minister and politicised the defence force, Paul Papalia decided enough was enough.

'I have been very sensitive to the potential for minorities in society to be scapegoated and isolated and in my opinion be wasted as a potential weapon against terrorism and a source of intelligence,' he says. 'People are isolating these people for their own gain, and scapegoating for their own gain and what that does is make it more dangerous for Australia, so I see that as a threat to the nation.'

An important point of reference for Papalia had always been his grandfather Vincenzo, who arrived in Australia as an Italian immigrant before World War II. He had been a soldier in the Italian army in World War I and then moved to America before settling in Western Australia, got into the land-clearing business in the booming south-west farming region and eventually owned a pub at Collie and a couple of city bars.

Then World War II came along and he was interned, which broke his heart and his health. 'It took him away from his family but significantly damaged him and he never really recovered. He had a breakdown, died reasonably young and lost everything.'

Papalia's father Frank, a labourer, moved to Brunswick near Burekup, not far from Bunbury where the young Papalia had an idyllic country life as the second of four boys. His mother, Edna Moore, was a local farmer's daughter. When he was 15 he decided to join the navy to relieve his parents of the burden of his education and so at the end of Year 10 he enrolled at the navy college and completed his schooling in uniform. At 18 he joined the fleet and after five years 'driving ships around the ocean' the 23-year-old decided to try out for the clearance divers. This is the navy's special forces unit who have to swim, dive and perform at a very elite level. Their primary role is explosive ordnance disposal but they are also trained to perform a wide variety of underwater roles.

Clearance divers served in Vietnam and in both Gulf wars and they performed hazardous missions in the explosives-laden waters around the port of Umm Qasr in southern Iraq. Dozens of navy divers have served with the SAS, but despite undertaking and passing all the courses required for selection, inter-service rivalry has thus far prevented them from receiving the fabled sandy-coloured beret and winged dagger badge of the regiment. That is reserved for the army members only.

In the early days of the SAS counterterrorist function the army lacked experience in 'closed circuit' diving, so navy divers were brought in to assist. This risky form of diving involves a breathing gas containing oxygen and it recycles exhaled gas so is much more compact that conventional scuba gear. The initial plan was for the sailors to perform the entire CT diving task, but that was canned and the navy was asked to provide personnel for the selection course.

The following year a large number of sailors passed selection and for all intents and purposes joined the SAS. They would undertake standard reinforcement training including a parachute course and then go on-line with the CT squadron. They just weren't beret-wearing members of the SASR.

According to some estimates about 60 navy divers served as fully beret-qualified members of B Troop 1 Squadron on CT duties throughout the 1980s.

One of those men, Michael Wulff, has for years been seeking recognition and assistance for the sailors damaged by their SAS service. Wulff has documentary evidence in the form of a letter from the Central

Army Records Office that shows the sole reason the sailors were never given berets was because they were not members of the Australian Army. He served as a CT operator with B Troop from 1985 to 1986 but there is no recognition of that service ever having occurred despite the fact that he is on a disability pension resulting from injuries sustained during that time.

He wrote to the defence minister in 2004 seeking the awards and recognition of his service in SASR as presented to his army colleagues with whom he very proudly served.

'I have an 11-year-old son to whom I want and need to be able to prove my service in this very proud elite Regiment that has, and still to this day, serves Australia magnificently,' he wrote.

Wulff has accused the Australian Defence Force of blatant discrimination over the issue. His only response has been a tersely worded letter from Army Records Office relaying a message from a major inside the Special Operations Command.

'ABCD Wulff attended and passed the 2/84 selection course, but will not receive a beret as he is not Army,' the unnamed major wrote.

Paul Papalia has also grappled with this fundamental injustice. As he was wheeled into surgery for the seven knee operations he underwent as a result of his SAS work, he found it difficult to comprehend why he, and navy men like him, could not be given a beret. In addition to the patrol, parachute and reinforcement courses, he had also passed the arduous and rare sole swimmers course, but to place the sandy beret on his head he would have had to resign from the navy and join the army.

'It wasn't something I would contemplate really.'

He recalls often being run down by the army guys in the SAS as 'a scruffy matlo' (seaman). 'I was always proud that our blokes had the capacity to maintain a sense of humour. I love the regiment blokes and they do have a sense of humour, but I think our blokes always took the piss out of themselves a bit in any situation they were in. They made a good contribution when they were there because they tended to take the edge off things. It is very easy to take yourself too seriously and believe a lot of the propaganda whereas if you have people who are willing to knock you down a little bit, we didn't have berets, we were matlos.'

Most of the navy divers were actually proud to be separate from their army mates, particularly when one of them topped a close-quarters battle course or extreme fitness test.

'They stood out in the regiment in their capability.'

When he arrived at Swanbourne in 1989 there were about eight navy divers in the CT squadron. When the east coast CT capability, Tactical Assault Group east (TAG east) in Sydney was set up, virtually the entire water troop was made up of navy divers.

Papalia says there was nothing complicated about his reasons for working inside the SAS. It was simply to be the best.

'I don't see how you'd want to be, at that time, a clearance diver and not want to serve in the regiment,' he says.

He served as water operations troop operations officer until the end of 1989 when he transferred to 1 Squadron where he stayed until the end of 1990.

'By that stage it was almost accepted practice that a navy officer wouldn't get to be a troop commander, they would just be officers,' he says.

A couple had reached such lofty heights in the early days when large numbers of divers were in the regiment, but it had become a matter of prestige or, more precisely, army prestige by the early 1990s.

He has no regrets from his time with SAS, describing it as a 'fantastic' experience. He picked up a suite of skills, such as weapons handling, that he would never have learned in the navy and he was also able to impart his superior knowledge of diving and the risk of 'death excursions under pressure' to a large number of soldiers.

'I feel I gained the most value from just getting through that selection and reinforcement process and being educated as to how powerful the mind can be,' he says. 'You learn very quickly that your body can go a lot longer than the mind. That was an incredibly valuable lesson . . . You are actually pushed to the limits of your capabilities.'

The SAS selection process combined with the extreme water operations provided him with an unshakeable sense of self-assurance. 'You know you can achieve things that could otherwise possibly appear daunting. That is an incredibly valuable thing, just to learn and know it inside and have that be part of yourself means there are very few things you think you can't achieve.'

Following his SAS service he returned to the navy and was posted to the explosive ordnance detachment on a ship before going on a six-month mine warfare course in the UK.

In 1992 he went to Iraq with the United Nations to work as an explosives disposal specialist. This was the start of the UN campaign to rid Saddam Hussein of weapons of mass destruction (WMDs) and his job was to blow the stuff up. His team would travel to manufacturing sites and use explosives to destroy stockpiles of chemical weapons.

For seven months he spent six days a week out in the desert destroying chemicals including the nerve agents sarin and mustard gas.

'This stuff had been exposed to extensive periods of time in extremes of weather and also the shock of the Gulf War; the sites had been bombed extensively,' he says.

'Travelling around a site where early in the morning the big drums were steaming with things and you didn't really know what they were — that was a great experience for me.'

Despite the hazardous nature of the work, he had just two minor incidents where he had to be cut out of chemical suits contaminated with mustard agent.

'Mustard nerve agent generally does not penetrate these suits, but mustard would work its way through after six hours, so each time you'd come back you'd be checked by other members of the team and if you were contaminated they would just cut you out of the suit.'

During his time in Iraq the unit to which he was attached destroyed tens of thousands of rockets and other explosives. The list included 6000 122-mm rockets with 8 litres of sarin inside each one as well as 13,000 155-mm mustard-filled artillery projectiles.

Because none of the nations involved in the UN operation would trust the other with their explosive techniques, the team had to do a lot of improvising. In one case some mustard-filled projectiles had casings that were a couple of centimetres thick.

'We had to access it without destroying the projectile and spreading mustard agent everywhere and it took us a long time to figure out how to do it,' he says. 'In the end we placed a small charge in the burster tube which was enough to break the burster tube open without blowing the entire projectile apart so you didn't have mustard agent going everywhere.'

With bombs, they constructed improvised explosive devices using empty beer cans, with shaped charges to blow small, neat holes in the casings to drain the chemical agent.

'That meant we needed to have a lot of empty beer cans which was not a bad thing,' he recalls with a smile.

The challenge was greatest with Saddam's stockpile of Scud missiles. Iraq had used these massive missiles to bombard Israel and Kuwait during the Gulf War. Fortunately they had thin casings and the team developed a cardboard standoff so that the scientists could test the contents before the weapon was destroyed. Inevitably the Scuds contained sarin nerve agent.

The work was hazardous but for Paul Papalia it was 'top end' stuff, just like being in the SAS. 'It was what you wanted to do because it was real; you don't want to train to practise all the time.'

The team often wondered how much of this material there was in Iraq. 'On reflection it looks as though we got most of it.'

He returned from Iraq in March 1993 to take command of clearance diving team 4 in WA. He was then given command of HMAS *Bunbury* and in 1995 married Gillian. Their first son was born in 1997.

'That started to change the way I viewed the world too,' he says. Their second son was born one weekend and he was away and back at sea on the Monday. That was the straw that broke the camel's back. He wanted family stability, but the travel was becoming a drain and he knew the next step in a naval career would be the east coast.

The family was about to up stumps and move to Vanuatu so he could work in a maritime advisory job, when they decided, 'That's it.' They vowed to stay in the west at all costs.

Then Papalia was approached by a mate to re-join diving team 4 as its executive officer. He jumped at the chance and, as fate would have it, his timing was excellent. The team went to the US for three months and then to Kuwait to join the invasion of Iraq in 2003.

The 30-man team deployed to a naval base in Kuwait that was occupied by 5000 American troops preparing to invade Iraq, eventually moving into northern Kuwait for the start of hostilities.

'There were missile strikes not far from us, close enough for us to be rocked in the desert,' he says. 'We were fortunate to be incredibly well equipped, we had access to the internet via satellite communications, could log on and email people and receive intelligence updates.'

A few days later they arrived at the southern Iraqi port of Umm Qasr to begin work in earnest. The city had not been fully secured, snipers were active and tank battles raged in the distance. The key task for the divers was deactivating hundreds of sea mines left behind by the Iraqis.

'Our blokes were the only ones who dived on live mines, but we also did ordnance disposal,' he says. 'We were better equipped than anyone else. We had our own vehicles, weapons, communications, we had 17 trained diver medical technicians in our detachment, which is kind of like the patrol medics the regiment has and we had the capacity to do a lot more but we were constrained in some ways by the nature of the command structure.'

They were frustrated at every turn by the American officer in charge of the unit, so the upshot was they did virtually no ordnance disposal. Fortunately Papalia hooked up with an old British mate who was a lieutenant colonel in the Royal Marines based further north near Iraq's second city, Basra, on the Shatt al-Arab waterway.

'I let him know that we had all these capabilities and they were very anxious to use us. Ordnance disposal was very limited and what they had they were concentrating on the combat role,' Papalia says. 'So we got a lot of ordnance disposal, maritime ordnance, out to the west of Basra and that was mostly our role there. It was frustrating, we could have done more. There were minefields in towns like Umm Qasr and other smaller towns around the peninsula and kids were blowing their legs off while we were there. We could have gone and cleared them, but they wouldn't let us do it because they perceived it to be a potential expansion of our role beyond the initial combat phase.'

This was extremely frustrating for Papalia and the others because it would have put their skills to good use and would have been very valuable from a hearts and minds perspective as well. But the higher command in Canberra and their political masters did not see it that way, so that was that.

When the team sought permission to set up medical clinics with British doctors to treat some of the thousands of people in hospitals around the place, that was also refused in Canberra. 'Same reason, they saw it as potential expansion in the post-combat phase, but it would have been really valuable at the time.'

Despite his strong desire for more quality family time, Papalia says he could not have refused the Iraq job after training with the men for a year and after 24 years in the navy without a single operational task apart from boat people patrol.

But in early 2004 it was finally time to go so he resigned his commission and left the navy for good.

He and Gillian had some property in Bunbury, which they developed, and they were already operating a couple of laundromats in the city. The family was going along fine when one day he received a phone call out of the blue from Labor MP and state education minister Mark McGowan, who was a former navy lawyer and acquaintance.

He asked Papalia if he would consider running for the seat of Peel that had become vacant after WA Premier Alan Carpenter sacked cabinet minister Norm Marlborough over his secret dealings with disgraced former premier Brian Burke.

'We asked Mark how long we had to decide and he said "tomorrow".'

Both Papalia and his wife had long been fed up with the Liberal government in Canberra and his political angst had been festering ever since his boat people days off northern Australia. He was certainly motivated for a political career. It was just a matter of deciding what was best for the family.

In the end they agreed and he joined the ALP that day. After a tweaking of the membership rules and with Carpenter's support he won the pre-selection two weeks later from a field of 11 candidates.

'Once that pre-selection rubbish was out of the way the support was overwhelming.'

One of the biggest challenges for the family was preparing the two boys, aged 10 and seven, for the media circus and the change of focus in their dad's life.

'When I won pre-selection I said, "I want to shield my family from the camera", but if you say you are married with kids, the next question is, "Where are they?" So we figured the best thing at the pre-selection was to get that out of the way, so we took my wife and boys to Kings Park with Alan and did a doorstop with all the press in Perth and my boys are standing there completely overawed.'

Papalia went on not only to win the seat on 3 February 2007 but also, unexpectedly, to increase Labor's majority by 1.09 per cent. He was sworn in when the WA State Parliament resumed on 27 February 2007.

In his maiden speech Papalia told the story of his grandfather's painful experience of being interned as a potential terrorist in his new country.

'I love my country and will willingly do anything to defend it against a threat,' the new Member for Peel told the parliament. 'However, I am gravely concerned when minority groups are used as scapegoats and targeted for political purposes. I believe the best way to defend this country against internal threats is to promote inclusiveness.'

Papalia regards his military service as a major asset in his new career.

'It gives you a mental fortitude, I guess, a conviction you can achieve what might not otherwise have been the case, then you've got all the other benefits of detailed planning, risk analysis and risk assessment. That is one of the greatest thing they offer in the regiment. I employed that as a patrol boat captain, in conflict, I use it every day.'

He regards teamwork and team spirit as vital ingredients in politics as well. It seems unlikely that he will become a political hater. 'I have respect for people on all sides, all types of politics. I went to war and I didn't hate the people on the other side, so I'm not going to hate the people on the other side of the chamber.'

chapter thirty-eight

THE NEAR POLLIE

Pete Tinley knew he would cop a razzing when he went to the stirrer's parade at Campbell Barracks during the fiftieth anniversary celebrations of the SAS in September 2007, and he wasn't disappointed.

As a former major and regimental operations officer, he had been one of the key officers who helped secure some plum roles for the unit during the US-led campaigns in Afghanistan and Iraq. Yet here he was just a few years later the Australian Labor Party candidate for the federal seat of Stirling in suburban Perth and therefore a supporter of a troop draw-down in Iraq.

Apart from abuse and the odd 'communist' reference from some Vietnam-era soldiers and vehement anti-Whitlamites, most of the barbs were good humoured and not intended to be to be spiteful. Fortunately the tall, imposing Tinley has broad shoulders and a sunny disposition, so he took it all in good humour.

Most military personnel are by nature conservative and in the broad sweep of history, conservative governments have tended to give soldiers greater resources and more work. That was certainly the case with the Howard government, which dramatically boosted defence spending, including half a billion dollars on the special forces, and handed them plenty of operational work from East Timor to Afghanistan and Iraq.

Tinley knew that his decision to run for Labor would rattle a few cages in the military, but he was committed. After 17 years in the SAS he had learned the wisdom of rolling with the punches and sneaking in through the back door rather than breaking down the front one.

That ability to adapt goes right back to the SAS selection course, which he completed twice — as a digger and an officer — when young men are tested to the limit through 22 days of food- and sleep-deprivation.

'The SAS selection course is the starting point, or the genesis if you like, for personal growth,' he says. 'It's the point where you discover your personal inventory of skills and talents.'

During selection most candidates experience an epiphany, a moment when the decision is taken to leave their former self behind. Tinley's moment arrived as a wave of energy that swept over him, a determination to do what he could with what he had.

'It's almost like a survival thing. You give up on effort you've put behind you, you don't worry about it, and you give up worrying about what's going to come to you in the next challenge, and you just live for the moment,' he says. 'And a lot of guys have taken that sort of stuff into the field where you don't worry about what is happening next, you fight the moment. It's that capacity to concentrate and focus on that particular point, that level of excellence that makes the SAS quite different from other organisations. The mission is paramount, the mission is above all else and that's it.'

He joined the ALP in 2001 as part of his transition from the military to civilian life. The military takes a heavy toll on families and he had been divorced in the late 1990s before going to Staff College in 2000. He knew his next stepup army ranks would be in Canberra and he was not prepared to put an entire continent between himself and his two young sons permanently. So he returned to Perth, intending to take up a reserve posting on the road to transitioning out.

However, the incoming commanding officer SASR, Lieutenant Colonel Gus Gilmore, asked him to be his operations officer. He jumped at the chance, but his path out of the army would not be reversed.

'That's one of two distinctions I will make about people who make a successful transition. Those who use the years, and I do mean years, depending on their time in service, prior to their eventual separation to shape what they want,' he says.

'The other aspect of it is that those guys who've been successful have been drawn out of the place, as opposed to pushed out of the place. They've been drawn out by a passion for the next challenge and for me it was starting a small business.'

In Tinley's case the *Tampa* adventure, 9/11, Afghanistan and Iraq delayed his departure by five years, and what a five years they were.

When he arrived in the Middle East to begin planning Australia's contribution to the US-led coalition's operations in Afghanistan, Tinley became a salesman as much as a military planner. While Gilmore sold the merits of the SAS to the American marines' Brigadier General Mattis and other force commanders, Tinley walked the corridors of land headquarters in Kuwait telling anyone who would listen about the merits of the SAS. The son of a salesman put his skills to good use.

There was considerable pressure on both men not only to deliver the government's intent of a meaningful contribution, but also to ensure the SAS was not placed on POW escort duty or search and rescue, as in the Gulf War.

'That would have locked us out for the next one [Iraq] as well.'

The rapid pace of the Northern Alliance advance down through Afghanistan meant that speed was of the essence. 'We had to get in behind whatever was going and fast.'

The men eventually won the SAS the crucial job of supporting Mattis's headquarters from Forward Operating Base Rhino. The troops became Mattis's eyes and ears and made a lot of powerful friends in the US military, virtually guaranteeing them a crucial role in the Iraq operation.

As Tinley left the Middle East in February 2002, he saw that US planners in Kuwait had turned their heads west away from Afghanistan and towards Iraq.

More than a year before John Howard told the Australian people that their troops would be going to Iraq, Major Peter Tinley already knew about 'Plan 10/3 Victor', the American contingency plan for the invasion of Iraq.

Formal planning for that mission began in mid-2002 and in October he was dispatched to Central Command in Florida and other US bases, such as Fort Campbell in Tennessee, to help position the SAS in the front row of the invasion plan.

When he arrived at Fort Campbell, home to the Fifth Special Forces Group, Tinley became aware that a lot of the information about Iraq was coming from just one place in the Pentagon. That was a special office established by Secretary of Defense Donald Rumsfeld and his 'neo-con' deputy Paul Wolfowitz, who was a principal architect of the Bush administration's Iraq policy.

Tinley was convinced that the intelligence from that office was being shaped to support the invasion plan. Alarm bells sounded in his head because none of the material that he saw, and he saw a lot, post-dated 1996. He assumed that others further up the chain must have known something that he didn't. Surely no one would go to war based on intelligence information that was more than six years old?

'Rumsfeld and Wolfowitz were running a special office out of the Pentagon, which shaped the intelligence, there's no question — talk to anyone, I talked to other guys over at the CIA,' he says.

Not that it made any difference to a professional army officer. 'Once you put one hand on the Bible and the other in the air when you join the army you say you'll go where you're told to go and you'll do your duty. I don't think anybody in Australia would want anything different because the alternative is pretty chaotic.'

Despite this, Tinley now says that he and his colleagues were always sceptical about finding Scud missile launchers, which was their primary mission in Iraq's western desert. It did have an upside for the diggers: at least they would be unlikely to face the threat of weapons of mass destruction. They still had a strong belief that Saddam possessed and would use tactical chemical or biological weapons.

Tinley's observations support pre-war intelligence gleaned by British sources that all but ruled out the possibility that Saddam had any WMDs.

This material, seen by numerous Australian officers, including some on exchange with British forces, was ignored by the American, British and Australian governments, which by late 2002 had staked their entire justification for invasion on one issue and one issue alone — WMDs.

'We were always sceptical that we were going to find Scuds when we wouldn't actually get anything out of the American intelligence system,' Tinley says. 'In your planning you're looking for actionable intelligence and targetable locations. Geography's everything. You always say, "Where?" and we had had air defence issues we had to knock out. We suspected all along that we were unlikely to find Scuds because none had been seen for a long time.'

Apart from a strong sense of duty he was determined to put his own stamp on the intense operational planning to ensure its success.

'Call it ego if you like, but I felt a sense of obligation to make sure that I put my stamp and my view on it all to help achieve a successful outcome in both those conflicts,' he says. 'I couldn't imagine having not done it. It would be a failure on the part of the culture.'

The Iraq operation was the second time in his career that Tinley had been part of what was clearly a political deception.

In August 2001, six months after he had joined the ALP and in the middle of a federal election campaign, he was in the bush at Lancelin near Perth with Gilmore helping out with a selection course, when a 44,000-tonne Norwegian container ship called the *Tampa* hove to in the Indian Ocean alongside a sinking refugee boat and rescued 438 desperate souls trying to reach Australia.

Prime Minister John Howard saw this as a golden opportunity to play hard-ball and wedge the Labor opposition at the same time. When it became apparent that the captain of the *Tampa*, Arne Rinnan and his tiny crew were under duress from the large number of refugees, and were determined to land them at the nearest Australian port, Christmas Island, the government activated its elite SAS counterterrorist force.

Gilmore and Tinley were ordered back to Swanbourne to prepare the TAG to go to the island and to prevent any refugees from setting foot on Australian soil.

Tinley and most other senior military officers were in furious agreement that the ship could have been stopped and boarded by the navy and that using the SAS was complete overkill.

'We looked at the credible threat and we looked at what was going to be achieved on the *Tampa* in the normal course of your tactical planning and . . . "Whoa, have we got an overmatch of capability here! A poor old box ship and a few refugees looking for a feed and a place to call home, well I'm going to throw the counterterrorist force at them, stand by",' he says.

After seizing the ship, the SAS men did a sterling humanitarian job liaising with the ship's crew and assisting the refugees, including providing medical help, cleaning them up and feeding them, but it was their role as political soldiers that left a sour taste in many mouths.

One of the most unsavoury incidents involved the Norwegian ambassador to Australia, Ove Thorsheim.

Gilmore was on board the *Tampa* so Tinley was on the phone to special operations commander Major General Duncan Lewis in Canberra. Tinley, who was located in the island's former Government House, believed Lewis was receiving his orders directly from Howard. Those orders were relayed by radio from Tinley to Gilmore and the squadron commander on the ship.

Tinley was seeking guidance about what to do with Ambassador Thorsheim. He was told to stop the ambassador from boarding the ship and was left in no doubt that the order had come from the very top of the Australian government, the prime minister himself.

'We were invading the sovereign soil of the Norwegian country, a foreign country, on a flagged vessel of Norway. We were inhibiting the movement of an internationally protected person in the body of the ambassador of Norway who wanted to get on to the ship, which to my understanding was his universal right.'

The big fear in Canberra was that a request for asylum would be made directly to the ambassador. So a go-slow began and then suddenly and inexplicably the rigid hull inflatable boat (RHIB) that had been working perfectly and was due to carry Thorsheim to the *Tampa*, suffered a mechanical fault. And when the ambassador finally reached the ship he was prevented by an armed SAS soldier from accepting a letter from the asylum-seekers.

Tinley says the senior SAS men on the *Tampa* mission, the officers and the sergeants, knew they were engaged in a cynical political exercise. Initially there was some suggestion that pirates might have been involved or that some of the asylum-seekers who had pressured Captain Rinnan might have been armed, but it soon became apparent that it was simply a group of pathetic and hungry refugees.

The military term for boarding a hostile vessel is 'ship underway capability' and the SAS has finely honed skills in this area. They have been used against suspected drug vessels, fish poachers and now a 40,000-tonne container ship.

'When we got there and it had to be done the guys just thought it was a waste of their resources and a waste of their time,' he says.

The common feeling among the blokes as they left Christmas Island and returned to Perth was, 'What was that all about?'

In his view, none of the men felt 'used', because they are employed to be used by government, but they understood clearly that the *Tampa* job was a blatant political exercise.

Tinley's first marriage had foundered for a host of reasons.

'Not the least of them was going away for seven months of the year,' he says, 'and the ego that you can sometimes develop in SAS. It hasn't got a mortgage on egos but it's got the down payment sorted out. That has to be continually managed because that's the competitive nature of the person who goes there.'

He has since remarried and has another child and lives around the corner from his first wife and the boys. 'I shared care for the boys because

349

I take the responsibility of parenting really seriously and we've got two houses, one home, so those boys transition between two houses but they're geographically very close. It is seamless, but not without its struggles.'

In late 2001 Tinley had no idea that politics would feature in his future. Sure, he had joined the ALP, but running for office was not on the radar.

By April 2005 the time had come to quit the army. Finally he was going to realise his dream of starting up and running a small business where he could apply his special forces pedigree.

'So I started a manufacturing business, a little start-up company manufacturing paving and concrete products for the building industry,' he says.

He thought he understood risk until he went into business.

'You get on a helicopter in Kandahar and you can put a box around the risk and sort of assess where you're going, assess the risk of whether you're going to get shot at or not,' he says. 'When you go to start up a business and you underwrite it with your family home and a couple of investment properties you've cobbled together over 20-odd years and that's your family's future, nothing keeps you awake more at three in the morning than wondering whether you're going to make wages this week.'

Tinley was inspired to make a run in politics by former federal Labor leader Kim Beazley and former WA Labor Premier Geoff Gallop. It was Beazley who phoned and asked him to run for the Liberal-held marginal seat of Stirling in the northern suburbs of Perth.

He soon realised that a fight for a marginal seat required full-time effort. In February 2007 he gave up the business to go campaigning for the federal election.

'It was a fantastic adventure but I've got to say my wife runs that business now. As she says, "You start things, I'll finish them."'

He has no family history in politics and he comes from conservative stock.

When he told his father that he had been pre-selected to run in the 2007 election, his father said, 'Oh, good.'

'For [the seat of] Stirling,' Pete Tinley added.

'What's happened to the bloke that's there now? Is he retiring or something?'

'No, Dad, I'm running for the Labor party.'

'Well, I'll never vote for you.'

'Well, lucky you don't live in Stirling!'

As he wore out shoes doorknocking and campaigning he came across many inspirational stories of individual endeavour.

One that shone like a beacon was a woman who began a schools volunteer program in the back of her house with no money.

'She now has seven full-time staff and two part-time staff covering 1700 volunteers providing one-on-one mentoring from Year 1 to Year 12, in 135 schools. So I'm fighting like hell because she wants to roll it out as a national model — it's a great story and a great achievement. I run into those all the time. And that one person does make a difference.'

Tinley lost his bid for the seat of Stirling in the 2007 election that swept Kevin Rudd to power federally. But in true SAS fashion, he is determined to succeed. He is now working for a small mining supply company in Perth and planning another bid for political office as an ALP candidate at the next federal election.

Despite his defeat, the first Rudd government budget included a one-off $10 million grant to the SAS Resources Trust, honouring an election promise made by Rudd and Tinley during the campaign.

FULL CIRCLE

chapter thirty-nine

THE OPEN DOOR

The Chief of the Australian Defence Force, Air Chief Marshal Angus Houston, acknowledges that retaining SAS soldiers is a major challenge for the defence force.

Houston regards the expensively trained Australian SAS as among the finest special forces units in the world.

'Therefore I am very keen to retain as many of them as I can,' he says. 'We try to look after them to the very best extent we can but as you know, at the moment we have a very high level of operational tempo and in the special forces world in particular we have been pushing them pretty hard over recent years. They have been on some form of operation almost continuously since 2001 and they have given a very good account of themselves, they've done a magnificent job for Australia and I think they've enhanced Australia's reputation as a country that produces very fine military people and in particular very fine special forces.'

Houston also acknowledges that the army needs to be more flexible if it hopes to retain a higher percentage of SAS soldiers, particularly officers. He is aware that many at the major/squadron leader level find the adjustment into other areas of the military extremely difficult.

'There are many who make the transition very successfully and go on to bigger and better things,' he says. 'But just as many others say, "This is fine, but really what I want to do is stay down here at the tactical level", and what they do is, they might spend a short time in Canberra and then go back to the tactical level. And most of the time the sort of approach is flexible enough to accommodate their requirements. That is something that we have to manage a lot more.'

The same philosophy applies to those returning to the regiment after a stint out in the world, the so-called 'retreads'.

Houston says the ADF is keen to get them back.

'We greatly value these people. You know, I always say to people who are leaving that I see, "Look, if it doesn't work out the way you want it to work, please do come back and re-enlist", and a lot of people do, not just in special forces, right across the board,' he says. 'We have people for example who go to airlines to be pilots who just don't like airline flying because it's a lot more, I suppose, pedestrian than flying in a military jet or a military helicopter or even a military transport plane and they decide they want to go back to that. And we get that in all three services.'

As far as the future of Australia's special forces is concerned, Angus Houston has a clear vision. It will be about tailoring forces to suit particular jobs.

'I think bringing the Commandos into the special forces has been a huge success, we've seen the fruits of that amalgamation in Afghanistan, where SAS and commandos and indeed the Incident Response Unit, they all work together in a very seamless way,' he says.

'Clearly what we have is a task force there at the moment in Afghanistan that is tailored to the task and I think what you'll see in the future, with the sorts of operations we're doing, like Afghanistan, where we're deploying special-type people it will always be a tailored force that goes, not necessarily a unit.

'More and more now, and you see it with the Overwatch Battle Group in Iraq, what we've got is an outlet, a unit that has been tailored for the task that it's been given and it comprises the elements that you need to deliver the required effects. I am very, very comfortable with the structure of our Special Operations Task Force in Afghanistan and I think to a large extent it's going to be pretty typical of the sorts of special operations forces that we will use in the future. We'll always adapt them, we'll always adjust them depending on the circumstances that we face at the time and the effects that we have to deliver.'

By early 2008, the former head of Australia's Special Operations Command (SOCOM), Duncan Lewis, had detected a definite slowdown in the 'leakage' rate of SAS troops to private industry.

'In the years between 2001 through 2004 there was a massive expansion of that private security sector,' he says. 'There's probably been a bit of a stabilisation in the labour market, if you like, in that area. But having said that, the retention of high-calibre very expensive soldiers is and will always be one of the principal considerations of our special forces commander and of our military commanders in general.'

It is not just a challenge for special forces. 'If you look at navy there's a big leakage . . . currently, people going to work on oil and gas platforms and so on. So it moves around a bit — sometimes you've got pilots because the airlines are hiring and so on.'

The high standard of training, combined with the fact that they come as a 'free good', is another reason why military personnel are so attractive to private sector employers.

They are a no-cost resource in a booming economy because taxpayers have already paid for their training and the private corporations get the benefit.

'It's astonishing how much effort, time and money is put into training military personnel when compared to other walks of life,' Lewis says. 'Even when I compare it to the public service, we have training sessions in the public service, very good training sessions, but they are far less than you have in a military environment. This rigid training regime of the military is a thing of excellence. It's really surprised me on the outside looking back in.'

It is not all one-way traffic. Government intelligence and law enforcement agencies also benefit from some 'free goods' of their own. Lewis is regularly in touch with his vast network of old mates of both Australian and other nationalities and on more than one occasion they have provided him with some valuable information.

'You'll often hear people say "Oh, the military club is the biggest club in the world", and that's probably true,' he says. 'I was on the Golan Heights during the '82 war in Lebanon. I worked for a Russian. It was amazing because at that time it was the height of the Cold War and my boss was a Russian and he's a wonderful man! He could have walked into any Australian military unit, so long as he could knock the edge of his accent; he would have been able to pass off as a very credible military officer.

'Because we were all in the same kind of business, you had enormous empathy and understanding of this guy even though we were at the height of the Cold War. So it's not only among allies, but it can often work in more strained circumstances where you will have a relationship with somebody who's been through the same sort of experience as yourself.'

Such relationships are magnified in the special forces community where bonds are forged under extreme circumstances and the common hardships can be traced back to the selection course.

'Special forces around the world all have a very stiff selection process and everyone remembers their selection,' he says. 'That's the common bond and you can always compare notes and say, "Well, my selection course was harder than yours." For private sector security companies the special forces service on a soldier's CV is a virtual guarantee of quality.'

According to Lewis the community is small enough that if a bloke were a 'dud' then word would pass around very quickly and he wouldn't have lasted long in the SF world anyway.

'If he's served for some time in the special forces you're guaranteed what you're getting,' he says. 'I think a lot of employers find that quite attractive because it saves you, if you like, the experimental phase of employing someone to see if they're any good or not. A lot of the young fellows who have gone off into the commercial security business have been found to be very attractive by employers for that reason.'

He admits that his own 'free goods' network is growing and that he gets the occasional phone calls at odd times of the day or night from unusual corners of the globe.

'Government's got its own intelligence tentacles quite obviously, but even if the information is corroborating what you've heard through official channels and you're getting just another corroboration that yes, x is happening or y is happening then that's very helpful. We don't have any formal reporting linkages or anything like that, but certainly somebody who is travelling the world and whom I know and who sees something and who rings up, then that's a "free good".'

It is also a feature of the post 9/11 world that pivotal strategic positions inside the special forces of non-western allied nations can be filled by such people as Terry O'Farrell, not on exchange but as an officer of that foreign army.

Lewis regards O'Farrell as a very fine special forces officer who is delivering a much-needed capability to a close ally of Australia in the campaign against terrorism.

'To find our people doing that for what I'd describe as very good causes, developing capability and assisting friendly governments in the development of their own forces, I think that's a very good thing,' he says.

He does sound a note of caution, saying, 'You've got to be very careful around some of this stuff because there are all sorts of complications to do with contractual arrangements and exactly what they're involved in and so on. But in the case of Terry, he's working for a recognised government and doing a wonderful job.'

O'Farrell believes that the growing power of the global network will require governments to be imaginative if they want to keep their people.

'I think the worrying thing for the Australian Army is that whilst there are a few of us here like myself who have done their time, more importantly there are a lot of younger guys here in the early to mid-thirties,' he says.

Dr Nick Reynolds says it is perfectly natural for the bonds forged under the sort of duress that special forces troops operate in to endure beyond their military careers. He says that, like pilots or other military professionals, the elite soldiers will only leave if the military stops giving them what they want. RAAF pilots, for example, tend to drift to the airlines when their next promotion will result in driving a desk rather than an aircraft.

'Special forces is like the Formula One of the military, so they get a lot of satisfaction from that role,' he says. 'When they come to the end of that particular role, if they have to get transferred out or have to go to different postings, that is when they will start looking for something more beneficial. If you think of what an elite athlete goes through, they don't necessarily do it for the excitement or the adulation, they do it because they want to be the best they can. A lot of the special services people have that desire to be the best they can in that particular field.'

He says that is what makes them successful in other walks of life.

'They tend to make their own way in the organisation. They are not ones to sit back and wait for opportunities.'

chapter forty

COMING HOME

The email arrives early in 2008.

'Great news for me. I'm bugging out of here and rejoining the regiment.'

The gloss has worn off. George has had enough of Abu Dhabi after little more than two years. He is finishing up as a contractor to the United Arab Emirates special forces and has accepted an offer to return to the SAS in Australia.

He and Audrey have sold their luxury cars, packed up their boxes, had their round of farewell parties and are heading back to Perth.

George will drop to about half of what he earned in Abu Dhabi and will be demoted a rank, becoming a corporal rather than the sergeant he was when he left the army in 2005. He doesn't care. He can hardly wait.

So what has caused this change of heart? He says it all stems from satisfaction and professionalism.

'I seriously tried my hardest to be happy here but the analogy I'd use, it's like playing for Dapto Dogs on the reserve bench after playing for Australia. There's no comparison between working here and working back there,' he says.

He agrees that money and lifestyle were originally the key attractions. Now he says, 'The money here is really good but the satisfaction is really low. It would take more than money to make this place sustainable because it's a pretty good place to live but ultimately you're in an Arab country, you have to be nice. You can't just give someone the forks when you're driving down the road. You can't say anything to an Arab here no matter what they do and it's very frustrating and that's in civilian life as well as at work. We can't even tell a private soldier ultimately what to do; he can just walk away and do what he likes.'

He also concedes that the five-star hotel style of expatriate existence gets a bit wearing. 'It's all very pleasant but it would be nice to be able to do your own thing entirely and not worry about other people's sensitivities and all that.'

Being demoted a rank in the SAS is customary practice for 'retreads', as they are known, who return after a spell in civilian life.

It is supposed to stop feathers being ruffled and noses being put out of joint among those who have stayed doing the hard yards in the meantime, but it also acts as a major disincentive when it comes to enticing 'retreads' back to the SAS, which has lost so many expensively trained people to the private sector in recent years.

George is taking a characteristically optimistic view of the demotion.

'It's a beautiful thing actually because when I left I was a sergeant patrol commander and was acting troop commander and my duties, because I've done that job for just over three years, were becoming more closed and more desk-like, like an operations sergeant or something along those lines. And that wasn't really what I wanted to do.'

He concedes that it probably won't be long before he gets promoted again, but says, 'The upside for me is that it puts me back firmly on the deck so there's no chance of being a deskbound Johnny or anything like that. I can actually get out and move with the boys again.'

He is hoping to become a patrol commander again and spend a good few years being operationally active. 'There's a window of opportunity; for me there's a definitely small window of opportunity. I've been out of the regiment for two years, I'm 41 years old, if I wait too long there's no way I could ever go back there.'

This time around he says he feels happy about becoming a 'deskbound Johnny' once he is too old to be operational.

'I'll go through the point where my body is useful then I'll just use my influence on people who can be influenced in a positive way. I can stay active but it's just that the more senior and older I get I won't walk the hills anymore, I'll sit in a forward operating base and influence those who walk the hills.'

As for becoming an officer, he says, 'I've thought about that but I don't know that I'm ready for the dark side!'

He says Audrey, who has never been an SAS wife before, was 'a bit dumbfounded' when he told her he wanted to rejoin but gave him 100 per cent support.

'She was a bit worried. It's a very strange thing, she's worried that I'll get killed or worse become an amputee and I don't really understand that,' he says, laughing.

For her part, Audrey says she was 'a bit surprised'.

'I knew that he wasn't getting a huge amount of job satisfaction here but I didn't realise how much he actually missed what he used to do. And as soon as we had a conversation and I realised how much he did miss it, it was just an easy decision to go home. Because coming here, for me, was just about earning a little bit of cash and I wanted a break from what I was doing. So it was a good opportunity and what was initially quaint doesn't remain quaint, it just becomes annoying and boring and you miss home. So it was an easy decision but of course I worry about what's going to happen to him.'

She reassures herself that he is excellently trained and will look after himself.

'I look at how well the Australians always do overseas and I know they've lost a few in recent times but compared to the number of boys who are there and the kind of work they do, they do phenomenally well.'

She won't miss the expatriate life, although George is certain that she will get Louis Vuitton withdrawal symptoms.

'I think we will certainly miss the financial position,' she says, 'and I'll miss the fun — it's a good opportunity when you are here because all your friends want to come over and visit you and you get to enjoy the fun aspect of Dubai, what it offers, the tax-free shopping.'

However she has really missed her own network of friends at home.

'People here are transient. They come and they go and you might develop a friendship and then those people are going home or you're going home. It's a false sort of a lifestyle.'

With George expecting to be away for four months or so every year, Audrey knows she will miss having him home every night. 'It's been fabulous. It's like working part-time here! He's home most days by 2.30. After a while, though, you kind of get bored with it, because there's no challenge in what you're doing.'

Most of the other former SAS wives have been very supportive of their decision. 'Some of them will tell you horror stories about what life is like as an SAS wife and others are really positive about it and I think I'm not the kind of person to look for the negative in the situation. I just want Georgie to be happy and satisfied in what he's doing and if I can support that then I'm more than happy.'

George has a good laugh about some of the cultural frustrations he has experienced in the Middle East, which will provide him with years of anecdotes back home. 'I was saying to the blokes here, when I have a bad admin day in Perth I'll send them an account and they'll just be in tears wishing it was them.'

Yet he says he would certainly encourage others to spend a couple of years doing what he has done.

'I wouldn't say it was time wasted or I hate this place or anything like that at all,' he says. 'What I'd do though, and am going to do, is give them an outline on how to approach living here, how to maximise your effort out of it and what to expect. It's been good, it's chilled me out massively, it's given Audrey and me time to travel and see and do and spend like we never would have. And I feel fresh and keen and ready to go again and I think it's a good thing.'

He adds, 'If it was just about money we'd stay here until the cows came home but it's not. We've got to be happy in our hearts and souls.'

INDEX

The Amazing SAS

IAN MCPHEDRAN

For the soldiers and officers of Australia's Special Air Service (SAS) Regiment, this is not just their professional motto, but a creed that shapes their lives. The SAS is among the world's most respected special forces units, a crack team of men from the Australian Defence Force who can be relied upon to handle the most difficult, strategically sensitive and dangerous of military tasks.

Now *The Amazing SAS* provides a thrilling insight into the way this country's SAS soldiers are selected and trained, and reveals fascinating details about recent SAS deployments: East Timor, the 2000 Olympic Games, the *Tampa*, the Afghanistan campaign and the regiment's action-packed mission in Iraq.

The Amazing SAS draws on interviews with General Peter Cosgrove, Prime Minister John Howard, Chief of Army Lieutenant General Peter Leahy, former SAS commanding officers Gus Gilmore and Tim McOwan, and many SAS soldiers and officers.